Visigothic Spain 409

A HISTORY OF SPAIN

Published

*Iberia in Prehistory**
Maria Cruz Fernandez Castro

The Romans in Spain†
John S. Richardson

Visigothic Spain 409-711
Roger Collins

The Arab Conquest of Spain, 710-797
Roger Collins

The Contest of Christian and Muslim Spain 1031-1157†
Bernard F. Reilly

The Spain of the Catholic Monarchs 1474-1520
John Edwards

*Spain 1516-1598: From Nation State to World Empire**
John Lynch

The Hispanic World in Crisis and Change, 1598-1700†
John Lynch

Bourbon Spain, 1700-1808
John Lynch

Spain in the Liberal Age: From Constitution to Civil War, 1808-1939
Charles J. Esdaile

Forthcoming

Caliphs and Kings 789-1033
Roger Collins

Spain 1157-1312
Peter Linehan

Spain: 1939 to the Present
Javier Tusell

* Out of print
† Print on demand

Visigothic Spain
409–711

Roger Collins

Blackwell
Publishing

© 2004 by Roger Collins

350 Main Street, Malden, MA 02148-5020, USA
108 Cowley Road, Oxford OX4 1JF, UK
550 Swanston Street, Carlton, Victoria 3053, Australia

The right of Roger Collins to be identified as the Author of this Work has been asserted in accordance with the UK Copyright, Designs, and Patents Act 1988.

All rights reserved. No part of this publication may be reproduced, stored in a retrieval system, or transmitted, in any form or by any means, electronic, mechanical, photocopying, recording or otherwise, except as permitted by the UK Copyright, Designs, and Patents Act 1988, without the prior permission of the publisher.

First published 2004 by Blackwell Publishing Ltd

Library of Congress Cataloging-in-Publication Data

Collins, Roger, 1949–
  Visigothic Spain, 409–711 / Roger Collins.
    p. cm. — (A history of Spain)
  Includes bibliographical references and index.
  ISBN 0-631-18185-7 (alk. paper)
  1. Spain—Civilization—To 711. 2. Spain—History—Gothic period, 414–711. 3. Visigoths—Spain. I. Title. II. Series.

DP96.C653 2004
946'.01—dc22

2003017277

A catalogue record for this title is available from the British Library.

Set in 10.5/13pt Garamond
by Graphicraft Limited, Hong Kong

For further information on
Blackwell Publishing, visit our website:
http://www.blackwellpublishing.com

Contents

List of Maps		vii
Introduction: Visigothic Spain in the Twenty-first Century		1

Part I A Political History

1	From Empire to Kingdom, 409–507	11
	A Turning Point	11
	The Visigoths	15
	The Gothic Conquest of Hispania, 456–507	26
2	The Imposition of Unity, 507–586	38
	A Fractured Kingdom	38
	The Reign of Leovigild, 569–586	50
3	The Catholic Kingdom, 586–672	64
	Conversion and Reaction, 586–590	64
	Changing Dynasties, 590–642	69
	Kings and the Political Elite, 642–672	81
4	The Visigothic Twilight, 672–710	92
	Court Conspiracies, 672–681	92
	The Uneasy Throne, 681–710	102
5	The End of the Visigothic Kingdom	117
	The Coming of the Arabs	117
	The Last Kings, 710–713	130

Part II Society and Culture

6	Books and Readers	147
	The Legacy of Africa	147
	A Golden Age	161

7	Archaeology: Cemeteries and Churches	174
	Goths in the Ground	174
	A Visigothic Architecture?	186
8	Archaeology: Rural and Urban Settlements	197
	Country Dwellers	197
	Towns in Transition	213
9	Law and Ethnic Identity	223
	The Fog of the Law	223
	Gothia and Hispania	239
Bibliographical Essay		247
Index		254

Maps

1 The provinces of Visigothic Spain 12
2 Towns and rivers 39
3 Archaeological sites 175

In memory of my father
John Howard Collins
(1919-2003)

Introduction: Visigothic Spain in the Twenty-first Century

The Visigothic period, from the early fifth century to the beginning of the eighth, has both gained and lost from recent changes in scholarly taste and methodology. While it could never be described as overwhelmingly popular, its history was one of the subjects that used to benefit from something like an official seal of approval, not just in the time of General Franco but for much of the twentieth century. This was thanks to the dominant ideology of the time encouraging study of periods in the Spanish past in which the central power of the state was strong, and in which political unification was a favoured goal.[1] For the medieval centuries this led to an almost exclusive interest in a succession of monarchies seen as contributing to the reuniting of the peninsula under strong royal and Christian leadership, with the concomitant destruction or ejection of those racial and cultural elements regarded as alien to the true Spanish identity or *Hispanidad*.

Success or failure in the *Reconquista*, the military recovery of Spain from Muslim Arab rule, was the bench mark against which individual kings or even whole dynasties could be judged. The approved line of succession ran from the Asturian monarchy (ca.718 to 910), to that of León (910 to 1037), and culminated in the kingdom of Castile (1037 onwards). Other peninsula states that were independent of or hostile to Castile in the high Middle Ages, such as the kingdoms of Aragón, Navarre, and Portugal, were hardly considered worthy of serious study. The loss of pace in the *Reconquista* and the weakening of Castilian royal authority in the second half of the fourteenth and much of the fifteenth century also condemned most of that period to scholarly

---

[1] Jocelyn Hillgarth, "Spanish Historiography and Iberian Reality," *History and Theory* 24 (1985), pp. 23-43.

neglect.[2] Only the emergence of the *Reyes Católicos* in the late fifteenth century, with the ensuing elimination of the Muslim kingdom of Granada and the beginning of the Spanish overseas empire, saw the return of history to the right track, on course for the Golden Age of the Hapsburg period.

The Visigothic centuries gained honorary membership of this elite sequence of approved periods and regimes, despite the fact that the supposed moral deficiencies of the last phase of its history were held responsible for the failure to resist the Arab conquest of 711. However, this regrettable lapse in competence was more than compensated for by other features of the Gothic legacy. In particular, it was under the Visigothic monarchy that the Iberian peninsula was unified for the first (and in practice the last) time. Although Roman *Hispania* had been ruled by a single authority, this was only as separate provinces of a much larger political entity that was of non-Spanish origin. It was the Visigothic kings who first created a monarchy that was purely Spanish in its geographical extent, and which at least in theory controlled the whole land mass of the peninsula. This became an ideal toward which medieval Castilian kings could aspire, though never attain.

At the same time, the intellectual, legal, and liturgical legacy of the Visigothic church contributed uniquely to the formation of a distinctively Spanish learned culture, at least until the various elements of it were suppressed in favour of modish ultramontane equivalents from France and Italy from the later eleventh century onwards.[3] So, if the Visigoths could be blamed for letting the Arabs in, they also set the agenda for the many generations of Asturian, Leonese, and Castilian kings who claimed to be trying to restore what they had lost.

It was not just twentieth-century Spanish historians who liked the Visigoths. The smack of firm government resounded through the law books, both civil and ecclesiastical, that they created, and virtually everything toward which they aspired had to do with increasing the central power of the state and of the church. At the same time, thanks to the lack of literary historical narratives from the period,

---

[2] See Roger Collins, "Angus MacKay and the History of Later Medieval Spain," in Roger Collins and Anthony Goodman (eds.), *Medieval Spain: Culture, Conflict and Coexistence* (Basingstoke and New York, 2002), pp. vii–xvi.

[3] Bernard F. Reilly (ed.), *Santiago, Saint-Denis, and St. Peter: The Reception of the Roman Liturgy in León-Castile in 1080* (New York, 1985).

there was little by way of detailed information on the realities of political life to contradict the desired image of church and state working hand in glove to build up their authority in a mutually supportive fashion. The Visigothic period, and the normative law texts that provide so much of the evidence upon which our understanding of it is based, could therefore be idealized by authoritarian regimes in twentieth-century Spain. Thus in the decree of May 6, 1969, establishing the new Museo de los Concilios y de la Cultura Visigótica in Toledo, General Franco praised the Visigoths for giving the Spanish their "national love of law and order." It probably came as a surprise to Spaniards then as it would now to feel that anyone might think they had a "national love of law and order," but this is just one example of how the Visigothic myth was manipulated.

This has not done the Visigothic period any favors now that political and other conditions have altered. The most marked and immediate change that took place in Spanish university departments of history in the aftermath of the Franco period was the emergence of interest in regional identities as opposed to national ones. At the same time, public criticism of the methodological backwardness of the historical establishment began to appear even in the daily papers by the early 1980s. The intellectual agenda of *Hispanidad*, and the obsession with strong central government and national unity, all gave way to the study of the history of regions and then of micro regions. Much of this is now being funded by autonomous regional governments, and in consequence some of it is published in local dialects, real and imaginary.

The Visigothic period, relegated to the field of ancient history once more, might have expected to receive some punishment for its previous popularity with centralists, but worse still is the fact that it has proved to be shockingly lacking in good regionalist credentials. As just mentioned, there is a lot of evidence for what secular and ecclesiastical rulers in Toledo were thinking in those centuries, but exceedingly little to show what was happening on the ground in Galicia, León, the Basque country, Navarre, and so on.[4] Archaeology can compensate, but the lack of literary texts makes it very difficult to put any flesh on very bare bones. A few scholars have managed to

---

[4] A rare exception would be Francisco Salvador Ventura, *Hispania Meridional entre Roma y el Islam: economía y sociedad* (Granada, 1990).

work the Visigothic period into a chronologically broader survey, of the *longue durée* variety once popular with French historians of the *Annales* school, but most are happier to start their surveys in the centuries after 711.

Rather than be allowed to go into a peaceful intellectual retirement until fashions change once more, the Visigothic period has in recent years instead been required to contribute to a project that is currently in vogue among Spanish medieval historians; this is the study of feudalism. It used to be held that Castile, unlike Aragón, was singularly deficient in traces of any kind of feudal system, and that this was further evidence of its unique and distinctively Spanish character. In the light of the earnest desire for Europeanization, a macro counterpoint to micro regionalization, that has swept over Spain since Franco, and the vogue for French historiographical methodology, a reexamination of this issue under new management has led to a plague of conferences on feudalism, following on from the all too predictable discovery that Castile too could be called truly feudal. Thus, as has rightly been pointed out, Spanish historians have been desperately seeking to make their country's past feudal at a time when their counterparts in the rest of Europe are trying to rid themselves of the concept and all it stands for.[5]

As it has never been suggested that "the feudal system" existed in the seventh century, let alone the fifth, and that therefore the study of feudalism has not formed a part of the historiography of Merovingian Gaul, Ostrogothic Italy, or Anglo-Saxon England, it might have been hoped that the Visigothic period in Spanish history would escape embroilment in this new scholarly obsession. Unfortunately, as if to prove that such things are contagious, a hunt has been started for evidence of what has been called "protofeudalism," an ancestral form of the later phenomenon. Belief in this now seems to be obligatory, but has not been helpful to the serious study of this period.[6]

---

[5] Peter Linehan, "The Toledo Forgeries *c.*1150–*c.*1300," in *Fälschungen im Mittelalter*. (6 vols. *Monumenta Germaniae Historica, Schriften* 33, Hanover, 1988), vol. 1, pp. 643–74, especially pp. 643–6.

[6] Luís García Moreno, "El estado protofeudal visigodo: precedente y modelo para la Europa carolingia," in Jacques Fontaine and Christine Pellistrandi (eds.), *L'Europe héritière de l'Espagne Wisigothique* (Madrid, 1992), pp. 17–43, who proclaims that there exists *unanimidad internacional en adjetivar de protofeudal a la formación social y política encarnada por el Reino de Toledo a principios del siglo VIII* (p. 17). I think not.

"Protofeudalism" is not the only linguistic horror spawned by the current desire of Spanish historians to prove themselves good Europeans. The most prominent sign of the dominant taste for French methodology is the difficulty in avoiding the word *espacio* or "space" in recent writings on almost any period. Conceived as a way of seeing history in terms of a series of overlapping political, social, and economic categories, this may once have been liberating, but its novelty value and intellectual utility have long been exhausted. What survives is a kind of jargon that reduces the comprehensibility of almost anything that employs it. Thus a kingdom has to be called *un espacio monárcico*, "a monarchical space," and daily life is lived in *espacios cotidianos* or "daily spaces."[7]

While the Visigothic period in general may be rather out of favor, good work has continued to be done despite the difficulties just described, and many useful studies have been published. Particularly valuable has been a series of new critical editions of several of the major texts produced in these centuries, not least the historical ones.[8] In that sense research on the period is now much better equipped than it was in the past, when reliance had to be placed upon a range of often very old and frequently defective editions, not all of which were easily accessible.

Another long-term weakness of the old tradition of historical research in Spain was its deeply entrenched geographical isolationism. This applied not least to the Visigothic period. All aspects of the society were examined in an exclusively Hispanic context. Comparisons with equivalent societies of the same period, such as Merovingian Francia or Lombard Italy, were never made, and their history was not taught. This encouraged the maintenance of the highly idiosyncratic agenda revolving around the identification of the true elements of "Spanishness" and the moralizing explanations for the success of the Arab conquest, which justified it: Spain was unique and so there was no point wasting time looking for parallels or methodologies from

---

[7] It would be unfair to single out examples in that this phenomenon is in danger of becoming universal in Hispanic historiography.

[8] For example Carmen Cardelle de Hartman (ed.), *Victoris Tunnunensis Chronicon cum reliquiis ex Consularibus Caesaraugustanis et Iohannis Biclarensis Chronicon* (= *CCSL* vol. CLXXIIIA, 2001), José Carlos Martín (ed.), *Isidori Hispalensis Chronica* (= *CCSL* vol. CXII, 2003), A. Maya Sánchez, *Vitas Sanctorum Patrum Emeretensium* (= *CCSL* CXVI, 1992).

outside the peninsula. This has changed since the 1980s, again for both better and worse. Really valuable collaborative and comparative international projects that have broadened intellectual horizons have been undertaken.[9] On the other hand, while much excellent work is being done in local studies, there exists a real danger that the current vogue for purely regional history could make the wider Hispanic perspective of earlier generations look positively broad-minded.

After a long period of apparent stagnation, in which the orthodoxy of the received wisdom of the late nineteenth century went unquestioned, studies of the civil law of the Visigothic period are asking challenging questions of the evidence and are starting to undermine old certainties. Some important new discoveries have been made, resulting in the nature and purposes of the seventh-century Visigothic law code known as the *Liber Iudiciorum* or "Book of the Judges" being seen in a new light.[10] The critical edition of this made in 1902, and long regarded as an invaluable aid in the study of this period, may become more of a hindrance than a help, as its editor sought to standardize a text whose real significance may lie in its variants and in the apparent errors of the individual manuscripts containing it.[11]

The question of what constitutes best editorial practice has not become as controversial as it probably should. While there have been several new editions of theological and other literary works of the period in recent years, the assumption remains that their texts should be normalized to make them look as if they had been written by classical authors of the first century AD.[12] In part this derives from a far too optimistic assessment of the level of classical learning in late Visigothic Spain, for which there is all too little real evidence, and in part from an unwillingness to take the testimony of the manuscripts seriously. While all too few are of Visigothic date, most of them are

---

[9] A good example is the Spanish-Italian conference whose acts are published in Javier Arce and Paolo Delogu (eds.), *Visigoti e Langobardi* (Florence, 2001), and also some of the volumes produced by the *Transformation of the Roman World* project that have Spanish content.

[10] Leading the way is Yolande García López, *Estudios críticos de la "Lex Wisigothorum"* (Alcalá de Henares, 1996).

[11] Karl Zeumer (ed.), *Leges Visigothorum* (= *Monumenta Germaniae Historica, Legum sectio I, vol. 1*, Hanover, 1902).

[12] Particularly stimulating are the arguments of Roger Wright, "On Editing 'Latin' Texts Written by Romance-speakers," in his *Early Ibero-Romance* (Newark, DE, 1994), pp. 109–26.

much closer in time to the authors of seventh-century Spain than was Cicero.

While the Visigothic kingdom has left us far fewer original administrative and legal documents written on parchment than its Frankish neighbors, and the only detailed study of them remains unpublished, there is weighty compensation in the form of 100 or so texts of this kind scratched on slate. While their existence has been known for several decades, the quantities discovered have gradually increased, and the errors made in the earliest attempt to edit them have been corrected in an authoritative new version and an accompanying study.[13] The purposes served by the slate documents are far wider than those of their surviving equivalents on parchment or papyrus. The durability of the medium has preserved ephemeral doodles, curses, and school exercises that otherwise would have long since been obliterated. These materials have hardly begun to be integrated into the wider study of this period; they offer exciting new possibilities for further research.

From the context of the discovery of some of them in rural settlement sites of Visigothic date, these slates must count as archaeological as well as historical and literary evidence, and thus as part of a new wave of discovery in this field. Important excavations in urban centers such as Mérida, Cartagena, and Tarragona have proved extremely revealing of conditions in their Visigothic counterparts. Equally important have been sites in the countryside of what were once significant early medieval towns, such as *Reccopolis* (Zorita de los Canes in the province of Guadalajara) and *Ercavica* (Tolmo de Minateda, near Hellín in the province of Albacete). Rural settlements of Visigothic date have also begun to be discovered in increasing numbers, despite the technical difficulties of locating them.[14]

All is not entirely rosy in the archaeological garden. Variations in funding and in local and regional government enthusiasm can encourage or retard work on this period. Money that would be better spent on excavations is often put into fatuous restoration of

---

[13] First and not always very acurately edited in Manuel Gómez-Moreno, *Documentación goda en pizarra* (Madrid, 1966), but now to be consulted in Isabel Velázquez Soriano, *Las pizarras visigodas. Edición crítica y estudio* (Murcia, 1989), or in the much more expensive but possibly now more accessible eadem (ed.), *Documentos de época visigoda escritos en pizarra (siglos VI-VII)* (2 vols., Turnholt, 2000).

[14] For references and further details on these sites see chapter 8 below.

monuments to make them look appealing. Too many restored monuments look as if they were built the day before yesterday, and the decisions made as to the idealized state to which they are to be reconstructed usually conflict with taste and common sense, and can lead to the destruction of important evidence.[15] Publication of archaeological results also remains a problem. A few crucially important sites have been excavated but never published, even decades later, depriving other scholars and the interested public of vital information.[16] It would be wrong to end on a negative note when so much good work is being done, but non-publication is worse than neglect, in that sites thus affected are in effect destroyed to no purpose and with no benefit.

Because there is so much that is ongoing in both the historical and the archaeological study of Visigothic Spain, some of the conclusions offered in this book must be considered provisional. The book itself should be seen as a report on various aspects of the new work being done on the period, with some doubtless idiosyncratic interpretations and judgments on the part of its author being thrown in to help stir the pot. It falls into two parts, with the first providing a historical overview and the second more of a survey of different key features of this society in its three centuries of existence and of the evidence that has to be used to evaluate them. Its author is more than delighted to find that he now disagrees with well over half of his own former views on most matters here discussed.

---

[15] Examples may be found in Roger Collins, *The Oxford Archaeological Guide to Spain* (Oxford, 1998); Spanish translation as *España – Guía arqueológica* (Madrid, 1999).
[16] See pp. 211–12 below.

Part I
A Political History

1
From Empire to Kingdom, 409–507

A Turning Point

If a date had to be set for the ending of Roman imperial rule in the Iberian peninsula, the autumn of 409 would be as good a one as any. On either September 28 or October 12 of that year – an all too typical contradiction between two contemporary sources makes it impossible to choose between them – a loose and recently formed alliance of "barbarians," who had spent the previous three years making their way from the Rhineland and across Gaul, came through the passes over the the Pyrenees into Spain.[1] These invaders are reported to have been made up of three distinct ethnic components: the Alans, the Sueves, and the Vandals. The latter group was subdivided into the Silings and the Hasdings. Both Sueves and Vandals were thought by the Romans to be Germanic peoples, originating in lands to the east of the Rhine.[2]

The Alans, on the other hand, would have been seen as far more recent and exotic arrivals in the West. They were one of the peoples of the steppe of probably Iranian origin, who were mainly to be found in the area of the northern Caucasus and the lower Don in the third and fourth centuries. Some of them may be assumed to have moved westward in the years following the arrival of the Huns on

---

[1] Orosius, *Historiarum adversum paganos libri VII*, VII. 40, ed. C. Zangemeister (Vienna, 1882; reprinted Hildesheim, 1967), pp. 548–52; Hydatius 15th year of Arcadius and Honorius, *The Chronicle of Hydatius and the Consularia Constantinopolitana*, ed. R. W. Burgess (Oxford, 1993), p. 80; on Hydatius see also Carmen Cardelle de Hartmann, *Philologische Studien zur Chronik des Hydatius von Chaves* (Stuttgart, 1994), and Steven Muhlberger, *The Fifth-Century Chroniclers* (Liverpool, 1990), pp. 193–266.
[2] Tacitus, *Germania* II. 4 and XXXVIII. 1–3, ed. J. G. C. Anderson (Oxford, 1938).

Map 1 The provinces of Visigothic Spain

the fringes of the Carpathians in the 370s.[3] Others of their number seem to have become subject to the Huns on the plains north of the Danube soon afterwards, and yet others were driven southward into Roman territory. How those Alans who moved west came to find themselves associated with the Vandals and the Sueves on the the east bank of the river Rhine opposite Mainz in late 406 remains entirely unknown.

In the winter of that year the river froze over, and the three groups crossed into Roman territory where, despite initial resistance by some Frankish allies of the empire, they were able to force their way into the otherwise undefended Gallic provinces. Following a three-year period in Gaul, of which virtually nothing is recorded, they reached the western Pyrenees in the autumn of 409, and were able to cross unopposed,

---

[3] Ammianus Marcellinus XXXI. ii. 12-25 and iii. 1-3, ed. J. C. Rolfe, vol. III, pp. 386-96. On the Alans in this period see Vladimir Kouznetsov and Iaroslav Lebedynsky, *Les Alains* (Paris, 1997), pp. 35-54.

possibly as the result of deliberate treachery on the part of Roman units supposed to be defending the passes across the mountains.[4]

These imperial troops were in the pay of a rebel emperor, Constantine III (407-11), who had been set up by the army in Britain in 407 and had then made himself master of much of Gaul and Spain in the ensuing period of confusion.[5] Whether the Spanish priest Orosius, writing his *Seven Books of Histories Against the Pagans* in 417, was right in suggesting that Constantine's soldiers deliberately allowed the Vandals and the others across the Pyrenees in order to conceal the looting of the civilian population they themselves had been carrying out is impossible to tell. But the Roman government of the legitimate western emperor Honorius (395-423) was never able thereafter to reimpose its authority on all of the Spanish provinces.

As can be seen from what was happening elsewhere in this period, the migrating armies that were the Vandal, Sueve, and Alan confederacies were probably seeking to reach some form of accommodation with the Roman government, by offering to provide military service in return for regular pay and supplies and some degree of integration into the imperial administrative structure. This is what Alaric and his Gothic confederacy had been trying to persuade the emperor Honorius to agree to up to the sack of Rome in 410, and some of his successors were able to make such arrangements with the imperial government on at least two occasions in the succeeding decade.[6]

Roman military power had come increasingly to depend on the employment of soldiers, both individuals and whole units, drawn from the populations who lived beyond the empire's borders or who had been permitted to settle in it by treaties of federation. Such groups as the Vandals, driven into imperial territory, could provide valuable resources of military manpower relatively cheaply for Rome, but in such periods of disturbance there were more potential soldiers looking for government subsidy than either were required or could be afforded by the depleted imperial treasury. For their part, such relatively large bodies of non-Roman soldiers in a potentially hostile

---

[4] Orosius VII. 40, ed. Zangemeister, pp. 551-2.
[5] *PLRE* vol. 2: Constantinus 21, pp. 316-17.
[6] For the events of these years see Peter Heather, *Goths and Romans, 332-489* (Oxford, 1991), pp. 193-224; also Roger Collins, *Early Medieval Europe, 300-1000* (2nd edn., London, 1998), pp. 47-60.

new land needed to make some kind of agreement with the imperial administration for their own security as well as employment. They were not able to maintain themselves as armies without access to regular food supplies, and they could not disperse widely over the countryside if faced by a military threat from hostile Roman forces.

The Alans, Vandals, and Sueves, after a brief but savage period of looting and destruction, seem to have made a treaty of federation with a Roman government. The two main Spanish literary sources for the history of this period, Orosius, an exact contemporary, and Hydatius, a bishop who wrote a short chronicle in northwest Spain around the year 468, agree that a period of famine, starvation, and cannibalism followed the entry of the Alans, Sueves, and Vandals into Spain in 409.[7] While the two chroniclers' sympathies lay with the suffering civilian population, what they describe implies that the invaders were having to take short-term and desperate measures. Once they had taken what food was available and had reduced the inhabitants to starvation, they either had to move on, to inflict similar misery on other untouched areas, or to change the nature of their relationship with the Roman ruling classes. As they had devastated their way across Gaul between 406 and 409 and were at this stage unable to cross into North Africa, the latter policy was the only alternative left to them if they were not to join the civilians in starvation.

Conditions in Spain at the time meant that the ensuing treaty of federation had to be made with a rebel imperial regime that had been set up in the peninsula in 409. The emperor with whom they made the agreement was called Maximus, and his rule was centered on Tarragona and Barcelona on the Mediterranean coast, an area not then directly threatened by the presence of the invaders.[8] Maximus had been created emperor by Gerontius, one of the generals of Constantine III, who had rebelled against his former master and in 410/11 was besieging him in Arles.[9] In the circumstances, neither Gerontius nor Maximus was in a position to resist the Alans, Sueves, and Vandals, and might in any case have hoped to make use of them in an attempt to overthrow Constantine III and gain control of Gaul.

---

[7] Hydatius, 15th-17th years of Arcadius and Honorius, ed. Burgess, p. 82; Orosius VII. 41, ed. Zangemeister, pp. 552-4.
[8] On Maximus see *PLRE* vol. 2: Maximus 4 and Maximus 7, pp. 744-5.
[9] *PLRE* vol. 2: Gerontius 5, p. 508.

In practice this was not to be. In the winter of 410/11 the Visigoths withdrew from Italy, and the army of the legitimate emperor Honorius was thus free to try and reestablish his rule in Gaul. This was achieved quite rapidly in the course of 411. Gerontius was forced to abandon the siege of Arles and retreat toward Spain, only to be killed by his own men, while Constantine III had to surrender to Honorius, who had him executed. The ephemeral regime of Maximus on the Catalan coast collapsed and he had to take refuge with his new Alan and Vandal allies in the interior of the peninsula, while expecting an attack by Honorius's armies.[10]

This was slow in coming because conditions in Gaul remained chaotic, and it was not until 416 that the western imperial government, dominated since 411 by the *Magister Militum* or Master of the Soldiers Constantius (died 421), was in a position to try to regain control of the Iberian peninsula.[11] This operation was to be carried out not by imperial forces, but by those of Rome's new ally, the Visigothic king Wallia (415-19). The campaign that he launched on behalf of the emperor Honorius against Maximus and his Alan, Suevic, and Vandal federates saw the Visigoths make their first appearance in Spain.

The Visigoths

To attempt a synoptic history of the Visigoths in the centuries preceding this point would not be easy. This is not just due to the size and complexity of the subject, but results from the continuing high level of scholarly disagreement about it. Above all this focuses on the central questions of who "the Visigoths" actually were, and what kind of an entity did they form? The fact that the name probably ought to be put in inverted commas may give some indication of the difficulties to be faced in trying to establish even the most basic consensus on these issues. The difficulties of definition in trying to answer such questions apply equally to all comparable research into the nature and composition of the other Germanic and non-Germanic peoples to be found in the historical sources relating to these centuries. In the case of the Alans, Sueves, and Vandals, the evidence relating to

---

[10] Heather, *Goths and Romans*, pp. 219-24.
[11] For Constantius see *PLRE* vol. 2: Constantius 17, pp. 321-5.

them is so limited in extent that it has seemed better to wait until the Visigoths entered the story before trying to tackle the difficulties involved in trying to make sense of the character, composition, and development of the so-called barbarian peoples.[12]

A few decades ago there would seem to have been no difficulty to be faced in trying to answer such questions. The various peoples who settled in the territories of the western Roman empire from the fourth century onward would have been taken to be just that: separate and coherent ethnic groups, united by their common culture, history, and genetic inheritance. In terms of their government, they would have been seen either as being led by war leaders elected from within their own number in times of military need, or as being permanently ruled by dynasties of kings of ancient lineage, whose authority might stem from their special relationship to or descent from the gods whom the people worshiped. Such a population group was usually called a tribe. Some elements of the culture of each tribe might be shared with others. In particular, several of them shared a common language, such as proto-Germanic or Gothic, but no doubt with dialectical differences to match their political separateness. While their particular tribal histories could include long-term rivalries and feuds between them, the mutual comprehensibility of their speech would be expected to provide a sense of Germanic solidarity in the face of the alien civilization of Rome.[13]

According to such an interpretation, the histories of these peoples had long been transmitted orally, but came to be written down only in the period after their establishment inside the frontiers of the former Roman empire. As such, they testified to the long-term survival of each individual tribe over centuries, and to the great distances that most of them may have traveled in the course of their existence, either buffeted by conflicts with their neighbors or taking advantage of Rome's increasing weakness. Some of these histories also seemed

---

[12] On the Alans see Kouznetsov and Lebedynsky, *Les Alains*, pp. 11-34; on the Sueves Wilhelm Reinhart, *Historia general del reino hispánico de los Suevos* (Madrid, 1952) remains the only monograph, but see the four articles devoted to them in E. A. Thompson, *Romans and Barbarians: The Decline of the Western Empire* (Madison, WI, 1982), pp. 137-229. On the Vandals the main treatment is still that of C. Courtois, *Les Vandales et l'Afrique* (Paris, 1955).

[13] e.g. Franz Altheim. *Die Krise der alten Welt* (3 vols., Berlin-Dahlem, 1943), vol. 1, pp. 83-116.

to be confirmed by what earlier generations of Roman authors, such as Tacitus, had written about the empire's previous contacts with the various Germanic peoples.

From such a perspective there was nothing inherently incredible about the narrative that could be composed from a mixture of Roman and Germanic sources about the history of the Visigoths, which would have been presented along the following lines.[14] Their origin in Scandinavia, probably southern Sweden, where Götland remains a regional name, could be dated to around the first century BC. This period of genesis was followed by a migration of the tribe across the Baltic to northeastern Germany, beyond the Elbe, in the course of the first century AD, and then a gradual southerly movement, gravitating toward the Danube. The first significant impact of the southward-migrating Goths on the Roman empire, the frontier of which was fixed on the southern bank of that river for much of its course, occurred in the mid-third century. Following their crossing of the Danube and a dramatic victory over the emperor Trajan Decius in 251, the Visigoths remained within the empire, looting and destroying for 20 years, until expelled by Claudius II Gothicus (268–70) and Aurelian (270–5).[15]

Likewise, a second Gothic people, who would become known as the Ostrogoths, followed a similar pattern of migration southward out of Scandinavia over the same period, but adopting a more easterly line of march than their Visigothic relatives. They eventually fetched up in the steppes of southern Russia along the shores of the Black Sea, having subjected a number of indigenous peoples in the region, thereby creating a Gothic empire. The Visigoths, finally pushed out of Roman territory in the early 270s, then established themselves between the Danube and the larger realm of their Ostrogothic cousins to the northeast, while continuing to threaten the imperial frontier.[16]

It was generally accepted that all of this was changed by the appearance of the Huns, a nomadic confederacy from Central Asia,

---

[14] The classic presentation of the once generally accepted view being described here is that of Ludwig Schmidt, *Geschichte der deutschen Stämme bis zum Ausgang der Völkerwanderung: die Ostgermanen* (2nd edn., Munich, 1933).

[15] For a good overview of the historiography see Peter Heather, *The Goths* (Oxford, 1996), pp. 1–18.

[16] On this "Ostrogothic Empire" see T. S. Burns, *A History of the Ostrogoths* (Bloomington, IN, 1984), pp. 18–38.

whose sudden attack around 370 led to the collapse of the Ostrogothic kingdom, then ruled by Athanaric, and the flight of some of the survivors into Visigothic lands to the southwest.[17] Under these pressures the Visigoths too soon packed their bags and begged to be admitted into the Roman empire. Once this had been conceded by the emperor Valens (364-78) in 376, the Gothic refugees quickly began to be exploited by the local imperial officials in the Danube region, upon whom they had to rely for supplies. The ruthless ill-treatment to which they were subjected led the Visigoths to revolt, aided by some smaller groups of Ostrogoths, who had accompanied them into the empire in 376. In attempting to suppress this Gothic revolt, Valens was defeated and killed at the battle of Adrianople in 378, leaving the Visigoths masters of much of the eastern half of the Balkans. Under the next emperor, Theodosius I (379-95), whose home had been in Spain, the various Gothic groups were soon brought to sign a treaty with the empire, and thereafter served in his armies in a series of civil wars fought against rival emperors in the West in 388 and 394. In the process they were reunited under the leadership of Alaric, a member of the ancient ruling house of the Balt dynasty.

Following Theodosius's death, Alaric tried to play off the imperial regimes in the two halves of the empire, now ruled by the infant sons of the late emperor, to secure a position for himself and an assured source of pay and supplies for his Visigothic followers. In the course of his attempts to coerce the western government, he led his forces into Italy in 408, and to stave off a crisis brought on by the emperor's refusal to compromise, he sacked the city of Rome in 410, shortly before his own death from natural causes. Alaric's successor Ataulph (410-15) led the Visigoths out of Italy into Gaul later that year.

This account of Gothic history seems a simple and comprehensible enough tale, and it is one that can easily be illustrated, as it always used to be in historical atlases and textbooks, by a long arrowed line that snakes all across Europe, from Scandinavia, through Germany and Hungary, into and across the Balkans, on into Italy and then France, finally ending in Spain. This line represents the movement of the Visigoths from their first home to their last, and all their travels as a migratory people in between.

---

[17] E. A. Thompson, *A History of Attila and the Huns* (Oxford, 1948), pp. 20-4.

Simplicity was at least the main virtue of this presentation of events, which also chimed in perfectly with the ideologies of the days in which it came to prominence, in which German and Roman were seen as two opposed cultural polarities. In this ideological perspective, which was highly influential in the first half of the twentieth century, a vigorous young Germanic civilization, untainted by the corruption of its decaying neighbor, first drove back Roman attempts to expand into its own homelands east of the Rhine and north of the Danube, and then, as Rome declined into extinction, came to supplant it across the whole of western Europe.[18]

This kind of thinking remained popular, and not just in Germany, until the end of the Second World War. It may then have had some of the ideological stuffing knocked out of it, but the interpretation of the composition and movements of Germanic peoples that it sustained remained in force, albeit in an increasingly fossilized form, until new views began to be advanced in the final decades of the century. It has been only in the last 10 to 15 years that these alternative interpretations have begun to gain widespread scholarly support, but achieving a complete consensus on these issues is still hampered by disagreements over points of detail.

There are many reasons why the old view of early Gothic history is no longer tenable. For one thing, the names that are conventionally used to distinguish the two bodies of Goths - "Visigoths" and "Ostrogoths" - are anachronistic. In the texts that were written in Italy and Spain in the sixth and seventh centuries, both groups are just referred to as Goths. More significantly, quite different names for them were used before the fifth century. In the Roman sources of the mid-fourth century, two confederacies were identified as dominating the region north of the Danube and the Black Sea prior to the rise of the Hun hegemony, and these were known as the *Teruingi* and the *Greuthungi*.[19] The former is often seen as being ancestral to the Visigoths and the latter to the Ostrogoths, but the contemporary narrative of the Roman historian Ammianus Marcellinus, among others, makes it clear that only certain elements of both of these groups

---

[18] For an overview of the historiography see Malcolm Todd, *The Early Germans* (Oxford, 1992), pp. 256-69; see also Walter Goffart, "Two Notes on Germanic Antiquity Today," *Traditio* 50 (1995), pp. 9-30.

[19] Ammianus Marcellinus, *Res Gestae* XXXI. iii. 1-xiii. 19 *passim*, ed. J. C. Rolfe (3 vols., London and Cambridge, MA, 1952), vol. 3, pp. 394-482.

crossed into Roman territory in the 370s, leaving others still settled north of the Danube.[20]

To cut a long story short, it is now generally accepted that the self-identification of the people who are now known as the Visigoths (and who would have thought of themselves as just being Goths) was the product of the years that followed the battle of Adrianople in 378. In this confused period all sorts of individuals and groups from a wide variety of cultural, genetic, and linguistic backgrounds were welded together, largely through recruitment by and service under the emperor Theodosius I. They were deliberately not integrated into Roman society in the Balkans, and were kept on a military footing under a leadership of their own, probably to maintain their mobility and loyalty to the emperor. By around 392 immediate leadership of this confederacy was being exercised by Alaric, who took advantage of the emperor Theodosius's death in 395, and the succeeding division of the empire, to establish the independence of his following, as effectively a mercenary army that was prepared to take service with whichever imperial regime offered the best terms.[21] There is no real evidence that Alaric belonged to any long-established ruling house, with or without a supposedly divine ancestry.[22]

It would be tempting to think that there ought to be marked and obvious differences between a Roman army and a barbarian confederacy in this period, but this would not be true. Throughout the fourth century the empire had recruited increasing numbers of its soldiers from Germanic and other peoples beyond its frontiers. In terms of material culture, Roman influence had been so pervasive that there was little to distinguish imperial troops from those recruited from outside the empire, either in terms of their weapons or of their dress and appearance.[23]

---

[20] Ibid. XXXI. iv. 1-5, pp. 400-3.
[21] Herwig Wolfram, *History of the Goths*, trans. Thomas J. Dunlap (Berkeley, CA, 1988), pp. 117-50.
[22] P. Grierson, "Election and Inheritance in Early Germanic Kingship," *Cambridge Historical Journal* 7 (1941), pp. 1-22.
[23] Walter Pohl, "Telling the Difference: Signs of Ethnic Identity," in W. Pohl and H. Reimitz (eds.), *Strategies of Distinction: The Construction of Ethnic Communities, 300-800* (Leiden, 1998), pp. 17-69. Patrick Amory, *People and Identity in Ostrogothic Italy, 489-554* (Cambridge, 1997), pp. 277-313 and 338-47. On Late Roman military equipment and dress see Pat Southern and Karen R. Dixon, *The Late Roman Army* (London, 1996), pp. 89-126.

Religion was also not a major differentiating factor, in that all of the Germanic groups found inside the imperial frontiers from the late fourth century onward seem to have been Christian.[24] This may seem rather surprising, but no indications exist to the contrary, and, to take the most pertinent case, the Visigoths were praised by Orosius for not looting ecclesiastical vessels and for not harming those of the citizens who had taken refuge in churches in the course of their sack of Rome in 410.[25] Whether they were so sensitive in practice is another matter. Orosius's argument would have been entirely undermined had the Goths been generally thought of as being pagans.

The social composition of a German confederate force would also not have distinguished it from its imperial equivalent. Roman armies, when moving their bases, whatever may have been true of the early empire, would by this period have always been accompanied by the families of the soldiers, and a great variety of camp followers, making them again indistinguishable from non-Roman units.[26] In such terms a Roman army on the march was no different to a Germanic "people" supposedly migrating.

In fact it is necessary to abandon the imagery and terminology of migration when looking at the movements of "barbarians" in this period. For one thing, there was no self-evident incentive for such people to move from what had been their traditional homelands, where their ancestors were buried and where, to judge by later parallels, their gods would have been linked to particular sacred places.[27] While Roman civilization served as a lure for individuals or small groups who might hope to enrich themselves through imperial service (and then possibly return home with the proceeds), this is not the same as the physical uprooting of a whole society. Only certain extreme pressures, economic, climatic, or military, could lead to a large-scale abandonment of their settlements by the bulk of the population.

---

[24] E. A. Thompson, "Christianity and the Northern Barbarians," in Arnaldo Momigliano (ed.), *The Conflict between Paganism and Christianity in the Fourth Century* (Oxford, 1963), pp. 56–78; see also D. H. Green, "Problems of Christianization," in idem, *Language and History in the Early Germanic World* (Cambridge, 1998), pp. 275–90, and A. Schwarcz, "Cult and Religion among the Tervingi and the Visigoths and their Conversion to Christianity," in Heather (ed.), *The Visigoths*, pp. 447–59.
[25] Orosius VII. 39, ed. Zangemeister, pp. 544–8.
[26] Southern and Dixon, *Late Roman Army*, pp. 85–6.
[27] Green, *Language and History*, pp. 13–29.

Some such pressures were clearly exerted in the 370s, possibly from all three causes, but it is still important to note that many of the inhabitants of the lands north of the Danube did not abandon their lands to enter Roman territory, even if this involved their becoming subject to the Huns, whose "empire" depended upon the continuing existence of large elements of earlier populations in the lands north of the Danube and the Black Sea.[28]

It makes more sense to see new ethnic identities being formed among those who had, for whatever reasons, been forced to leave their homeland, who had been thrown together in a new location, and who had come to adopt a new and predominantly military lifestyle.[29] As previously mentioned, the so-called Visigothic confederacy in the Balkans after the treaty of 381 was a permanent military force in the service of the emperor and was generally supplied by the imperial administration or was permitted to requisition from the civilian population. This was quite different to the self-sufficient agrarian lifestyle of the peoples north of the Danube, who were not normally on such a permanent war footing, except when under attack.[30]

If it be accepted that a new Gothic identity was created in the eastern Balkans in this period, just as a second one, that of the so-called Ostrogoths, would also emerge in the very same area about a century later, it should be asked what gave it its distinguishing characteristics. The old view that saw the Visigoths as the *Teruingi* under a new name would not have found this a question in need of asking. But Alaric's confederacy of Goths, which took shape in the 390s, was actually made up from elements not just of *Teruingi* and *Greuthungi* but also from several other ethnic groups from both north and south of the Danube. Furthermore, this confederacy would subsequently pick up and drop off components of itself in the course of its movements through the western Balkans, Italy, and Gaul between the years 405 and 415.[31] Its composition was thus both varied and constantly changing.

---

[28] Heather, *The Goths*, pp. 109-29.
[29] Peter Heather, "The Creation of the Visigoths," in idem (ed.), *The Visigoths from the Migration Period to the Seventh Century* (Woodbridge, 1999), pp. 43-73.
[30] Michel Kazanski, *Les Goths (Ier-VIIe après J.-C.)* (Paris, 1991), pp. 39-55.
[31] J. H. W. G. Liebeschuetz, "Alaric's Goths: Nation or Army?" in John Drinkwater and Hugh Elton (eds.), *Fifth-century Gaul: A Crisis of Identity?* (Cambridge, 1992), pp. 75-83; Heather, *The Goths*, pp. 174-8; see also Wolfram, *History of the Goths*, pp. 150-71, who emphasizes the importance of the period up to 416 in the processes of "Visigothic ethnogenesis."

What, therefore, provided the sense of identity and continuity that kept this grouping of disparate elements united? Several of the most influential modern scholars who have been studying these processes, for which they have coined the term "ethnogenesis," have come from the University of Vienna, and hence have come generically to be called "the Vienna School."[32] For them the answer to the question of what gave a confederacy such as that of Alaric its sense of identity was the existence of what they call a *Traditionskern*, or core tradition. This provided the sense of a common history for the group, stretching back into the distant past, and was primarily embodied in the existence of an ancient royal lineage, whose dynastic traditions became those of the people they ruled. Allied to and supporting this central ruling family was an inner core of a warrior elite, which formed an aristocracy.[33] Other historians have disputed this interpretation, preferring, for example, to see the *Traditionskern* as being provided by the presence of a wider social group of families of middling economic and social standing.[34]

It must be admitted that neither view is entirely satisfactory, as there is no evidence at all, other than for claims made at much later dates, that Alaric and his successors were linked in any way to the former rulers of the *Teruingi*. The latter do not seem in any case to have had permanent war leaders of the kind represented by Alaric.[35] Similarly, none of the various and often rival leaders of the Goths in the years immediately following the entry into the empire in 376 and the battle of Adrianople in 378 can be shown to be related to Alaric. He emerges as if from nowhere in 392. Nor can the long-term survival of significant sectors of either the upper or the middle echelons of this society be established across the divide represented by the years around 376 to 392. Neither an aristocracy nor a hypothetical class of "yeomen" can thus provide the core on which a sense of common identity and shared tradition might be based.

---

[32] See the works by Wolfram and Pohl previously referred to; for criticism of the approach adopted see A. C. Murray, "Reinhard Wenskus on 'Ethnogenesis', Ethnicity, and the Origin of the Franks," in Andrew Gillett (ed.), *On Barbarian Identity: Critical Approaches to Ethnicity in the Early Middle Ages* (Turnhout, 2002), pp. 39-68.

[33] See Wolfram, *History of the Goths*, pp. 36-116.

[34] Heather, *The Goths*, pp. 299-321.

[35] Herwig Wolfram, "Athanaric the Visigoth: Monarchy or Judgeship. A Study in Comparative History," *Journal of Medieval History* 1 (1975), pp. 259-78.

It is worth noting too that arguments about the movements of the *Teruingi* in the centuries before 376 remain equally porous. Central and Eastern European archaeologists have tried to link the material remains of two specific cultures with the literary evidence relating to the prehistory of the Goths, and they believe that this substantiates the idea that a coherent body of people moved from the area south of the Baltic to the Danube and the Black Sea in the course of the first three centuries AD.[36] Virtually everyone would now discard the idea of a prior origin in southern Scandinavia. However, this archaeological argument depends in part upon purely negative evidence, such as the lack of weapons burials in the two cultures.[37] In the absence of literary sources, it is also impossible for us to know if a sense of common identity existed between the two archaeologically defined populations.

For present purposes, however, it is enough to accept that the Goths who came to make themselves masters of Spain in the course of the fifth century derived from a confederacy of different ethnic groups that was brought together and given a new common sense of identity in the Balkans in the last quarter of the fourth century. They formed a mercenary army that tried to secure employment for itself from successive imperial regimes, and when this was not forthcoming, was increasingly obliged to look to its own interests.

An obvious question is that of the probable size of this and other such confederacies, not least as this has an important bearing on the understanding of what happened when the Visigoths finally came to settle permanently in Spain. The figures that are normally quoted suggest that the Visigoths may have numbered around 100,000, while smaller confederacies, such as those of the Alans, Sueves, and Vandals, are more likely to have been in the order of 20,000 strong.[38] There are no firm quantitative grounds for making these or other estimates of population size, which depend upon a handful of statements in early sources, and no real reliance should be placed in them.

Even if only from the vantage of common sense, it must be recognized that a group such as that of the Goths, almost continuously on the move between 392 and 419, and for most of that time depending

---

[36] For a helpful overview of these arguments see Peter Heather and John Matthews, *The Goths in the Fourth Century* (Liverpool, 1991), pp. 51-101; also Heather, *The Goths*, pp. 11-50.
[37] Heather, *The Goths*, pp. 23, 72-3.
[38] A. H. M. Jones, *The Later Roman Empire* (3 vols., Oxford, 1964), vol. 1, pp. 195-6.

on its own resources, could maintain its coherence only as long as it was able to support itself materially. If food was not being provided from the granaries of the Roman state, drawing primarily on the resources of Africa, it would have to be acquired locally and by force. Far smaller quantities of supplies would have been available under such circumstances, and these would depend on seasonal and other conditions. It is very hard to believe that a body of people as large as 100,000 could support itself in such conditions, and in a hostile environment. It is probably more realistic to see the Visigothic confederacy as being no more than the size of a small Roman army. Together with family members, this may have amounted to something in the region of 30,000 people at most. The number of the Vandals, Alans, and Sueves would certainly have been fewer, as their history would suggest; 10,000 might not be too conservative an estimate in their cases. If these numbers seem small, it is important to remember that by this period there were few if any larger military forces that might challenge them.

It may still be wondered why a clear ethnic distinction seems to have existed between Goths and Romans, and also why it was that various Roman emperors, legitimate and otherwise, needed to make use of the military services offered by the Visigoths (as for convenience we shall continue to call them, not least to help distinguish them from the second Gothic confederacy, that of the Ostrogoths). The second of these questions is the easier to answer, in that as the history of the fifth century unfolds, it becomes harder and harder to find traces of the presence of a specifically Roman army, in either the eastern or the western half of the Empire.[39] Units that had existed at the beginning of the century disappear rapidly, especially in the West. The army in Britain, one of the largest concentrations of military forces in the western provinces, was taken to Gaul by Constantine III in 407 and does not seem to have survived his fall in 411. The smaller number of troops in Spain were withdrawn by Gerontius to fight in Gaul in 410, and were not returned to the peninsula following his killing.[40] Thus by around 416, while there were still imperial armies commanded by generals appointed by the emperor to be found in

---

[39] Southern and Dixon, *The Late Roman Army*, pp. 179-80; Collins, *Early Medieval Europe* (2nd edn.), pp. 80-99.
[40] Orosius VII. 42, ed. Zangemeister, p. 556.

Italy and Africa (until 432) and in parts of southern Gaul, the Roman units that had once had their bases in Britain, Spain, and northern Gaul had all been withdrawn from those provinces or had been disbanded. Into the vacuum thus created came the mercenary armies of the so-called barbarians.

The Gothic Conquest of Hispania, 456-507

Alaric's successor Ataulph (410-15) is said by the contemporary Spanish historian Orosius, who was quoting a former friend of the king, to have contemplated the creation of a Gothic state, thus replacing *Romania* by *Gothia*.[41] However, he decided instead to put his forces at the service of the Roman state. He married Galla Placidia, the half-sister of the emperor Honorius, who had been carried off in the sack of Rome in 410, and he began negotiating a military role for himself and his following with the imperial government. These plans may already have been far advanced when he was murdered in 415 in Barcelona, in a short-lived coup led by a personal enemy.[42] The murderer, Sigeric, was himself killed a week later.

That Ataulph was in Spain at this time probably means that the arrangements for Gothic military service in the peninsula, which were finalized under his successor Wallia (415-19), had already been made by the time of his death. Under Wallia, who returned Galla Placidia to her brother's court, the Goths carried out a series of campaigns for the emperor in the Iberian peninsula, to eliminate the Alans, Sueves, and Vandals, and to put an end to the regime of the usurping emperor Maximus.[43] The details of this war have not been preserved, but the Visigoths proved highly effective, destroying the Alans and the Siling Vandals, before being withdrawn from Spain in 419 to be established in Aquitaine in southwestern Gaul as the result of a new treaty with the empire.[44]

---

[41] Orosius VII. 43, ed. Zangemeister, p. 560. On this see J. M. Wallace-Hadrill, "Gothia and Romania," in idem, *The Long-Haired Kings and Other Studies in Frankish History* (London, 1962), pp. 25-48.
[42] Orosius VII. 43, ed. Zangemeister, p. 561.
[43] Wolfram, *History of the Goths*, pp. 170-1.
[44] T. S. Burns, "The Settlement of 418," in Drinkwater and Elton (eds.), *Fifth-century Gaul*, pp. 53-63.

It has been suggested that the imperial government, dominated by the *Magister Militum* Constantius, had become worried by the success of the Goths and feared that they would merely take over from the Vandals and Sueves as the new masters of the Iberian peninsula. On the other hand, if that was the case it would have to asked why they were given control of the important Gallic province of *Aquitania Secunda* instead. It is more likely that the Roman administration felt that military problems facing southern Gaul were of greater and more pressing importance than what by then may have seemed no more than mopping-up operations in Spain. It could have been the growth of the threat from the *Bagaudae* north of the Loire in these very same years that influenced imperial policy into moving the Goths from Spain to Aquitaine.

While the presence of *Bagaudae* does not seem to have been a problem affecting Spain at this time, it would soon become one. So it is worth trying to understand what was meant by this term, which appears in a number of fifth- and sixth-century chronicles.[45] Unfortunately, these references are far from informative, in that they tend to do no more than mention the presence of *Bagaudae*, the damage they may have caused, and their violent suppression by military forces in the pay of the empire, without ever once defining the term itself. Its significance must have been self-evident or well known to contemporary readers. In consequence a number of suggestions have been made as to what the word may have meant.

That the *Bagaudae* were a class or group and that they represented some form of threat to the Roman landowners is clear enough from the mention of the destruction they wrought and the urgency of the military steps taken to counter them. Beyond that there is less agreement, and they have been seen as standing somewhere on a spectrum that extends from starving peasants to class-conscious social revolutionaries.[46] In reality they are most likely to have been bandits, drawn from a number of different social classes, including

---

[45] J. F. Drinkwater, "The Bacaudae of Fifth-century Gaul," in Drinkwater and Elton (eds.), *Fifth-century Gaul*, pp. 208-17.

[46] J. F. Drinkwater, "Patronage in Roman Gaul and the Problem of the Bagaudae," in A. Wallace-Hadrill (ed.), *Patronage in Ancient Society* (London, 1989), pp. 189-203; E. A. Thompson, "Peasant Revolts in Late Roman Gaul and Spain," *Past and Present* 2 (1952), pp. 11-23, and idem, "Some Recent Studies of the Bacaudae," in idem, *Romans and Barbarians*, pp. 221-3.

slaves and dispossessed small farmers, driven by the political and economic upheavals of the time into joining ever-expanding gangs of those unable any longer to support themselves from their own resources. Although not a well-known phenomenon in western Europe, such large-scale bandit gangs are frequently encountered in the history of other parts of the world during comparable periods of political and economic disturbance.[47]

It is one way in which a rural population can try to support itself when normal patterns of production and economic exchange have broken down over a wide area or an extended period. By combining to raid those, such as the landowners and the town-dwellers who still controlled food supplies and other resources previously acquired from the countryside, the rural population could maintain itself in conditions that had temporarily made agriculture and marketing impossible. Similarly, such a large-scale combination was a possible reaction in times when the rural population's own resources were being taken from them by force by other armed gangs, such as unemployed mercenary units or unpaid government soldiers. Once a certain critical momentum had been reached, such groups of bandits would be able to raid the estates of the landowning classes, attack and sack towns and other settlements, and even try to take on professional troops in battle or guerrilla warfare.

Britain had passed out of imperial control in 410, and Gaul north of the Loire seems to have been left to look after itself from 406 onwards. The unchecked growth of bandits in this area is thus not surprising, and the relative lack of large aristocratic estates in the region meant that the reimposition of order was less of a priority for the imperial government than would have been the case with the wealthier provinces in the south.[48] The fear of the extension of the Bagaudic threat across the Loire may thus explain the decision to establish a permanent military presence, as provided by the Goths, in the southwest in 419.

---

[47] The best-documented cases of this phenomenon are to be found in the history of China, particularly in the periods of dynastic decline and replacement. See Frederic Wakeman Jnr. *The Great Enterprise: The Manchu Reconstruction of Imperial Order in Seventeenth-Century China* (2 vols., Berkeley, CA, 1985), vol. 1, chs. 3–4 and 7–8 for some interesting parallels.

[48] E. A. Thompson, "The Settlement of the Barbarians in Southern Gaul," reprinted in idem, *Romans and Barbarians*, pp. 23–37.

Meanwhile in Spain, the remnants of the Alans took refuge with the Hasding Vandals, and some later references suggest they retained their ethnic distinctiveness within the confederacy until both disappear completely from the historical record in 535.[49] Of the Siling Vandals no more is heard. The Sueves, who seem to have been established in garrisons in the northwest of the peninsula, may have been quite untouched by the Visigothic campaigns of 416 to 419, which were probably concentrated in the areas to the south and east. They retained their hold on northern Lusitania and Galicia in the aftermath of the Gothic withdrawal.

The Hasding Vandals, now swelled by the influx of Alan and other fugitives, were the main beneficiaries of the premature termination of the Gothic attempt to regain Spain for the Roman government. They made themselves masters of much of the peninsula in the absence of further military opposition. Not until 422 would another attempt be made to eliminate them. On this occasion an imperial army was sent from Italy under the *Magister Militum* Castinus, which was intended to cooperate with Gothic auxiliaries provided by the new king of the Visigoths, Theoderic I (419-51). The latter was less interested in the Roman alliance than his predecessor, and whether with his connivance or not, his detachments failed to support Castinus, who was defeated by the Vandals in the province of Baetica and forced to withdraw.[50] The only achievement of his campaign was the capture of the fugitive emperor Maximus, who was taken to Ravenna and executed. Direct Roman rule in the peninsula was thereafter confined to the coastal parts of the province of Tarraconensis and the mid to lower Ebro valley.

Castinus himself went on to serve as the military leader behind the short-lived regime of Johannes, who was made emperor following the death of Honorius in 423. Refused recognition in the East, he was overthrown in 425 by an expedition sent from Constantinople, which installed a new western emperor in the person of Valentinian III, the son of Honorius's sister Galla Placidia and of Constantius, the military supremo of Honorius's last years, who had himself briefly been emperor in 421.

---

[49] Courtois, *Les Vandales*, p. 229: a silver *missorium* of Gailamir (530-3), the last Vandal king, is inscribed: GAILAMIR REX VANDALORVM ET ALANORVM.

[50] Hydatius, 28th year of Honorius, ed. Burgess, pp. 86, 88; *PLRE* vol. 2: Castinus 2, pp. 269-70.

The weakness of Johannes's regime and the rivalries of military commanders in Italy, Africa, and Gaul in the first five years of the reign of Valentinian III meant that no attention was given to further attempts to reimpose imperial rule in Spain. However, the jockeying for power between rival Roman military commanders did have a significant impact upon the Vandals, who by now were the unchallenged masters of most of the Iberian peninsula. In 427 a civil war broke out between Boniface, the Count of Africa, and Felix, Master of the Soldiers in Italy, possibly as the result of a plot by Aetius, the commander in southern Gaul. Although the first expedition Felix sent against his rival was defeated, the threat of a second may have led to Boniface entering into an agreement in 428 or 429 with the Vandal king Gaiseric, to bring his forces into Africa.[51]

Soon after, Aetius's role in setting Felix and Boniface against each other was revealed, but in May 430 he was able to murder Felix and seize power in Italy. The imperial court, led by Galla Placidia, the emperor's mother, turned to Boniface, and he withdrew his army from Africa for a confrontation with Aetius. He won the battle but died soon after from wounds received, and control over the now much diminished empire in the West fell into the hands of Aetius, who continued to exercise it until his murder by the emperor himself in 454. One consequence of all this was the removal of the last Roman military presence, and the introduction into the African provinces of the Vandals and Alans, who completed their conquest with the capture of Carthage in 439.[52] Their possession of Africa was recognized by a treaty with the empire in 442.

What does seem clear, though, is that initially the Vandals did not give up their position in Spain. In the aftermath of the transfer of their forces to Africa in 429, various Suevic bands moved into the south from Galicia, where they had been confined since 411/12, but the Vandal king sent a detachment of his army back, and the over-optimistic Sueves, led by Hermigar, were defeated near Mérida in 430.[53] This, however, was the last Vandal involvement in the peninsula. Faced with the need to impose themselves by force in Africa and until 442 by the threat of imperial attempts to eliminate them,

---

[51] *PLRE* vol. 2: Bonifatius 3, pp. 237–40.
[52] Courtois, *Les Vandales*, pp. 169–74.
[53] Hydatius, 5th year of Theodosius II, ed. Burgess, p. 90.

the Vandals concentrated all their efforts on making themselves masters of their new territories, leaving Spain to the Sueves, now the sole survivors in the peninsula of the invaders of 409.

Under their kings Rechila (438-48) and his son Rechiarius (448-55), the Sueves established themselves in Mérida (439) and extended their rule over most of the west and the south of Spain, with only the province of Tarraconensis remaining under direct imperial control. This was exercised in the emperor's name by a succession of military commanders, of whom several are known.[54] Among the problems now faced by the latter were outbreaks of Bagaudic activity in the middle Ebro valley, in which a number of towns seem to have been sacked.[55]

In the 430s and 440s, the imperial government based in Ravenna became concerned almost exclusively with preserving its control over southern Gaul, and by extension Tarraconensis, and was even willing to concede Africa to the Vandals in 442. The invasion of Gaul by the Huns under Attila in 451 undermined the authority of Aetius, leading to his murder by the emperor in 454, which in turn resulted in Valentinian III's own assassination as an act of revenge in 455. In the period of chaos that ensued the Sueves raided the province of Carthaginiensis, perhaps as a preliminary to its complete conquest. Imperial attempts at a diplomatic solution were rejected, and the Suevic king launched an attack on the province of Tarraconensis, but his ambition proved fatal not only to himself but also to his kingdom.[56]

In the disorder following the elimination of Valentinian III and with him the Theodosian dynasty in 455, a Gallic aristocrat called Avitus took the throne with Visigothic military backing.[57] Sharing the perspective of Aetius on the primary importance of retaining direct rule over southern Gaul, he allowed or encouraged his Gothic allies, now ruled by Theoderic II (453-66) to counter the new Suevic threat to Tarraconensis. In 456 Theoderic led his army into Spain against Rechiarius, although the latter was his brother-in-law. The Sueves were completely defeated at a battle on the river Orbigo near Astorga.

---

[54] These include Astyrius (441-3), Merobaudes (443), Vitus (446), Nepotianus (458/9-61), and Arborius (461-5): *PLRE* vol. 2, p. 1289, and individual entries for each of them.
[55] Hydatius, 17th and 19th years of Theodosius II, ed. Burgess, p. 96.
[56] Ibid. 4th and 5th years of Marcian, ed. Burgess, pp. 104.
[57] *PLRE* vol. 2: Avitus 5, pp. 196-8.

In the subsequent flight Rechiarius was captured and executed, and the Suevic monarchy disintegrated.[58] A number of rival warlords are reported fighting among themselves and against the Goths in the course of the next decade, before an evidential silence descends for nearly a century.[59] It seems, though, that the remnants of the Sueves and their feuding rulers were driven back into northern Lusitania and Galicia in the aftermath of 455, while the Visigoths took direct control of most of the rest of the peninsula, other than for the coastal regions of Tarraconensis and parts of the Ebro valley, which still remained under imperial rule.

The last emperor to visit the Iberian peninsula was Majorian (458-63), whose primary concern was the launching of an attack on the Vandals, who, after they had carried out the second sack of Rome in 455, were now regarded as the main threat to the very diminished imperial interests in the West. According to some of the few surviving entries from a sixth-century chronicle that may well have been written in Zaragoza, Majorian arrived in Spain in 460.[60] He made a formal entry or *adventus* into *Caesaraugusta* (Zaragoza) in that year, but does not seem to have interfered with Visigothic control over most of the peninsula. The fleet that he was preparing for the invasion of Africa was captured in the harbour of Cartagena in a surprise attack by the Vandals, and the emperor was forced to abandon his plan.[61] Returning to Italy in 461, he was deposed by his Master of the Soldiers, Ricimer, who was of mixed Suevic and Gothic origin, and Majorian was executed.[62]

Roman rule in the Ebro valley and on the Mediterranean coast was finally terminated by the Visigothic king Euric (466-84), who murdered

---

[58] Hydatius, 5th and 6th years of Marcian, ed. Burgess, pp. 104, 106.
[59] The few available references to the doings of the rival Suevic warlords of the years 456-64 will be found in the final section of Hydatius's chronicle. Attempts have been made to identify an early sixth-century Suevic king "Veremundus" on the basis of an inscription found at Vairão, between Oporto and Braga in northern Portugal, but this can only refer to the Leonese king Vermudo II (982-99).
[60] See Carmen Cardelle de Hartmann (ed.), *Victoris Tunnunnensis Chronicon cum reliquiis ex Consularibus Caesaraugustanis et Johannis Biclarensis Chronicon* (= *Corpus Christianorum Series Latina*, vol. CLXXIIIA, Turnhout, 2001): Victor 23a, p. 10; see also the *Commentaria Historica* by Roger Collins, ibid., pp. 96-7.
[61] Hydatius, 4th year of Leo and Majorian, ed. Burgess, p. 112.
[62] Ibid. 5th year of Leo and Majorian, ed. Burgess, p. 112. For Ricimer see *PLRE* vol. II: Fl. Ricimer 2, pp. 942-4.

his brother Theoderic II in 466.[63] At the time southern Gaul still remained the primary area of Visigothic occupation, and Toulouse served as the administrative center and principal royal residence, despite the conquest of much of Spain in 455/6.[64] As imperial rule in the West further declined in the 460s and 470s, more Gallic territory was acquired by Euric by war or by treaty, culminating in the Gothic occupation of Provence and the Roman cession to him of the Auvergne in 474. Following the deposition of Romulus in 476, Euric's generals rapidly overran the remaining parts of northeastern Spain still administered directly by the empire.[65]

By about 480 at the latest the Visigothic kingdom in Gaul had come to extend from the valleys of the Loire and the Rhône to the Pyrenees and now also encompassed all of the Iberian peninsula, except for Galicia, which remained in the hands of the Sueves. Euric himself died of natural causes in 484, and the kingdom he had so greatly enlarged was inherited by his son Alaric II (484-507). Under the new king some major, if poorly recorded, changes took place. The *Consularia Caesaraugustana*, or "Consular(-dated) Chronicle of Zaragoza," contains an entry assigned to the year 494, reporting that "in this consulship the Goths entered Spain." A second one, for the year 497, adds "in this consulship the Goths acquired settlements (*sedes acceperant*) in Spain."[66]

While these brief statements raise more questions than they answer, it has generally been accepted that they record a process of the relocation of Visigothic settlement out of southern Gaul and into Spain, taking place in the mid-490s. It should firmly be noted that this can not be corroborated archaeologically. The royal court, however, remained at Toulouse, and following Alaric's marriage to the daughter of the Ostrogothic king Theoderic, who had made himself ruler of

---

[63] *PLRE* vol. 2: Euricus, pp. 427-8.
[64] Ana María Jiménez Garnica, *Orígenes y desarrollo del Reino visigodo de Tolosa* (Valladolid, 1983) remains the only book devoted to the Visigothic kingdom of Toulouse, but there is a susbtantial treatment of it in Wolfram, *History of the Goths*, pp. 172-246.
[65] *Chronica Gallica A. DXI*, items 651 and 652, ed. T. Mommsen, *Chronica Minora*, vol. 1, *MGH AA* vol. IX, pp. 664-5.
[66] Entries taken from this source are to be found as marginalia in some of the manuscripts containing the chronicles of Victor of Tunnunna and of John of Biclarum. On this text see *Victoris Tunnunnensis Chronicon*, ed. Hartmann, pp. *115-*124; for the two entries - Victor, 71a and 75a - see pp. 22-3; also the *commentary*, pp. 100-1.

Italy in 493, economic and political interests became even more strongly focused on southern Gaul.[67]

What had happened in the intervening decades to the descendants of those warriors who had followed the Gothic king Ataulph out of Italy in 410/11 is not easy to say. Were the followers of Alaric II still little more than an occupying army, distributed in garrisons across the major towns and cities of southern Gaul and to a lesser extent Spain? Or had there been a major social transformation in the course of the fifth century, involving a redistribution of Roman senatorial estates, which had turned the upper levels of Gothic society into a landed aristocracy? What roles were played by those who would have called themselves Goths but who did not belong to the upper stratum of this society? May they have become the dependents of those Visigothic nobles who wished to build up their own individual military followings, or did there now exist a class of Gothic peasant proprietors, freely owning small amounts of land?

None of these questions can receive a certain answer. The issue of whether the Goths benefited from a redistribution of Roman estates that they farmed directly, or whether they only received the taxation due on such lands, and thus remained as no more than a garrisoning army of occupation, has aroused much scholarly debate.[68] This has focused above all on the meaning of the term *Hospitalitas*, which was used to describe divisions carried out at the behest of the Roman imperial government between the local civil aristocracy and incoming barbarian "guests" in various parts of the western empire at different times in the course of the fifth century.

In the case of Gaul, this involved the assigning to the Goths of two-thirds of Roman estates. That this formally took place can be established from a variety of sources, but what it involved in practice is much less easy or even impossible to determine. An expropriation of land on such a scale would have been totally unprecedented, and it is hard to see what legal justification could have been used to validate it. An adjustment in the payment of tax, with two-thirds of what was owed on each estate going directly to designated Gothic recipients, rather than to the imperial government's increasingly inefficient fiscal

---

[67] Jiménez Garnica, *Orígenes y desarrollo*, pp. 97-130.
[68] Walter Goffart, *Barbarians and Romans* A.D. *418-584: The Techniques of Accommodation* (Princeton, NJ, 1980).

administration, might seem the more logical explanation. Even so, the available evidence does not prove that this is what actually happened, and some of it may support the older view of a physical distribution of land.[69] The reassignment of tax revenue theory would, however, make more sense of the cryptic references in the *Consularia Caesaraugustana* to the movement of Goths into Spain in the 490s, as it is otherwise not easy to see why at that period they would have been so willing to move from what by the other interpretation would have been well-established farming properties in Gaul.

Whatever happened, and whatever their causes, these events coincided with a period of political turmoil in the peninsula that is only dimly recorded in a handful of entries in the *Consularia*. In relation to the year 496 it is reported that "Burdunellus became a tyrant in Spain," and in the following year he was "handed over by his own men and having been sent to Toulouse, he was placed inside a bronze bull and burnt to death."[70] "Burdunellus" means "Little Mule" and may be only a nickname. To say that he tried to establish a tyranny would almost certainly imply that he tried to set himself up as emperor, though where he did so is unfortunately not recorded. The distinctively Zaragozan character of some of the *Consularia*'s information may suggest that it was in this city, or at least in the Ebro valley, that Burdunellus made his bid for local authority. His bizarre execution, while unparalleled, seems to belong to the Roman tradition of the public humiliation and degrading killing of failed political rivals.[71]

This was not the only case of its kind in this period. For the year 506 the *Consularia* reports that the Goths took Dertosa, and killed "the tyrant Peter," whose head was then sent to Zaragoza for public exposure.[72] Lacking in clarity and context as these two episodes may be, they certainly seem to indicate that Visigothic royal authority in Spain was far from widespread and securely established, and that

---

[69] S. J. Barnish, "Taxation, Land and Barbarian Settlement in the Western Empire," *Papers of the British School at Rome* 54 (1986), pp. 170-95.
[70] *Victoris Tunnunnensis Chronicon*, ed. Hartmann: Victor 74a, 75a, p. 23; commentary, pp. 100-1.
[71] On the survival of Late Antique forms of exemplary punishment for political offenses, such as a failed bid to seize the throne, see Michael McCormack, *Eternal Victory: Triumphal Rulership in Late Antiquity, Byzantium and the Early Medieval West* (Cambridge, 1986), pp. 80-130.
[72] *Victoris Tunnunnensis Chronicon*, ed. Hartmann: Victor 87a, p. 27; commentary, p. 102.

local rulers could try to set themselves up in various parts of the peninsula – a phenomenon that was equally marked in the sixth and seventh centuries (and for a long time after the Arab conquest as well). In the light of the very limited nature of the evidence relating to Spain in the fifth century, it is very likely that Burdunellus and Peter were not the only rebels who attempted to establish a "tyrannical" local regime in this period.

It was not from threats such as these, however, that the Gothic kings had most to fear. While they had conquered much of Spain in 456 as allies of the emperor Avitus, and had close ties with the military dictator Ricimer, who dominated the imperial government from 463 up to his death in 472, a succession of independent Roman warlords had established control over much of Gaul north of the Loire, and there were frequent clashes between them and the Visigoths. More significantly, the breakdown of local order in this region gave some of the Franks, another Germanic confederacy, the opportunity to expand their power westward from the area of the lower Rhine, where they had been established since the mid-fourth century.[73]

Clovis, one of a small number of rival Frankish leaders, proved particularly successful, in ca.486 eliminating Syagrius, the last of the independent Roman rulers in northern Gaul, and thus making his Merovingian Frankish kingdom the new northern neighbors of the Visigoths in the valley of the Loire. Clovis and his followers next expanded eastward at the expense of the Alamans, and then southward down the Rhône, greatly reducing the territory and power of the kingdom of the Burgundians.[74] By the beginning of the sixth century the Goths had become the next likely targets of Clovis's expansionary ambitions.

While diplomatic efforts were made, not least by the Ostrogothic king Theoderic, to contain Clovis, war between him and Alaric II broke out in 507. The Burgundians allied themselves with the Franks. In a battle fought at Vouillé near Poitiers, the Visigothic army was defeated and king Alaric was killed. In the aftermath the Franks and Burgundians rapidly overran most of the Gothic kingdom in Gaul. Toulouse fell, and Frankish forces briefly reached as far as Barcelona.[75]

---

[73] Edward James, *The Franks* (Oxford, 1988), pp. 35-77.
[74] Ian Wood, *The Merovingian Kingdoms 450-751* (London, 1994), pp. 41-9.
[75] *Chronica Gallica A. DXI*, items 688-91, ed. Mommsen, pp. 665-6.

Further losses were prevented by the armed intervention of the Ostrogoths, who overran Provence in 508 and forced Clovis to withdraw from Septimania, the region between the lower Rhône and the Pyrenees, which thereafter remained the sole enclave of the Visigothic kingdom in Gaul up till the Arab conquest.

It may be that the outcome of the battle of Vouillé had to some extent been determined by the processes so obliquely referred to in the *Consularia*, and that significant movements of Visigothic forces out of Gaul into Spain in the 490s left the Gallic part of the kingdom more vulnerable to Frankish assault. In any event, the loss of Toulouse and most of their Gallic territories in 507/8 meant that it would be in the Iberian peninsula that the Visigothic kings would have to rebuild their weakened authority.

2

The Imposition of Unity, 507–586

A Fractured Kingdom

The defeat by the Franks at Vouillé in 507 of an apparently strong and expanding Visigothic kingdom, which had hitherto been the dominant power in southern and eastern Gaul, was followed by a period of weakness and instability. In itself, the outcome of the battle was not surprising. Victory or defeat in such conflicts could depend upon a variety of short-term factors, such as the superior generalship of one of the two commanders. The outcome of a battle could be conditioned by differences in morale between the two armies, but it certainly did not reflect any long-term moral superiority of one side over the other, as is sometimes implied.

But for all of the chance or accidental factors that affected the result, military victory often had dramatic and far-reaching consequences in the early medieval centuries. The Visigothic kingdom in Spain would be destroyed in 711 in ways that were very similar to these events in 507 that put an end to its existence in Gaul. A single battle was crucial to the outcome in both cases. In the same way, the Vandal kingdom in Africa, which for several decades was regarded as the most potent force in the western Mediterranean, was obliterated as the consequence of little more than one battle fought against the imperial expeditionary force in 533.[1] In a not dissimilar way, the long-term struggle between the Ostrogoths in Italy and the armies sent against them by the emperor Justinian was finally determined by two decisive imperial victories, in this case after more than 15 years

---

[1] Procopius, *History of the Wars*, IV. i. 1–iii. 28, ed. H. B. Dewing, *Procopius*, vol. II (Cambridge MA and London, 1916), pp. 210–35.

Map 2 Towns and rivers

in which the two sides had generally failed to come face to face in open battle.[2]

The fragility of most early medieval confederacies, discussed in the previous chapter, was a vital factor. The people was formed out of a larger mixed following that was centered around a small elite. The latter would normally consist of a ruling family, whose status might be hereditary, but in practice depended on an aura of success, above all in matters military, and an inner core of aristocracy. The latter would in most cases also claim heroic ancestry, as well as holding a commanding economic position within the society.[3] The mutual

---

[2] Ibid. VIII. xxxii. 1-36, and xxxv. 1-38, ed. Dewing, vol. V, pp. 374-89 and 406-19.
[3] E. A. Thompson, *The Early Germans* (Oxford, 1965), pp. 106-8; Herwig Wolfram, *History of the Goths*, trans. Thomas J. Dunlap (Berkeley, CA, 1988), pp. 89-116; also D. H. Green, *Language and History in the Early Germanic World* (Cambridge, 1998), pp. 84-120.

interdependence of the components of the ruling elite required the royal house to be seen to be generous in its gifts of land, slaves, treasure, and other resources to its noble followers, who in turn redistributed some or much of what they thus received to secure the continued allegiance of their own immediate supporters. Successful warfare, too, could play a crucial part, in that it provided opportunities for the members of the great families to emulate the deeds of their heroic forebears, real or imaginary.

A royal treasure was another important element in the sense of common identity that was fostered among the social elite, in that it represented not so much a measure of the wealth of the rulers of the people as tangible evidence of a shared history.[4] Thus, it was generally believed that the Visigothic royal treasure included items originally taken from the Temple in Jerusalem by the emperor Titus in 70 AD, which fell into the hands of Alaric when his men looted Rome in 410. While the distinguished past of these objects added to their allure, their primary effect was to remind the Goths of their more recent triumph together over the Romans. Redistribution of treasure captured from a defeated enemy publicized that event and also created a memory of it that could last for centuries.

Defeat in a major battle could thus be critical. If the king was killed, in such a society it would be expected that his immediate noble following should fight to the death around him. Thus in such a defeat, as well as losing its royal house's precious reputation for victory, the people might lose a high proportion of its relatively small social and military elite. If this was followed, as would happen in 711, by the fall of the royal capital and with it the loss of the treasure that represented the common history of the people, a deep demoralization could follow, in which centralized resistance to conquest might become all but impossible, leading to rapid general submission to the victors.

The Visigoths were spared such a fate in 507, largely thanks to the intervention of the armies of the Ostrogothic king Theoderic, who was anxious to prevent the Franks from reaching the Mediterranean. It may also be that the processes of Visigothic resettlement in Spain

---

[4] On the importance of such royal treasures see Matthias Hardt, "Royal Treasures and Representation in the Early Middle Ages," in Walter Pohl and Helmut Reimitz (eds.), *Strategies of Distinction: The Construction of Ethnic Communities, 300-800* (Leiden, 1998), pp. 255-80.

in the 490s, so tantalizingly hinted at in the *Consularia Caesaraugustana*, prevented the loss of Toulouse being as catastrophic a blow as might have otherwise been the case. Despite the demoralizing defeat at Vouillé and the death of the king, resistance to the Franks was organized and a new monarch was chosen, in the person of an illegitimate son of Alaric II called Gesalic.[5]

His regime proved short-lived, not least because Theoderic preferred the claims of Gesalic's young half-brother Amalaric, who was the son of Alaric II by his marriage to the Ostrogothic king's daughter Theodegotho. Following a defeat at the hands of the Burgundians and the sack of Narbonne, which he had made his capital, Gesalic was forced into exile in Africa in 511. He attempted to regain his kingdom in 513 but was defeated by Ibba, one of Theoderic's generals. Captured in flight (to the Franks?) on the river Durance, he was executed.[6]

His half-brother Amalaric was still a minor, and after the expulsion of Gesalic the Visigothic kingdom seems to have been directly controlled by governors appointed from Italy by Theoderic. Acts of ecclesiastical councils held in Tarragona and Gerona respectively in 516 and 517 are dated by regnal years of Theoderic, which seem to commence in the year 511. This would imply that after the expulsion of Gesalic he ruled the kingdom in his own right, and not just as regent for his grandson. The Second Council of Toledo, which was held in 527, is, however, dated as falling in the fifth year of Amalaric, which would imply that he began to reign in his own name in 522 or 523, prior to his grandfather's death in 526.[7] Such a view is also confirmed by a later narrative account of the period.[8]

In 531, in a conflict whose origins are not clearly recorded, Amalaric was defeated by the Franks and in the aftermath was killed in Barcelona. Flatly contradictory accounts of this state that he was murdered

---

[5] *PLRE* vol. 2: Gesalicus, pp. 509–10.

[6] E. A. Thompson, *The Goths in Spain* (Oxford, 1969), pp. 7–8.

[7] G. Martínez Díez and F. Rodríguez (eds.), *La Colección canónica Hispana*, vol. IV (Madrid, 1984), p. 346. There are no manuscript variants for *anno quinti* and only a minor one for the era date for the year, so the tradition that 527 was the fifth year of Amalaric seems secure. See ibid. pp. 271 and 284 for the regnal dates of the Councils of Tarragona and Gerona.

[8] Isidore, *Historia Gothorum* 39, ed. Cristóbal Rodríguez Alonso, *Las Historias de los Godos, Vándalos y Suevos de Isidoro de Sevilla* (León, 1975), p. 236, which gives no date for this, but says that Theoderic gave the kingdom to Amalaric prior to his death.

by a Frank or by some of his own men.[9] In any event, with his death the dynasty founded by the Visigothic king Theoderic I in 419, and which claimed descent from Alaric I, came to an end. An Ostrogoth called Theudis, who had formerly been an officer in Theoderic's bodyguard, and then his appointee as governor of Spain during the minority of Amalaric, was elected king. At some point in his reign he achieved a military success over an invading Frankish army, but he also lost Ceuta, a Visigothic enclave on the North African coast near Tangiers, to the Byzantines, and an expedition sent to recover it proved a disaster. He ruled until he was murdered, for reasons that are never explained, in 548.[10]

The period between the battle of Vouillé in 507 and the death of Theudis is normally seen as that of the Ostrogothic "interval" in Spanish history, and is one of the most obscure in the whole history of the Visigothic kingdom in the Iberian peninsula.[11] This is due primarily to the almost complete lack of contemporary sources. The only narrative accounts come either in the form of the *Ten Books of Histories*, written by bishop Gregory of Tours in the early 590s, which reflect a Frankish perspective and contain relatively little on Spanish affairs, or from the even later *History of the Goths* of bishop Isidore of Seville. The latter was writing the two extant versions of this work around 620 and 625 respectively, and although drawing on some earlier sources, he was far removed in time from the events of this period.[12] Moreover, Isidore, whose historical writings put into practice his expressed support for the stylistic virtue of brevity, kept his narrative, which was structured around the reigns of the kings he described, extremely short.[13] While there were contemporary historical works being written in Greek, above all the *History of the Wars* of Procopius composed in the 550s, these rarely included current events in Spain, although there are some brief accounts of episodes from the past.

---

[9] *PLRE* vol. 2: Amalaricus, pp. 64-5.
[10] Isidore, *Historia Gothorum* 41-43, ed. Rodríguez, pp. 238-44.
[11] Peter Heather (ed.), *The Visigoths from the Migration Period to the Seventh Century: An Ethnographic Perspective* (Woodbridge, 1999), p. 477.
[12] Roger Collins, "Isidore, Maximus and the Historia Gothorum," in Anton Scharer and Georg Scheibelreiter (eds.), *Historiographie im frühen Mittelalter* (Vienna and Munich, 1994), pp. 345-58.
[13] On the stylistic virtue of *brevitas* see Ernst Robert Curtius, *European Literature and the Latin Middle Ages*, trans. Willard R. Trask (Princeton, NJ, 1973), pp. 487-94.

One consequence is that it is very difficult for us to understand what Ostrogothic rule in Spain was really like, let alone what was felt about it at the time by the Visigoths and the majority Hispano-Roman population. That Theudis, whose name confusingly may actually have been Theoderic, was chosen king in 531 would argue that there was no significant resentment or conflict between the different groups of Goths. That he was indeed Ostrogothic is confirmed by Procopius's account of how his nephew, Ildebad, briefly became king of the Goths in Italy in 540/1.[14] The mutual interpenetrability of the two branches of Gothic society, due to their sense of a shared origin and early history, is also indicated by the earlier example of Eutharic, who was said to have been the direct descendant of the ruler of the Ostrogoths at the time of the Hun attacks in the 370s. He was found living among the Visigoths in 507 and was brought to Italy by Theoderic to marry his daughter Amalasuntha, and thus link the two royal lines.[15] He died in 519, but their son Athalaric succeeded Theoderic in 526.

Although forces sent from Italy intervened in 508 to save the Visigothic kingdom from the Franks, and again to eject Gesalic in 511 and 513, this does not seem to have resulted in a permanent stationing of Ostrogoths in Spain. Procopius records that Theudis drew his own immediate military following from the armed slave army, 2,000 men strong, of his wife, a wealthy Hispano-Roman aristocrat.[16] Tribute payments seem to have been sent from Spain to the Ostrogothic court at Ravenna in the period of Theoderic's personal rule, but possibly not after 523. Direct rule from Italy proved relatively short-lived, and Ostrogothic viceroys may have established a following for themselves among the Visigothic nobility by resisting some of the demands of their distant master in Italy. Procopius reports that Theudis, while serving as Theoderic's governor in Spain, refused to obey a summons to Ravenna, and the Ostrogothic king decided it would be unwise to try to make him do so by force, for fear of opening the way to a Frankish invasion or a Visigothic revolt.[17]

---

[14] Procopius, *History of the Wars* VI. xxx. 15-17, ed. Dewing, vol. IV, p. 142. The hope expressed was that Theudis would send military assistance to his nephew if he were chosen as king, but this was not forthcoming.
[15] *PLRE* vol. 2: Fl. Eutharicus Cilliga, p. 438.
[16] Procopius, *History of the Wars*, V. xii. 50-2, ed. Dewing, vol. III, pp. 130-1.
[17] Ibid. V. xii. 52-4, ed. Dewing, vol. III, pp. 132-3; see also John Moorhead, *Theoderic in Italy* (Oxford, 1992), pp. 190-1.

Much of a law issued by Theudis has survived in a single manuscript in León cathedral.[18] It is a palimpsest, which is to say the original text has been erased at a later date, in order to allow a different one to be written over it. Fortunately the erasing process was not carried out so thoroughly as to make it impossible for some of the undertext to be recovered. What is striking about the law thus revealed is not just that it was promulgated by king Theudis, of whom no other legal texts survive, but it seems uniquely to have been preserved in its original state. Visigothic royal laws that are to be found in the various extant codes of the fifth and seventh centuries have preserved only the central part of their texts, with the preambles and concluding sections having been excised in the interests of greater brevity. Concerned with legal costs, this law of *Flavius Theudis Rex*, dated at the end of the document to November 24 in the fifteenth year of his reign (probably 545), is thus the only one from this period to have survived in its full or complete form, although there are some lacunae in its text.

The wider significance of the chance survival of this law lies in the evidence it provides for continuity in legal and administrative thinking and practices in Spain that were of Roman imperial origin. It was issued at Toledo, a hitherto relatively obscure provincial town, but which had become the capital of the Visigothic kingdom by the end of the reign of Athanagild (554-67).[19] This text confirms, however, that it had become at least an occasional royal residence a generation earlier.

How effective the Gothic administration was in practice in the sixth century is very hard to determine. Theudis's own case would seem to suggest that power rested at a local level with the regional nobility, still largely of Roman origin, to whom were now added the families of the incoming Gothic elite. Marriages such as that made by Theudis to his unnamed Roman wife may have been more common than the continued existence of legal prohibitions on such unions would make us think. It was certainly one way in which the Roman and Germanic upper classes could start to fuse.[20]

---

[18] *CLA* vol. XI, no. 1637; for the text see Karl Zeumer (ed.), *Leges Visigothorum* (= *MGH LL*., vol. 1), pp. 467-9.

[19] Isidore, *Historia Gothorum* 47, ed. Rodríguez, p. 250.

[20] On the supposed legal prohibitions see Hagith Sivan, "The Appropriation of Roman Law in Barbarian Hands: 'Roman-barbarian' Marriage in Visigothic Gaul and Spain," in Pohl and Reimitz (eds.), *Strategies of Distinction*, pp. 189-203.

Royal resources proper will almost certainly have included the former imperial estates in Spain. As the Theodosian dynasty (379-455) had been of Hispano-Roman origin, these may not have been inconsiderable, but there is no way of knowing their actual extent or value. Such lands, and those families of servile status who were legally bound to them, will have provided the immediate resources of wealth and manpower for the new rulers, but these would have had to be supplemented by those of the Gothic and Roman aristocracy, the most important of whose members would have to have been brought into active cooperation with the kings, not least through the grant of offices and the provision of other rewards. While the Visigothic kingdom had been expanding, as it did for much of the fifth century, newly acquired estates and offices were relatively readily available, but after 507 the situation was reversed, with much territory having been lost.

Once established in Spain, the Visigothic kingdom was far more secure than it had been under Alaric II, not least in terms of its much smaller and more mountainous borders, but the opportunities for conquest and expansion became almost nonexistent, especially after the Gothic forces were expelled from Ceuta and the North African coast in the time of Theudis, and then when parts of the peninsula itself were lost to the empire from 551 onwards. The kings had less with which to reward faithful service, and their value to the regional aristocracies, competing for local status and authority, was consequently much reduced. The physical extent of the territory controlled by the Visigothic kings seems to have declined almost continuously from 507 to the beginning of the 570s.

The extinction of the "Balt" dynasty of Alaric I in 531 transformed the transmission of royal authority within the kingdom.[21] Election of the king became a reality and dynastic sentiment was thereafter never a strong force in securing the easy transmission of power from father to son. Only a degree of inertia, whereby those already benefiting from the current ruling house would be disinclined for change for fear of losing their gains from a redistribution of royal patronage, favored dynastic continuity. Even this sentiment was a weak one, as the members of the elite generally proved reluctant to see one of

---

[21] On the notional antiquity of the Balt dynasty see Wolfram, *History of the Goths*, pp. 32-5.

their number and his family establish any kind of monopoly on the royal office.

The choice of monarch was primarily in the hands of the nobility of the court, who provided the immediate entourage of the monarchs and whose own military following supplemented his. It was from their own number that the selection was most likely to be made. This may have disenfranchised those who were not close to the court circle, and who may have enjoyed regional rather than curial standing. In some cases in the history of the kingdom this could result in a provincial revolt and the creation of a rival monarch with a regional following, who challenged the authority of the king chosen by the court nobility. However, such a rebellion would normally draw on more limited military resources than those available to the centrally chosen candidate, and unless the latter proved militarily incompetent, provincial pretenders rarely succeeded in overthrowing them.

In 548 Theudis was replaced by Theudisclus, who had previously established his credentials as the commander of the army that had defeated a Frankish raid into the province of Tarraconensis.[22] Whether this should be identified with the attempt of the Frankish king Childebert I (ca.511-58) to capture Zaragoza, as described by Gregory of Tours, is uncertain.[23] But as the first major success of the Visigoths in their several wars against the Franks since 507, it should have made Theudisclus a natural candidate to succeed Theudis. However, he was murdered during a banquet in Seville in 549. According to Isidore, this was because of his seduction of the wives of several of his leading followers, but such supposed motivation is not uncommon in accounts of palace coups in Antiquity.[24]

Whether his successor Agila (549-54) was implicated in the plot is not known, any more than are the reasons for his selection as king. He seems to have been an unfortunate choice, in that he suffered a humiliating defeat when he tried to suppress a revolt in Córdoba, losing both his son and the royal treasure in the process.[25] The causes

---

[22] Isidore, *Historia Gothorum* 44, ed. Rodríguez, pp. 244-7.
[23] Gregory of Tours, *Libri Decem Historiarum* III. 29, ed. Bruno Krusch and Wilhelm Levison (= *MGH SRM* vol. I), p. 125.
[24] *Historia Gothorum* 44, ed. Rodríguez, p. 246.
[25] Ibid. 45, pp. 246-8.

and consequences of this episode are not easy to understand, as we are dependent almost exclusively on the brief account of the reign included by Isidore in his *History of the Goths*, the first version of which was written over sixty years later.

His narrative is chronologically unclear, which is regrettable, as there are a number of elements that have to be fitted together, and which will make sense only if we can be convinced that we have them in the right order. These separate pieces of the puzzle consist of the revolt in Córdoba, if that is what it really was. Secondly, there is another revolt against Agila, which took place in Seville and was led by a Gothic noble called Athanagild. Thirdly, there is the arrival in Spain of an imperial army, which was sent by the emperor Justinian I (527–65), and which led to the establishment of a Byzantine enclave in the southeast of the peninsula.

From the logic of Isidore's narrative, the chronological order of these events would seem to place Agila's disastrous campaign against Córdoba first. In the aftermath of this he withdrew to Mérida. Secondly, "after the passing of some time," came the revolt of Athanagild in Seville. Thirdly, because of the time it was taking to overthrow Agila, Athanagild is said to have asked for military help from Justinian, resulting in the dispatch to Spain of the imperial forces. Finally, the threat of a wider Byzantine conquest led Agila's own supporters to murder him and give the weakened kingdom to Athanagild.[26] The precise nature of Isidore's sources for these events and his personal understanding of them may not be known. One of them was certainly the short *History* of bishop Maximus of Zaragoza, written in the opening years of the seventh century, but this too must have been largely derivative from earlier texts.[27]

Isidore's narrative of the reign of Agila is deceptively clear and sensible. It implies that the demoralizing defeat at Córdoba and loss of the royal treasure, as well as the death of the king's son, undermined Agila's credibility and thus led to a challenge for the kingship from another member of the Gothic elite. The protracted and evenly balanced nature of this contest then resulted in an appeal for outside help, which in turn led to the arrival of a Byzantine army

---

[26] Ibid. 46, p. 248.
[27] On this see Collins, "Maximus, Isidore and the Historia Gothorum" (note 12 above).

and the establishment of the imperial enclave in the peninsula, soon to be followed by the elimination of Agila at the hands of his own followers.

Unfortunately, the contemporary Byzantine historian Procopius, who left his *History of the Wars* unfinished with his account of the fighting in Italy in 552, did not include any mention of these events in Spain, any more than did his Continuator Agathias. However, another exactly contemporary author, Jordanes, reported in his *Getica* or "On the Origins and Deeds of the Goths" that an imperial expedition was on its way to assist Agila against Athanagild even as he wrote.[28] Unfortunately, he did not date his time of writing as precisely as we might have liked, but it has been generally accepted that he finished his short book in 550 or 551.[29]

If this date is correct, it does not allow a lot of time for the sequence of events described by Isidore, who was also probably in error in attributing the appeal for imperial help to Athanagild rather than Agila. The latter case is also more inherently probable in the light of other imperial interventions in the West in these decades, which were all ostensibly in support of legitimate monarchs who had been overthrown or challenged. As it stands, Isidore's narrative makes the revolt in Córdoba the catalyst for all that was to happen, but it is actually more plausible to suggest that Agila's succession was challenged from the start by Athanagild, since Jordanes's evidence indicates that, for the appeal to be received in Constantinople and an expedition to be dispatched in 550/1, the challenge to the legitimate Visigothic king must have been made by 550 if not earlier.

Whatever its justification, the imperial intervention in Spain led rapidly to the seizure of a series of ports and fortresses along the southeastern and southern coasts of the peninsula, at least as far as Medina Sidonia, with Cartagena coming to serve as the administrative center of the new imperial province. Whether a Byzantine presence was established inland is less certain. There remains a possibility, though, that the revolt of Córdoba, briefly recounted by Isidore, was the result of the Byzantine presence, and that until it was recovered by the Visigothic king Leovigild in 572 the city formed

---

[28] Jordanes, *Getica* 303 (or LVIII), ed. T. Mommsen (= *MGH AA*, vol. V.i), pp. 135–6.
[29] *PLRE* vol. 3a: Iordanes 1, pp. 713–14.

part of the imperial territories.³⁰ This is neither confirmed nor denied by any source, but it is not entirely easy to see how the city and its inhabitants, if they had rejected Visigothic royal authority, would not have reverted to an imperial allegiance. However, it is also possible that some kind of local regime was established, perhaps like those so briefly attempted by the would-be emperors Burdunellus and Peter at the beginning of the century. Ultimately, there is no way of knowing.

Despite the initial success of their intervention, Justinian's forces do not seem to have been involved in any kind of large-scale bid to reconquer the whole of the Iberian peninsula for the empire. The Gothic Wars in Italy had been protracted, expensive, and highly destructive. More serious threats now existed on the eastern frontiers, and it is probable that the primary intention of the setting up of an imperial enclave along the coast of southeastern Spain was to establish a defensive cordon for the protection of recently reconquered Africa, as it was from these very shores that the Vandals had launched their successful invasion back in 429.

Despite the hostile presence of imperial troops in the south, and the suggestion of continuous conflict with them, little more is known of Athanagild's reign in any detail. He based himself in Seville for his wars against the Byzantines, but he died at Toledo.³¹ Despite the preoccupation of the Visigothic king with the military threat in the south, no further Frankish threats are recorded, but for the first time diplomatic ties seem to have been established with some of the rival Merovingian monarchs. In the 560s two of Athanagild's daughters were married to Frankish kings, the brothers Sigebert I (561–75) and Chilperic I (561–84), although the latter soon connived at the murder of his wife by his mistress.³² Athanagild himself died of natural causes in 568, the first of the Gothic kings so to do since 484.

---

[30] Thompson, *The Goths in Spain*, pp. 320–3; Warren Treadgold, *A History of the Byzantine State and Society* (Stanford, CA, 1997), p. 211 and note 21 on p. 929 criticizes Thompson's argument.

[31] There is a brief reference to the wars in the south and the king's base in Seville in the last item in the *Consularia Caesaraugustana*, which appears as a marginal note to the text of John of Biclarum; see *Iohannis Biclarensis Chronicon* 6a, ed. Carmen Cardelle de Hartmann (= *Corpus Christianorum Series Latina*, vol. CLXXIIIA), p. 61.

[32] Ian Wood, *The Merovingian Kingdoms 450–751* (London, 1994), pp. 120–36 for Merovingian family politics and the roles of queens.

After a five-month interregnum, a new king was elected in the person of Liuva, who died prematurely either in 571 or in 573.[33] Why he had no immediate heirs of his own is not known, but he had already ensured the continuation of his dynasty. In 569 he took the unprecedented step of dividing the kingdom, and giving one half to his younger brother Leovigild. The latter was established as king in Toledo, where he married Gosuinth, the widow of Athanagild. Liuva based himself in Narbonne, probably to counter Frankish threats.[34] No details are recorded of any campaigning in this region during his few remaining years, and on his death both parts of the kingdom were reunited under his brother.

The Reign of Leovigild, 569-586

Leovigild is generally regarded as one of the most effective of all the Visigothic kings, reestablishing royal authority in most parts of the peninsula, but it should be noted that we are much better informed about his reign than about those of any of his sixth-century predecessors. This is almost entirely due to the survival of a short chronicle which was written by a Gothic monk and later bishop of Gerona (by 592-after 614), known from the monastery he founded as John of Biclarum.[35]

According to the account later given of him by Isidore in his *De Viris Illustribus* or "On Famous Men," John was born in Santarem in modern Portugal. While still a young man, he went to Constantinople.[36] The reasons for this are not clear, but the fact itself typifies the continuing openness of Mediterranean society in the sixth century. Only a little earlier a monk from Pannonia, in the northwest of the Balkans, who had also traveled in Egypt, came to Galicia, where he

---

[33] Isidore, *Historia Gothorum* 48, ed. Rodríguez p. 250, gives his regnal length as three years. But John of Biclarum places the death of Liuva in the fifth year of Leovigild's reign: *Iohannis Biclarensis Chronicon* 24, ed. Carmen Cardelle de Hartmann (= *Corpus Christianorum Series Latina*, vol. CLXXIIIA), p. 64. See the historical commentary by Roger Collins, ibid. pp. 118-19 for a suggested explanation for these differences, also taking account of the regnal lists that give Liuva reign lengths of one to four years.
[34] Isidore, *Historia Gothorum* 48, ed. Rodríguez, pp. 250-2.
[35] See *Iohannis Biclarensis Chronicon*, ed. Hartmann, pp. 124*-128*.
[36] Isidore, *De Viris Illustribus* XXXI, ed. Carmen Codoñer, *El "De Viris Illustribus" de Isidoro de Sevilla. Estudio y Edición crítica* (Salamanca, 1964), pp. 151-2.

subsequently became bishop of Braga.[37] In the same period, merchants and other travelers from the eastern Mediterranean were still arriving in Mérida, where two of the later sixth-century bishops are also reported to have been of Greek origin.[38]

Among other things John almost certainly brought back from his visit to the imperial capital was a copy of the chronicle of an African bishop, Victor of Tunnunna. This was a continuation of one of the versions of a chronicle written by the mid-fifth-century Gallic author, Prosper, and it covered the years 444 to 565.[39] Victor included no information about Spain in his work. It is quite possible that in an attempt to rectify this absence of Spanish material, John himself added the entries that now form the *Consularia Caesaraugustana* as marginalia to his copy of Victor's chronicle, even though they never came to be properly integrated into the text.[40] He wrote his own chronicle as a continuation of that of Victor in the first decade of the seventh century, and in contrast to his predecessor devoted much of it to Spanish events.

By implication John refers in his work to the deaths of the emperor Maurice and of pope Gregory the Great in the years 602 and 604 respectively, thus suggesting he did not write his chronicle until after the latter event. His actual narrative, though, extends no further than 590, having begun, thanks to a chronological confusion in Victor, with the year 567. John is thus in a position to provide a contemporary account of the reigns of Liuva and Leovigild, and of the crucial opening years of that of the latter's son Reccared. His narrative of this period was subsequently used by Isidore of Seville in the longer version of his own chronicle, written in the mid-620s.

John himself had been in Constantinople for seven years from around 571/2, and in consequence he included quite a lot of information about events in Italy, Africa, and the eastern provinces of the empire in that period in his chronicle. Some of this is unique and not found in any other source. Unfortunately, where John's narrative of Byzantine affairs can be checked against other contemporary or near

---

[37] Ibid. XXII, pp. 145-6.
[38] *Vitas Sanctorum Patrum Emeretensium* IV. iii, ed. A. Maya Sánchez (= *Corpus Christianorum Series Latina*, vol. CXVI), pp. 31-3.
[39] *Victoris Tunnunnensis Chronicon*, ed. Carmen Cardelle de Hartmann (= *Corpus Christianorum Series Latina*, vol. CLXXIIIA), pp. 3-55.
[40] Ibid. pp. 115*-124*.

contemporary eastern historical texts, he is revealed as being both confused and imprecise in his chronology.[41] The nature of his errors would seem to preclude their being the result of the subsequent transmission of his work, even though this survives in only a single medieval manuscript.[42] It seems more likely that writing, as he seems to have been, thirty or more years after the events described, his memory could fail him. While there is no way of checking the validity of his information about Spain, for which he was in practice often the unique source, this weakness in his narrative has to be borne in mind, especially as the only other near contemporary historian, Isidore of Seville, was at least in part dependent on him.

The very existence of John's chronicle affects our perspective on the second half of the sixth century. Because no comparable narrative exists, it looks as if Athanagild's reign was lacking in events, and that no significant achievements can be credited to him. On the other hand, following the accession of Leovigild we are made aware, thanks to John, of a pattern of virtually annual campaigning that resulted on several occasions in significant military and diplomatic triumphs. Leovigild seems active and successful while his predecessors appear lethargic or incompetent, but it may all be a matter of the relative availability of information.

With all of that said, Leovigild's wars clearly produced results. Following John's account, something of a pattern emerges. Leovigild's first campaign is probably to be dated to 570, and involved a raid into the region of "Bastania" (classical Bastitania) and the driving off of imperial forces from Málaga that tried to stop him. In 571 a similar expedition into the south led to the recovery of "Asinoda" (modern Medina Sidonia) from its imperial garrison, which seems to have been slaughtered.[43] The following year saw the regaining of Córdoba, which had been out of Gothic hands since the time of Agila. John adds that Leovigild also captured many other cities and fortresses, perhaps in the Guadalquivir valley. He notes too that "a multitude of rustics were killed."[44] No explanation is given for this, but it was obviously a

---

[41] Ibid. historical commentary, pp. 111-29 for numerous examples of John's chronological errors and lack of precision.
[42] Ibid. pp. 13*-45* for the manuscript tradition.
[43] *Johannis Biclarensis Chronicon* 17, ed. Hartmann, p. 63.
[44] Ibid. 20, p. 63.

significant enough feature of the campaign to be thought worthy of inclusion in his very compressed account. While this may have been an act of intimidation, to persuade other rural communities not to provide any support for the imperial forces, there exists the more interesting possibility that John's *rustici* are what fifth-century sources would have called *Bagaudae*. In other words, they were elements of the rural population that, through economic hardship or the disturbed conditions engendered by the war between the Visigoths and the empire, had been driven into forming bandit armies that preyed on the estates of the great landowners and on urban settlements.

In 573 John records Leovigild's conquest of the region of *Sabaria*, a process again said to involve devastation. He also made his two sons from a previous marriage, Hermenegild and Reccared, his *consortes regni* or "partners in the kingdom," a development to which we shall return. The location of *Sabaria* has remained controversial, but John's calling its inhabitants *Sappos* has led to the plausible suggestion that the region may have lain between the Roman towns of Caprara and Salmantica (modern Salamanca).[45] This would imply that Leovigild was starting to turn his attention away from the south, at least for the time being.

The following year saw the king's first definite expedition into the north of the peninsula, when he overran *Cantabria* and "killed the invaders (*pervasores*) of the province." From a variety of early medieval references, it seems clear that at this time Cantabria was larger than the modern region of the same name, and extended from the Biscay coast in the vicinity of the present Santander, in a broad swathe southeastward into the upper Ebro valley and the Rioja.[46] In the *Life* of the Riojan hermit Aemilian, which was written by bishop Braulio of Zaragoza, probably in the 620s or 630s, this episode seems to be foreshadowed (albeit retrospectively) when the saint warns the members of "the Senate of Cantabria" of their imminent destruction when they resisted his calls for their repentance.[47]

---

[45] Ibid. 27, p. 65; for discussion of the location see the historical commentary, pp. 119-20.
[46] Ibid. 32, p. 66; see the historical commentary, pp. 121-2.
[47] Braulio, *Vita S. Aemiliani* 33, ed. Luís Vázquez de Parga (Madrid, 1943), p. 34; see Santiago Castellanos, *Hagiografía y sociedad en la Hispania visigoda: la Vita Aemiliani y el actual territorio riojano (siglo vi)* (Logroño, 1999), pp. 49-60.

Although Braulio's short text postdates the event by half a century or more, it may well be that he has recorded genuine traditions about a largely Hispano-Roman local aristocracy that had set itself up as the ruling elite in Cantabria, ignoring the Visigothic monarchy. Whether this was the product of the periods of weakness in royal power after 507 or following the civil war between Agila and Athanagild in the early 550s, or whether in fact the Visigothic kings had never imposed their authority on the region at any previous time, cannot be known. It is at least interesting to speculate about the possibility that this local senate was actually a reaction to the collapse of imperial power in the peninsula around 409. That it did not survive the events of the year 574 is made clear by both John of Biclarum and Braulio, with the latter indicating that many of its members were massacred.

In 575 another independent regime was terminated when Leovigild overran the *Aregenses montes* and captured the ruler of the region, Aspidius, together with his family. Although the area cannot be located with certainty, the placing of this campaign between one in Cantabria and another, in the following year, against the Suevic kingdom, makes it seem likely that it was somewhere on the eastern fringes of the modern province of Orense.[48] As in the case of *Sabaria*, there is no way of knowing whether Aspidius's authority was long-established or just a response to the weakening of the authority of the Visigothic kings in the sixth century. Although Leovigild is recorded as taking the wealth of the region and its ruler, there is for once no word of massacre and mayhem. On the campaign of 576 against the Suevic king Miro John gives no details, other than recording that he rapidly made a treaty with Leovigild and agreed to pay him tribute, even if only "for a short time."[49]

In 577 an expedition entered the region of *Orospeda*, where the towns and fortresses were captured, and very soon after "the rustic rebels" were "crushed" by the Goths, who thus made themselves masters of the province. A number of suggestions have been made as to where this region was located, without any of them gaining general support.[50] What may be significant is the lack of reference to

---

[48] *Johannis Biclarensis Chronicon* 35, ed. Hartmann, p. 67, and see the historical commentary on p. 123 (where for "western" read "eastern"!).
[49] Ibid. 39, p. 68.
[50] Ibid. 46, p. 69, and historical commentary pp. 126-7.

any local leadership and its elimination, which could imply that this was an area under Byzantine control. The reference here to *rustici rebellantes*, reminiscent of the mention of the slaughter of rustics in the Guadalquivir valley in 572, may reinforce the view that these were late sixth-century equivalents of the fifth-century *Bagaudae*, and thus that large-scale banditry was endemic in many parts of the peninsula at this time.

While the idea that this was territory previously held by imperial forces does not make it possible to locate *Orospeda* more precisely than somewhere within a large stretch of territory extending from the lower Guadalquivir valley to the coastal area north of Cartagena, it is worth noting that recent archaeological excavations in the southeast are starting to give slightly more depth to our understanding of the Byzantine presence. In particular, the "towns and fortresses" mentioned more than once by John of Biclarum could include some that can be shown to have received distinctively Byzantine defensive features. Recent excavations at Tolmo de Minateda, near Hellín in the Province of Albacete, have established what seems to be a phase of Byzantine refortification of part of the perimeter wall of the settlement, making it an example of the kind of imperial fortress to which John was referring.[51] It may be hoped that others will be found.

In the course of six years the Visigothic monarch had regained some of the territory lost by his predecessors in the south, and reimposed royal authority on a broad band of territory in the west and the north, extending from the Rioja to Galicia and *Sabaria*, at the same time eliminating various forms of regional self-government and bands of *Bagaudae*, while also bringing the Suevic monarchy into a tributary relationship. So it is perhaps not surprising to find that in 578 he took a break from campaigning, and devoted himself instead to the foundation of a new city, which he named Reccopolis, apparently in honor of his son Reccared.[52] The latter, which is John's interpretation, may be a post-facto rationalization, and makes poor

---

[51] Sonia Gutiérrez Lloret and Lorenzo Abad Casal, "Fortificaciones urbanas altomedievales del Tolmo de Minateda (Hellín, Albacete, España): el baluarte occidental," in Isabel Cristina Ferreira Fernandes (ed.), *Mil Anos de Fortificaçoes na Península Ibérica e no Magreb (500-1500)* (Lisbon, 2002), pp. 133-44.
[52] *Johannis Biclarensis Chronicon*, 50, ed. Hartmann, p. 70; historical commentary, pp. 128-9.

sense linguistically. *Reccaredopolis* would have been perfectly feasible, and all other classical and late antique examples of such dedications would argue that the complete name would have had to have been used; otherwise why not *Constopolis* rather than *Constantinopolis*? It is also not easy to see why Leovigild would have wanted to honor his second son rather than his elder one Hermenegild. It might be suggested instead that what he intended was *Rex-opolis*, "The City of the King," rather than *Reccopolis*, "The City of Recc."

While John only places the new city rather generally in the region of *Celtiberia*, which would imply the central parts of the peninsula, its location has been deduced more precisely from the identification of a place called *Recupel* with the fortress of Zorita in the historical and geographical work of the ninth-century Arab author al-Razi. The discovery here of a small hoard of coins from the mint of *Reccopolis* seemed to confirm this, and various excavations have been carried out on the site, a small plateau on a bend in the Tagus about a mile from the village of Zorita de los Canes in the Province of Guadalajara. The earliest excavations in 1944/5 uncovered the foundations of a long thin building, 133 meters long, and between 9 and 13.5 meters wide, that paralleled the edge of the cliff that falls steeply away to the river immediately to the south. This was identified as a palace, even though there are no obvious parallels to it in other palatine sites of Antiquity and the Middle Ages. Unfortunately, the premature death of the excavator and the apparent loss of all his notes on the work has meant that this excavation has not been published and now never can be, leaving a subsequent generation of archaeologists only a small portion of this particular site on which to work.[53] So it is not known why this was identified as a palace, nor whether it could be dated with certainty to the period of Leovigild.

The year 579 saw the start of one of the most dramatic episodes of the reign, the revolt of the king's elder son Hermenegild in Seville. This is described by John of Biclarum as *domestica rixa* or "a domestic quarrel," in that he said it came about *factione Gosuinthae*, "at the instigation of Gosuinth."[54] While it is clear that he is placing

[53] Lauro Olmo Enciso, "Proyecto Reccopolis: ciudad y territorio en época visigoda," in Rodrigo Balbín, Jesus Valiente, and M. Teresa Mussat (eds.), *Arqueología en Guadalajara* (Toledo, 1995), pp. 209–23.
[54] *Johannis Biclarensis Chronicon*, 54, ed. Hartmann, p. 71; historical commentary, pp. 129–30.

responsibility on Leovigild's wife for driving her stepson into revolt, the nature of her influence remains ambiguous. Did she encourage him to rebel or was he driven to it in reaction to her influence or because of something she had done? Gregory of Tours reports that she had ill-treated Hermenegild's wife, Ingundis, who was her own granddaughter, because of her refusal to accept Arian doctrines.[55] This would support the view that it was her hostility that drove Hermenegild into revolt, and that his motivation was at least in part religious. This latter interpretation would seem confirmed by the way in which, little more than a decade later, the Visigothic prince came to be depicted by pope Gregory the Great (590-604) as a Catholic martyr.[56]

On the other hand, it has also been suggested that as Ingundis was the daughter of the Frankish ruler Sigebert I and of Brunechildis, daughter of the former Visigothic king Athanagild, after whom her and Hermenegild's son would be named, what Gosuinth was seeking was the establishment of a separate monarchy in the south for the heirs of her first husband. By this view Hermenegild rebelled under her encouragement. It has to be admitted, though, that this theory does not really convince: what was the need for Hermenegild to revolt when he was already subordinate ruler in the south and likely to inherit full authority there in the not too distant future?

On the other hand, there are problems with the view that the revolt was the product of reaction in the strongly Roman and thus Catholic south against the increasing attempts of Leovigild to impose a modified form of Arianism as the basis of ecclesiastical unity in the kingdom. For one thing, there is no definite evidence that such a policy was yet being followed. It would only be in 580 that a synod held in Toledo worked out a revised formulation of Arian Trinitarian doctrine, which made it more acceptable to Catholics, including at least one bishop.[57] Similarly, Gregory the Great's image of Hermenegild as a martyr who gave his life for his faith is both controlled by the ideological purposes of the *Dialogues*, in which the story appears, and is a perspective from the period following the Visigothic prince's

---

[55] Gregory of Tours, *Historiae* V. xxxviii, ed. Krusch and Levison, p. 244.
[56] Gregory the Great, *Dialogues* III. 31, ed. A. de Vogüé, *Grégoire le Grand, Dialogues* (3 vols., Paris, 1978-80), vol. II (1979), pp. 384-93.
[57] *Johannis Biclarensis Chronicon* 57, ed. Hartmann, pp. 71-2.

somewhat mysterious death. It does not in itself validate the view that it was the defense of Catholicism that motivated Hermenegild from the start. There are some grounds, from the logic of the various narratives of these events, for suspecting that his personal conversion from Arianism to Catholicism took place some time after the beginning of the revolt in 579, possibly even as late as 582.[58]

The role in all this of imperial diplomacy has remained opaque.[59] Whether there was any form of Byzantine influence working on Hermenegild is not known. He certainly sent his principal ecclesiastical advisor, bishop Leander of Seville, to Constantinople, where incidentally he met the future pope Gregory, then serving as papal envoy in the imperial capital. Whether or not the empire, now ruled by the emperor Maurice (582-602), had had any part to play in the instigation of the revolt, it may have been the prospect of Byzantine military intervention that led Leovigild to act against his son in 583.

That he had not done so before would seem to imply that the rebellion of Hermenegild was not originally seen as constituting a serious threat, beyond denial of his father's authority over the province of Baetica. In 581, rather than turning his attention southward, Leovigild had gone to campaign against the *Vascones* or Basques, founding another new town called *Victoriacum*, on the fringes of their territory.[60] However, the prospect of renewed imperial intervention, like that of 551 but from fortresses already established in the peninsula, may have seemed to be far more menacing. In 582 Leovigild began to prepare for war against his son and in 583 commenced the siege of Seville, including instituting a blockade of the Guadalquivir. The latter certainly prevented supplies arriving by water, but may also have been intended to stop imperial reinforcements coming up the river.

Seville fell in 584. Before it surrendered Hermenegild escaped, but only as far as Córdoba, where he was captured while trying to make his way to imperial territory. The submission of other towns and

---

[58] Roger Collins, "Mérida and Toledo, 550-85," in James, *Visigothic Spain: New Approaches*, pp. 189-219.
[59] Walter Goffart, "Byzantine Policy in the West under Tiberius II and Maurice: the Pretenders Hermenegild and Gundovald (579-85)," *Traditio* 13 (1957), pp. 75-118.
[60] *Johannis Biclarensis Chronicon* 60, ed. Hartmann, p. 72.

fortresses that had supported him followed rapidly, and the rebel prince was sent into exile in Valencia.[61] In 585 he was killed in Tarragona by some one called Sisbert, who himself "died a dishonorable death" in 587.[62] Although it is possible to speculate, we just do not know why Hermenegild was killed, why he was in Tarragona rather than Valencia, who Sisbert was, and why he met an equally unpleasant fate so soon after. It would seem unlikely that Leovigild was not somehow involved, but some suspicion has been cast on his second son and successor, Reccared.[63]

While, from a somewhat Machiavellian point of view, failed rebels, especially those with legitimate claims to authority, are an embarrassment and their subsequent elimination not entirely surprising, there may be more than *realpolitik* behind the killing of Hermenegild. The year 585 saw the first recorded Frankish assault on the Visigothic kingdom for many years, relations apparently having been tranquil if not harmonious since the time of Athanagild. The chance survival of a small collection of diplomatic and other letters emanating from the Austrasian or eastern Frankish court shows that the rulers of this kingdom were using the presence of Heremegild's young son Athanagild in Constantinople as a way of facilitating links with the empire.[64] This proved short-lived, in that his mother Ingundis had died at Carthage in 585/6 on the way to Constantinople, and the young Athanagild himself is never heard of again after ca.587.[65]

The Frankish kingdom of Austrasia was ruled by Childebert II (575-96), Ingundis's brother, and himself a grandson of the Visigothic king Athanagild. He and his family thus had strong personal motives for seeking revenge, but the raids on the Visigothic province of Narbonensis in 585 were the work of another of the Frankish rulers, Guntramn, king of Burgundy (561-92). There is a more detailed account of what happened in Gregory of Tours, who confirms John's view that the raids were a complete failure as far as the Franks were

---

[61] Ibid. 64-6, 68, pp. 73-4.
[62] Ibid. 83, p. 77.
[63] Luis Garcia Moreno, "La coyuntura política del III Concilio de Toledo. Una historia larga y tortuosa," in R. Gonzálvez (ed.), *El Concilio III de Toledo. XIV Centenario 589-1989* (Toledo, 1991), pp. 271-96.
[64] Elena Malaspina (ed.), *Il "Liber epistolarum" della cancelleria austrasica (sec. V-VI)* (Rome, 2001), *epp.* 27, 28, pp. 168-71.
[65] *PLRE* vol. 3: Athanagildus 2, p. 141.

concerned, and that in a counterattack Reccared took the fortress of *Ugernum*, near Tarascon, on the river Rhône.[66]

There remains the possibility that these Frankish expeditions were not just opportunistic and predatory, but were linked to the quarrel over the fate of Hermenegild and his family. That the former rebel is reported as being killed in Tarragona, rather than further south in Valencia, could mean that he had escaped from custody and was seeking to join the Franks. Alternatively, it is possible that Reccared, who had been entrusted with the defense of Narbonensis, suspected some such intention and secured his brother's elimination in order to prevent it. There is no way of knowing, but the killing of Hermenegild at the same time as the renewal of conflict with the Franks after several decades of peace is unlikely to have been purely coincidental.

The crushing of Hermenegild's revolt in 584 and the existence of more pressing military commitments in the Balkans and on the eastern frontier meant that imperial intervention on his side, if it had ever been planned, never materialized.[67] Leovigild was able to devote the final stage of his reign to the elimination of the independent Suevic kingdom in Galicia. Its ruler Miro had died near Seville in 583 while taking part in the civil war. John of Biclarum's words are here ambiguous and it is not certain whether Miro was there to support Leovigild, to whom he had become a tributary in 576, or to aid Hermenegild. In either case no active Suevic participation is recorded and it is likely that Miro's unexpected death, leaving the throne to his young son Eboric, led to the army's withdrawal.

Eboric's deposition in 584 by a Suevic noble called Audeca, who seized the throne and married Miro's widow Sisegutia, provided an excuse for Leovigild to intervene, probably by virtue of the treaty of 576. In 585 the Visigothic king "devastated Galicia, captured and deposed Audeca, and brought the Suevic people, treasure and land under his own rule."[68] Audeca was forcibly made into a priest, depriving him of any right to rule, and was sent into exile in the south. A revolt, led by a Suevic noble called Malaric, was suppressed

---

[66] Gregory of Tours, *Historiae* VIII. 30, ed. Krusch and Levison, pp. 393-7; cf. *Johannis Biclarensis Chronicon* 74, ed. Hartmann, p. 76.

[67] For the problems of the empire in this period see Michael Whitby, *The Emperor Maurice and his Historian* (Oxford, 1988), pp. 138-83 and 276-304.

[68] *Johannis Biclarensis Chronicon* 72, ed. Hartmann, p. 75.

by Leovigild's forces the very same year, and he was sent in chains to the king.[69] His eventual fate is not known. With this the Suevic kingdom disappears from the historical record. Although various attempts have been made, no subsequent distinguishing feature of the society and culture of Galicia has ever effectively been identified as a distinctively Suevic inheritance.

Following this final military success, Leovigild died in 586, leaving a largely united peninsula to his only surviving son Reccared. His reign is normally seen as having marked a turning point in the fortunes of the Visigothic monarchy. After decades of defeat, civil war, and disintegration, a strong king had finally reversed the almost continuous decline, had defeated all of the kingdom's traditional enemies, and had imposed his authority on virtually all parts of the peninsula.[70] Even if the imperial enclave still survived in the south, it did so in a much reduced form, and it would never thereafter present a significant military threat to his successors. Various forms of local self-government had been suppressed, as had the Suevic kingdom in Galicia. Only in respect of his religious policies, trying to impose a modified Arian theology as the basis for doctrinal unity, is Leovigild seen as anything less than successful. Even in this, it could be argued, he had the right idea in principle. The resolution of the religious conflict that divided the upper echelons of society in the kingdom was essential if a new sense of common identity and purpose was to emerge among the governing classes. Leovigild's mistake was to favor an imposed Arianism; Reccared's success lay in doing the same thing in support of Catholicism.

No doubt there is much to be said for such a view, even if it is largely based on an unreflective assumption that strong central government is a good thing in its own right. What also needs to be considered, however, is the price that may have had to have been paid and the damage done in the course of achieving it. As previously mentioned, the lack of a Spanish precursor to John of Biclarum means we lack a rounded picture of the reign of Athanagild, but even Isidore's brief reference implies that warfare with the imperial forces in the south was endemic there from the beginning of the 550s onwards. The relatively greater details available for the campaigns of Leovigild

---

[69] Ibid. 76, p. 76.
[70] For example, in Collins, "Mérida and Toledo."

indicate something of what this may have involved: sieges, massacres, destruction, disruption of economic and social life. Such features extended themselves into the west and the north from the middle of the 570s onward, while further damage was done to the south in the suppression of Hermenegild's revolt.

In the case of Spain, we lack the kind of substantial historical narrative of events that is provided in the case of the war of 535 to 554 between the Ostrogoths and the Byzantines in Italy by the writings of Procopius and Agathias. But it is known, both from these and other sources and confirmed archaeologically, that nearly 20 years of almost continuous warfare had the most profound and destructive effects on the social and economic order of Italy, marking a real break in many aspects of administrative organization, settlement patterns, and population sizes.[71] There may be grounds for wondering if more than 30 years of continuous warfare in Spain, from the revolt against Agila around 550 to the destruction of the Suevic kingdom in 585, may not have had equally dramatic effects on life in the Iberian peninsula.

As the Italian evidence shows, actual battles and sieges and the movements of armies may have been periodic and localized. Certain towns and regions might be particularly affected by them, but others could suffer equally from the general and widespread breakdown of order that such a state of endemic warfare generated. If it is correct to identify the *rustici rebellantes* that Leovigild slaughtered in 572 and 577 with what fifth-century writers would have called *Bagaudae*, it suggests that disruption was so intense that large-scale banditry was the best recourse for a significant body of the rural population. Similarly, although our sources present the destruction of such mechanisms for local government as the senate of Cantabria and the lordship of Aspendius as inherently desirable, this is a later and partial perspective. We do not know how much damage may have been done in the short term by the violence of the campaigns that led to their elimination, and beyond that in the medium term by the removal of what may have been very long-established forms of regional self-government, and their replacement by an alien military elite. In some of these regions Leovigild's campaigns in the 570s may have marked the real break with the Roman past.

---

[71] Chris Wickham, *Early Medieval Italy* (London, 1981), pp. 24–7.

This view of the impact of the reign of Leovigild, which sees it as marking the real caesura between Roman and Visigothic Spain, needs to be tested archaeologically, but the new evidence that is emerging to indicate that the Byzantine military presence was perhaps more extensive and that the militarization of society was more widespread than previously imagined may serve as a pointer in this direction.

3

The Catholic Kingdom, 586-672

Conversion and Reaction, 586-590

The accession of Reccared in 586 precipitated a short period of political activity, intended not least to resolve the continuing conflict in the kingdom over religious allegiance. Theologically the distinction between Arianism and Catholicism, which centered on the question of the equality and coeternity of the three persons of the Trinity, may appear rarefied. It is hard to know if this is how it would also have seemed to members of the laity in later sixth-century Spain. It has long been thought that the Visigoths retained their Arian beliefs, which they had acquired largely through the accident that this had been the dominant theology in the eastern empire when they were converted to Christianity in the fourth century, because these helped to reinforce their sense of distinctiveness from the majority Hispano-Roman population, which was almost entirely Catholic.[1] If so, this became in time a far less important determinant of that sense of identity. Goths were converting to Catholicism by the 560s if not before, as can be seen from the cases of John of Biclarum and bishop Masona of Mérida. At the same time, the Arian synod held in Toledo in 580 so modified its theology, effectively accepting the coeternity and equality of the Son while still denying that of the Holy Spirit, as to make it acceptable to some Catholics, including bishop Vincent of Zaragoza.[2] So the lines of demarcation between the two parties were

---

[1] J. M. Wallace-Hadrill, *The Barbarian West 400-1000* (3rd edn., 1967; revised version, Oxford, 1996), pp. 116-22.
[2] Isidore, *De Viris Illustribus* XXX, ed. C. Codoñer Merino, *El "De Viris Illustribus" de Isidoro de Sevilla* (Salamanca, 1964), p. 151: bishop Severus of Málaga wrote a treatise against Vincent, who had defected from Catholicism to Arianism.

breaking down even as the military and political unification of most of the peninsula was being achieved.

The existence of the two communities meant that most major towns would have had to have parallel Arian and Catholic churches and clergy. Likewise, rival ecclesiastical hierarchies existed, with bishops from the two denominations confronting each other in most if not all dioceses. Unfortunately, very little is known of the practicalities of Arianism in the Visigothic kingdom. That bishops of both parties coexisted in cities like Mérida is known, not least from the *Vitas Patrum Emeretensium*, a hybrid hagiographic work that ostensibly tried to provide a Spanish equivalent to the collection of Italian miracles contained in the *Dialogues* (593) of pope Gregory the Great, but which rapidly turns into a detailed narrative of the doings of the bishops of Mérida in the second half of the sixth century. It is thought to have been written around the 630s.[3] This text, in recounting the career of the Gothic Catholic bishop Masona (by 573-ca.600/610), indicates that an Arian bishop called Sunna was also present in the city. There is no way of knowing how many churches or clergy the Arian community had, nor of discovering what differences if any there may have been between the forms and language of their worship and that of the Catholics.

In the case of Mérida, Masona's principal difficulties are presented as coming both from his Arian episcopal rival and from king Leovigild, who eventually exiled him and put a more compliant Catholic bishop called Nepopis into the see. This followed an unsuccessful attempt by the king to force Masona into surrendering one of the principal relics of the city's patron saint, an early Christian martyr called Eulalia, to the Arians.[4] While the Arian establishment in the city lacked the local political weight to take on the Catholic bishop, it was able to use its clearly privileged access to the king in its bid to try and gain spiritual supremacy by acquiring the most revered objects of local popular devotion. Success in this would have given the Arians a monopoly on supernatural access to the martyr through her material relics.

---

[3] A. Moya Sánchez (ed.), *Vitas Sanctorum Patrum Emeretensium* (= *Corpus Christianorum Series Latina*, vol. CXVI), pp. i-x.
[4] Ibid. V. v-vi, pp. 56-71; on the significance of the struggle for control of the basilica and the relic see Roger Collins, "Mérida and Toledo, 550-585," in Edward James (ed.), *Visigothic Spain: New Approaches* (Oxford, 1980), pp. 189-219.

These issues of influence and communication lay at the heart of the difficulty in resolving the continuing religious divide, which seems from other indicators to have been becoming less and less meaningful in these years. Whatever may have been true in matters of comparative numbers of believers, and it could be that there were in practice very few Arians in Spain in comparison with Catholics, the association between the Visigothic elite and the Arian clergy made it hard for the monarchy to change its religious allegiance. To do so would involve a significant political risk. If the Gothic nobility supported the Arian hierarchy, it is unlikely the king would be able to act, even with the backing of the Catholic bishops and the Hispano-Roman landowners. At the same time, there must have been a growing recognition from all sides that this was a problem that needed solving.

Very similar difficulties had existed in some other western kingdoms earlier in the century. The Burgundian monarchy had initiated a dialogue with the Catholic episcopal establishment in the time of Gundobad (474-516), and had then converted under his son Sigismund (516-23).[5] Even the Vandals had seen their king tentatively explore the possibilities of theological reconciliation in the reign of Thrasamund (496-523), only for his successor to move too precipitately and trigger a reaction that led to his own death and the destruction of the kingdom.[6] There is some evidence that even Leovigild was moving toward the idea of accepting Catholicism as the basis for theological unity in the kingdom around the time of his death.[7] It is thus likely that many of the Visigothic lay aristocracy were coming to recognize the value of eliminating the religious division, but the problem lay in how to do this without precipitating violence. The Arian bishops, like their Catholic counterparts, are likely to have come from the ranks of the leading families and would have enjoyed a network of social and political connections, all members of which might fear loss of local influence and prestige if the main channels of communication between the regions and the court were switched from the Arian to the Catholic establishment.

---

[5] Ian Wood, *The Merovingian Kingdoms 450-751* (London, 1994), pp. 24-5, with references.

[6] C. Courtois, *Les Vandales et l'Afrique* (Paris, 1955), pp. 266-71 and 301-9.

[7] Roger Collins, "Donde esteban los arrianos en el año 589?" in R. Gonzálvez (ed.), *El Concilio III de Toledo. XIV Centenario* (Toledo, 1991), pp. 211-22.

In such circumstances, Reccared's own personal conversion to Catholicism in 587, just ten months after his accession, was clearly a highly significant symbolic act, as well as being the catalyst for the change necessary to bring the issue to a resolution. But if it were to lead to the elimination of the religious divide within the kingdom, it had to be accompanied by a real reconciliation of the Arian episcopal hierarchy and its powerful lay supporters. The latter in particular had to feel they were not in danger of losing patronage and status. How this was actually achieved is shrouded in evidential obscurity, but a crucial first step was undoubtedly the meeting between the king and an assembly of Arian bishops, held in the aftermath of the announcement of his conversion. No record exists of the decisions taken there, but this council must have initiated a process of discussing and resolving a wide range of questions, both practical and theological; by the time that the Third Council of Toledo assembled in May 589, most of these issues had already been settled.[8] This grand assembly itself, attended by the king and his new wife, queen Baddo, and by 72 bishops and many other lesser ecclesiastics and lay notables, primarily served as the means of formalizing decisions that had previously been made. It thus symbolized the reconciliation of the two churches, and in practice the elimination of Arianism from the Visigothic kingdom.

In such a process, however much consensus had been achieved, there were bound to be political and economic losers. Former Arian bishops were permitted to retain their episcopal rank and functions, sharing the dioceses with the Catholic incumbents, but the continuance in office of Arian metropolitans with province-wide authority could not be accepted.[9] Similarly, members of the secular aristocracy, at both court and regional levels, who had enjoyed royal favor under Leovigild, were not necessarily guaranteed its continuance from his son, especially as he immediately began using royal resources to patronize Catholic churches and monasteries, and to recompense those who had been deprived of their property under Leovigild. Discontented elements could only take to violence to try to reverse an imminent loss of status and power.

---

[8] Ibid. An English version, "King Leovigild and the Conversion of the Visigoths," forms item II in idem, *Law, Culture and Regionalism in Early Medieval Spain* (Aldershot, 1992).

[9] Ibid. pp. 4-5 (English version).

The first reaction came in 587 with a conspiracy to seize the throne on the part of a Gothic noble called Segga, with the backing of bishop Sunna, the Arian metropolitan of Lusitania. John of Biclarum reports that this plot was detected, and Segga had his hands amputated and was exiled to Galicia, while Sunna was also sent into exile, but outside the kingdom.[10] In his case the destination was the province of Mauritania (Tingitania), where he was later to be martyred while trying to convert the inhabitants to Arianism. These details of his fate are known from another account of this episode, given in the *Vitas Patrum Emeretensium*, which provides a more localized, Méridan perspective on it. According to this source, the conspirators included a number of Gothic counts, and their intentions also involved the murder of bishop Masona and that of Claudius, the Hispano-Roman duke of the province of Lusitania. The plot was betrayed by Witteric, one of the Visigothic counts, who would later become king.[11] The *Vitas Patrum* makes no mention of Segga, but combined with John of Biclarum's brief account, it is possible to see that this was a conspiracy with both court and regional ramifications, and represented the first attempt at a preemptive strike by those who felt threatened by the changes taking place following the death of Leovigild.

The year 588 saw what may have been a second such plot, though this may also have been invented to justify the elimination of some implacable opponents of the new order. According to John, a bishop Uldila, probably the Arian metropolitan of Toledo, and queen Gosuinth, widow of both Athanagild and Leovigild and the inspirer of the revolt of Hermenegild, were denounced to Reccared for treasonable conspiracy. The bishop was exiled, while as John puts it, "Gosuinth, always hostile to the Catholics, then gave up her life," leaving us to wonder if he means suicide, murder, or execution.[12]

The same year saw what is reported as a significant military success over a Frankish army invading the province of Narbonensis and besieging Carcassonne, one of the main frontier fortresses. This was won by duke Claudius, one of the targets of the Arian conspiracy of 587. Claiming that Claudius with only 300 men had put to flight 60,000 Franks, John compared this victory with that of Gideon over the Midianites. While such figures should be ignored, this and an

---

[10] *Johannis Biclarensis Chronicon* 87, ed. Hartmann, p. 79.
[11] *Vitas Patrum Emeretensium* V. x-xi, ed. Moya Sánchez, pp. 81-92.
[12] *Johannis Biclarensis Chronicon* 89, ed. Hartmann, p. 79.

earlier victory over a Frankish duke Desiderius in 587 must have given a considerable boost to Visigothic military morale and perhaps also something of a divine seal of approval to Reccared's new regime.

If so, it did not prevent a further attempt being made to overthrow it. This took place in 589, in the aftermath of the meeting of the Third Council of Toledo. It is not known if it was directly or otherwise linked to the recent political and theological changes, though this is a reasonable assumption. The principal protagonist was Argimund, the Gothic duke of Carthaginiensis. From John's words, he seems to have proclaimed himself king. His associates were executed and he himself was brought back to Toledo in chains. There he was "first interrogated with whips, then was scalped as a mark of his shame; next he had his right hand cut off, and was displayed throughout Toledo mounted on an ass, as an example to all that servants should not be presumptuous to their masters."[13]

Changing Dynasties, 590-642

With the account of the humiliation of Argimund in 590, John of Biclarum ended his chronicle, although he was probably writing it no earlier than around 604. From our perspective this is deeply regrettable, in that the remainder of the reign of Reccared is almost entirely obscure. Gregory of Tours took his historical narrative up to the year of his own death in 594, but had nothing more to say about Spain. In the Iberian peninsula the historiographical tradition was continued by Isidore of Seville, but the scale of his treatment of the period in his *History of the Goths* and in his chronicle is exceedingly brief. Both of these works of his exist in two versions: a shorter, earlier one composed in the reign of the Visigothic king Sisebut (611/12-20), and a somewhat longer one datable to the middle years of the reign of king Suinthila (621-31).[14] In the case of the chronicle two further versions

---

[13] Ibid. 93, p. 83. For such "exemplary" punishments, especially against failed usurpers, see Michael McCormack, *Eternal Victory: Triumphal Rulership in Late Antiquity, Byzantium and the Early Medieval West* (Cambridge, 1986), pp. 80-130.

[14] Cristóbal Rodríguez Alonso, *Las Historias de los Godos, Vándalos y Suevos de Isidoro de Sevilla. Estudio, edición crítica y traducción* (León, 1975); see also Roger Collins, "Maximus, Isidore and the Historia Gothorum," in Anton Scharer and Georg Scheibelreiter (eds.), *Historiographie im frühen Mittelalter* (Vienna and Munich, 1994), pp. 345-58.

have been detected in the manuscript tradition, representing intermediate phases in his transformation of the short form of the work into the longer one.[15] However, none of these texts provides more than the barest outline account of contemporary events.

From the final 85 years of the existence of the Visigothic kingdom, that is, from 625/6 to 711, only one contemporary historical work survives, the *Historia Wambae* or "History of (King) Wamba." This was written by Julian of Toledo, probably in the later 670s or soon after he became bishop in 680, and it just deals with events of the years 672 and 673. This text was intended to serve more as a work of rhetorical and political instruction than a piece of literary history, and it provides no information about Wamba prior to his accession or after his suppression of the revolt of count Paul in the province of Narbonensis in early 673.[16]

For the long periods not covered by contemporary Spanish historical writings, recourse has to be made either to later texts or to a handful of works composed outside the kingdom but which have some information on events in the peninsula. Of these the most significant is the anonymous chronicle written and compiled in Burgundy sometime after 659, and ascribed by scholars from the sixteenth century onward to a certain "Fredegar." There are no grounds for thinking this actually was his name, and indeed it was long believed that the work was written by more than one author. This Fredegar, or "Pseudo-Fredegar" as it would be more exact but cumbersome to call him, was primarily interested in Frankish events up to the year 642 when his chronicle abruptly stops, but he did manage to include some information on Spanish affairs. Generally, though, he preferred to provide picturesque stories rather than detailed historical narratives of the kind favored by Gregory of Tours. But at least he can be said to offer clues as to how events in Spain

---

[15] José Carlos Martín, "El Capítulo 39 del Libro V de las *Etimologías* y la *Crónica* de Isidoro de Sevilla a la luz de la tradición manuscrita de esta última obra," in Maurillo Pérez González (ed.), *Actas del III Congreso Hispánico de Latín Medieval*, vol. 1 (León, 2002), pp. 161-70.

[16] *Historia Wambae Regis*, ed. T. Mommsen, *MGH SRM* vol. V (1910), pp. 486-535; reprinted in *Corpus Christianorum Series Latina*, vol. CXV (1976), pp. 213-55. On this see Roger Collins, "Julian of Toledo and the Education of Kings in Late Seventh-Century Spain," which is item III in idem, *Law, Culture and Regionalism in Early Medieval Spain* (Aldershot, 1992).

were seen by a contemporary writing several hundred miles away in eastern France.[17]

There are later accounts of some aspects of Visigothic history, but few of these are close in time, and all look back to this period through the distorting glass of the Arab conquest and the ensuing destruction of the kingdom. Most concentrate on the events immediately preceding that cataclysmic episode, largely with an eye to determining where the blame for it should be laid.

Other contemporary sources may be more limited in scope and nature, but they tend to be more reliable than the fuller ones that date from after 711. Among such texts should included the acts of a succession of councils of the church in the Visigothic kingdom, held frequently though not regularly from 633 up to the later 690s.[18] A final council in this cycle of synods, which was held in Toledo in the first decade of the eighth century, has unfortunately not left any records of itself, though no doubt they once existed. Among the *acta* of the councils may be found occasional references to secular events, and many of the decisions taken by the bishops reflected issues of contemporary significance that had been put before them by the kings. These included the formulation of ecclesiastical sanctions that could be used in defense of the royal office against those who would try to take it by force, either in an act of usurpation or in breach of the agreed mechanisms for determining the succession to the kingdom.

The sense of insecurity and the frequency of the challenges to the king, especially when new to the throne, that emerge from such conciliar texts, are confirmed, not least by the detailed account of the first year of the reign of Wamba in Julian of Toledo's *History of Wamba*, and also by the evidence of yet other sources, such as coinage. Thus, two monarchs are represented in the Visigothic coinage, of whom no mention whatsoever is made in any literary

---

[17] On this work, its author(s), and the problems it poses see Roger Collins, *Fredegar* (Aldershot, 1996).

[18] The only modern critical edition of the councils of the Visigothic kingdom is that of Gonzalo Martínez Díez and Felix Rodríguez (eds.), *La Colección canónica Hispana* (5 parts in 6 vols., 1966-92). Unfortunately, this only extends as far as the *acta* of the Tenth Council of Toledo of 656. More than ten years later there is still no sign of the necessary final volume. Pending its appearance, the acts of the rest of these councils must be consulted in José Vives (ed.), *Concilios visigóticos e hispano-romanos* (Barcelona and Madrid, 1963), which is based on a smaller body of manuscripts.

source. One of these, called Iudila, is known from two coins; one minted in Mérida and the other in *Eliberri*, a Roman town close to Granada. As their style is closest to that of the coinage of Sisenand (631-6), it would seem that he held power for a short while in the province of Baetica, probably sometime in the early 630s.[19] The other case is that of a certain Suniefred, known only from a single coin minted in Toledo, which can be dated stylistically to the first half of the reign of king Egica (687-702).[20] These two examples show how very limited is our knowledge of what may have been quite major events in the history of the Visigothic kingdom.

Even the chronology of the kings is in some cases ambiguous or uncertain, though a systematic attempt was made to establish it by the German scholar Karl Zeumer in 1901.[21] While this has generally been accepted, in one or two cases it is in need of revision, and the dates offered here sometimes depart from those normally used. It has to be said, too, that in the light of the very limited nature of the evidence, a reconstruction of events, however much in outline, could be highly misleading and erroneous. But it must be attempted, in order to give at least some shape to the history of this period in the Iberian peninsula.

The obscurity of the reign of Reccared after 590, in comparison with its opening years, cannot really reflect a period of total tranquillity. Frankish threats remained, and Byzantine diplomacy was active in the western Mediterranean throughout the reign of Maurice (582-602). Isidore makes a general reference to campaigns fought against the Basques and against the imperial forces in the south, but gives no details. He enthuses over the king's good nature and kindly manner and appearance.[22] More concretely, he also refers to the restitution of property to individuals and of churches that had been confiscated by Leovigild. This, it may be assumed, was part of the continuing process of rewarding those who had suffered at the hands of his father's regime, something that might have involved depriving the latter's supporters of some or all of their gains. Even after the suppression of the revolts of 587 to 589 this could have left a discontented faction of

---

[19] G. C. Miles, *The Coinage of the Visigoths of Spain. Leovigild to Achila II* (New York, 1952), pp. 30 and 321, and plate XXII.
[20] Ibid. pp. 37-8 and 405, and plate XXXIV.
[21] Karl Zeumer, "Die Chronologie der Westgothenkönige des Reiches von Toledo," *Neues Archiv* 27 (1902), pp. 411-44.
[22] Isidore, *Historia Gothorum* 54, ed. Rodríguez, p. 264.

the nobility looking to reverse their recent losses. This would help to explain subsequent events.

On his death in 601, when he was probably still in his forties, Reccared left the crown to his only known son Liuva, who according to Isidore was then aged 18.[23] If so, he must have been born in 683. He was not Reccared's son by queen Baddo, who had been present at the Third Council of Toledo in 589, and his unnamed mother was described by Isidore as not being of noble birth. He may have been illegitimate, and the fact that Isidore makes such a point about his origins, while praising his personal virtues, might imply that this was used against him. In any event a coup in 603 by members of the nobility led to his deposition and death, probably in consequence of having his right hand cut off. With him ended the line of Leovigild.

Among the leaders of this coup was a count Witteric, who features in the *Vitas Patrum Emeretensium* as one of the men who had conspired against bishop Masona and king Reccared in Mérida in the aftermath of the Third Council of Toledo. As he was chosen king in 603, and was responsible for the killing of Liuva II, this coup has sometimes been seen as the prelude to an Arian revival.[24] There is no evidence to support such an interpretation, as it is unlikely that Isidore would have omitted such a detail, which to him would have been of the greatest significance. It is more probable that Witteric and his supporters were looking to redress the loss of power and wealth that they suffered under Reccared.

Witteric was regarded by Isidore, who otherwise disliked him, as a competent soldier, though in practice not a particularly lucky one. His reign was apparently marked by further conflicts with the Byzantine forces in the peninsula, which included the capture of some of them at Sagunto; whether this also involved the taking of the town itself is not stated.[25]

Another aspect of the reign is described by the Frankish chronicler known as Fredegar, who states that in 607 a marriage was arranged between Witteric's daughter Ermenberga and Theoderic II (596-613), ruler of the eastern Frankish or Austrasian kingdom, but that he sent her back to Spain unwed soon after she arrived at his court. This so

---

[23] Ibid. 57, p. 268.
[24] Wallace-Hadrill, *Barbarian West*, p. 121.
[25] Isidore, *Historia Gothorum* 58, ed. Rodríguez, pp. 268, 270.

infuriated Witteric that he organized an alliance against Theoderic, consisting of the latter's brother Theudebert II (596-612), king of Burgundy, the Lombard ruler Agilulf (590-616), and himself.[26] Nothing apparently came of this alliance in practice, and Witteric was murdered by a group of his own nobles in 610.

It is significant that Isidore makes no mention of these diplomatic activities on the part of Witteric or of his involvement in Frankish dynastic politics, which continued a tradition extending back to Leovigild and Reccared, who had attempted to negotiate a Frankish marriage for the latter in 584. This had failed only because of the murder of the chosen bride's father, the Neustrian king Chilperic (561-84), while she was actually *en route* to Spain for the wedding.[27] In the case of Ermenberga, Fredegar asserts that it was the influence of the Frankish king's Visigothic grandmother, Brunechildis, that led to the proposed marriage to Theuderic II breaking down. Isidore himself is unlikely to have been in royal favor in the time of Witteric and may have known little of what was happening in the court, and Fredegar's information is often of an anecdotal and personalized kind. The motives behind the proposed alliance and the reasons it collapsed may well have more substantial foundations than the physical appearance of one Visigothic princess.

In this respect it is noteworthy that the alliance against Theuderic II continued in being in the time of the next king in Toledo, Gundemar (610-11/12), and so can hardly have depended just or primarily upon the insult to Witteric's daughter in 607, especially as Gundemar must have been deeply involved in the plot that led to his predecessor's murder.[28] His own brief reign is significant on two counts. First it saw, at a synod held in the capital in 610, the transfer of the metropolitanate of the province from Cartagena, still in Byzantine hands, to Toledo. This made the hitherto rather obscure church of Toledo the primatial seat of Carthaginiensis, thus formalizing the close relationship that would develop between the bishops of the capital and the kings they served.

---

[26] J. M. Wallace-Hadrill (ed.), *The Fourth Book of the Chronicle of Fredegar* (London, 1960), IV. 32, pp. 20-1.

[27] Gregory of Tours, *Libri Decem Historiarum* VI. 45, ed. Bruno Krusch and Wilhelm Levison, *MGH SRM* vol. I, pp. 317-19.

[28] J. Gil (ed.), *Miscellanea Wisigothica* (Seville, 1972), pp. ix-xx and 3-49. See *epp.* XI and XII, pp. 31-7 for the continuing alliance against Theuderic II.

The second interesting feature of the reign is the existence of a collection of seven letters written by a count of the name of Bulgar, who was serving in the province of Narbonensis. Their survival is a matter of pure chance, in that they were put together with seventeen other letters of roughly the same period, perhaps to serve as models of literary style, probably in the ninth century in the kingdom of the Asturias.[29] King Gundemar himself is said by Isidore to have had led successful expeditions against both the Basques and the Byzantines, the latter involving the siege of a town whose name is not given.

Gundemar's death from natural causes led to the succession of Sisebut (611/12-20), one of the most learned of the Visigothic kings, who must also have been sufficiently competent militarily to have been chosen by the nobility who had supported his predecessor. He is said to have personally led two campaigns against the Byzantines, resulting in the capture of various towns, while his generals suppressed a rebellion amongst the Asturians and defeated the *Ruccones*.[30] The latter, who had been attacked by the Suevic king Miro in the early 570s, were probably located in Galicia or the western edge of the Asturias.

Fredegar speaks of Sisebut's defeat of a duke called Francio and the resulting recovery of Cantabria, which had been under Frankish rule. This has been seen as relating to the campaigns in the Asturias and against the *Ruccones*, but in this period Cantabria extended from the eastern borders of the Asturias to as far as the Rioja and the upper valley of the Ebro. This was the region conquered by Leovigild in 574, and no source suggests it had subsequently been overrun by the Franks. While allowing for the vagueness and imprecision of Fredegar, it may be allowed that some of this region had indeed come under Frankish rule, perhaps in the time of Liuva II and Witteric, and that its recapture was a triumph on the part of Sisebut's generals.

Sisebut was the dedicatee of the original version of Isidore's massive encyclopedia, the *Etymologiae*, and of his scientific treatise *De Natura Rerum*. Sisebut replied to the latter with a poem of his own composition on the subject of eclipses.[31] Such literary exchanges do not mean that Isidore was necessarily Sisebut's principal advisor, even

---

[29] Ibid. letters X to XVI, pp. 30-44.
[30] Isidore, *Historia Gothorum* 59, ed. Rodríguez, p. 270.
[31] Jacques Fontaine (ed.), *Isidore de Séville. Traité de la Nature* (Bordeaux, 1960), pp. 1-19 and 151-61.

in ecclesiastical matters. The bishops of Toledo were always in closer and more regular personal contact with the kings than those of Seville. In the second half of the reign the see of Toledo was in the hands of Helladius (615-633), who had previously been a member of the royal court and the holder of a high administrative office, before becoming a monk and then abbot of Agali.[32] Although he has left no writings, it is hard not to suspect that in most political respects his influence would have exceeded that of Isidore.

Certainly the bishop of Seville did not approve of one of Sisebut's policy initiatives, though whether he expressed this at the time is not known. This was the enforced conversion of the Jews, imposed early in the reign. Something very similar may have occurred in Francia in the reign of Dagobert I (623-38/9), who was said to have forced the Jews in his kingdom to convert, as the result of a request by the emperor Heraclius (610-41). If so, this is unlikely to have been the motive behind Sisebut's decision, which after the king's death was condemned by Isidore in his *Historia Gothorum*.[33] The means and consequences of reversing this policy were debated by the bishops of the kingdom at the first general council of the Visigothic church held thereafter – the Fourth Council of Toledo of 633.[34] While forced conversion was here implicitly criticized, those who had been impelled into becoming Christians were not to be permitted to relapse into Judaism because they had received the sacrament of baptism, which was irreversible.

On his death Sisebut was succeeded by a son called Reccared. This choice of name is significant in itself, in that it would seem to proclaim some kind of relationship to the former royal house of Leovigild and his descendants. Isidore does his best to skirt over the reign of Reccared II, assigning it a length of "a few days, before death intervened."[35] In so doing he obscured the regnal chronology of the Visigothic monarchy in these years, and may well have covered up

---

[32] Ildefonsus, *De Viris Illustribus* VI, ed. Carmen Codoñer Merino, *El "De Viris Illustribus" de Ildefonso de Toledo* (Salamanca, 1972), pp. 124-6.
[33] Isidore, *Historia Gothorum* 60, ed. Rodríguez, pp. 270, 272.
[34] IV Toledo, canons LVII-LXVI.
[35] Isidore, *Historia Gothorum* 61, ed. Rodríguez, p. 274. This reference to Reccared II is only to be found in the second, longer version of this work. The earlier version, to judge by its final words, was written very soon after Sisebut's death, and from its favorable tone, almost certainly during the reign of his son.

the young king's real fate. At any rate, it seems that, however he met his end, he reigned for more than a few days, probably for a year and two to three months.[36]

In 621 he was replaced by a new king of a different family, by the name of Suinthila, under whose rule the Byzantines were finally ejected from their remaining strongholds in the Levante. Cartagena, the administrative center of the imperial province, fell around 625, and may have been demilitarized, with the destruction of the city wall.[37] For this monarch Isidore produced revised and expanded versions of his *History of the Goths, Vandals, and Sueves*, and of his chronicle. In the former, completed in 625/6, Isidore gives some account of the king whom he describes as being "the first to rule all of Spain within the straits of Oceanus," in other words the whole of the peninsula.[38] Before acquiring the kingdom Suinthila had been one of Sisebut's military commanders, and had led the expedition against the Ruccones. As king he also conducted yet another campaign to try to put an end to Basque raiding. Like Leovigild before him, this led to his establishment of a new town called *Ologicus*, which is often thought to be on the site of the later Olite in Navarre, but this has not yet been confirmed archaeologically.[39] Whether such settlements were intended for occupation by pacified Basques, brought out of the Pyrenees or to serve as garrison centers for forces stationed to protect the region against subsequent raids, is not known, though the latter may be more probable.

Isidore extolled and idealized the virtues of Suinthila: "faith, prudence, industry, strenuousness in examination in the passing of judicial sentences, outstanding care in the exercise of rulership, munificence towards all, generosity to the poor, a disposition towards quick forgiveness; so that not only is he worthy to be called the ruler

---

[36] Regnal lists establish this longer period for his reign. Two separate versions give figures of one year, two months, and ten days, and of one year and three months. See Karl Zeumer (ed.), *Chronica Regum Visigothorum* (= *MGH LL* vol. I, p. 459). These command much higher respect than Isidore's weasel words. Accepting them has led to the chronological revisions made in this book, although Zeumer himself preferred to follow Isidore.

[37] M. Martínez Andreu, "La muralla bizantina de Cartago Nova," in *Del Conventus Carthaginiensis a la Chora de Tudmir* (= *Antigüedad y Cristianismo* 2, 1985), pp. 129-51.

[38] Isidore, *Historia Gothorum* 62, ed. Rodríguez, pp. 274, 276.

[39] Ibid. 63, pp. 276, 278; see Roger Collins, *The Basques* (Oxford, 1986), pp. 88-9.

of the people but also the father of the poor."[40] This, however, was the king under whom he was writing, and whose line might have been expected to have survived in the person of his son Riccimir (unusually, a Suevic name), who according to Isidore had been made co-ruler with his father. If so, however, this is not reflected in the coinage, which is all issued in the name of Suinthila alone. Conceivably Riccimir was still too young to exercise personal authority.

Whatever the truth or otherwise of Isidore's views on the king, they were clearly not shared by all. Fredegar reports that the nobility, from whose ranks Suinthila himself had risen, became increasingly hostile. In 630 one of them called Sisenand led a rebellion in the Ebro valley, having previously secured a promise of military assistance from the Frankish king Dagobert I (623-38/9). The latter's army had only just joined Sisenand at Zaragoza when Suinthila was overthrown.[41] His fate and that of his son and notional co-ruler are not recorded, not least because Isidore, having produced new versions of each of his historical writings in praise of the two previous kings, did not extend them any further. So we do not know what he thought of Sisenand or how he might have justified the coup of 631. It is possible, though, that this brief period of chaos also saw the short-lived bid of Iudila to make himself king in Baetica, something known only from the chance survival of two of his coins.

Fredegar's all too brief account of these events includes the interesting detail that Sisenand had promised the Frankish king Dagobert an item from the royal treasure of the Visigoths, a gold *missorium* or engraved charger that had been given to king Thorismund (451-3) by the patrician Aetius, in the aftermath of the defeat of the Huns by the Goths and Romans in 451. It is perhaps testimony to the role that such pieces played in preserving the historical memory of a collective such as the Visigoths, that the nobility prevented Sisenand from alienating it, and so he had to send Dagobert its weight in gold instead.[42] It has been suggested the resulting influx of gold led to an improvement in the quality of Frankish monetary emissions.[43]

---

[40] Isidore, ibid. 64, p. 278.
[41] Fredegar IV. 73, ed. Wallace-Hadrill, pp. 61-2.
[42] Ibid. p. 62.
[43] J. P. C. Kent, "The Coins and the Date of Burial," in Rupert Bruce-Mitford (ed.), *The Sutton Hoo Ship Burial*, vol. 1 (London, 1975), p. 600.

Whatever the reasons for Isidore's failure to revise his historical writings yet again, the reign of Sisenand may have seen the apogee of his political influence. Although it had been envisaged by the bishops attending the Third Council of Toledo in 589 that such kingdom-wide ecclesiastical assemblies should be held regularly thereafter, this had not happened. Admittedly, such hopes and intentions had been expressed at many of the great councils of the church in the time of the Roman empire and these too had been disappointed. So no particular blame attaches itself to the Visigothic bishops and kings for failing to turn this pious hope into reality. In practice, though, several provincial councils were held in the ten years after 589, and in most parts of the kingdom. But after 599 this activity ceases, except in Baetica, where a major council of the bishops of the province was held under Isidore's direction in 619 (the Second Council of Seville). Another one from the mid-620s is known but has left no records of itself.[44] Isidore himself may also have put together in these years the first version of a would-be comprehensive collection of acts of previous councils held in Spain, Africa, and Gaul, to be added to those of the great Ecumenical Councils of the imperial centuries.[45]

Not until December 633 was another council of the whole church of the Visigothic kingdom summoned to Toledo. It is perhaps significant that this followed the death of bishop Helladius of Toledo, probably earlier that year. It is possible that he was not keen for such a gathering that would be presided over by Isidore, by virtue of being the longest serving of the metropolitan bishops. On stylistic grounds it is also thought that Isidore may have been responsible for writing up the decrees or canons that the assembly passed, and therefore was no doubt also influential in the discussions that produced them.[46]

The council itself dealt with a very wide range of ecclesiastical issues of doctrinal, disciplinary, and liturgical kinds, but culminated in its final and seventy-fifth canon, "made under the judgment of God for the strength of our kings and the stability of the people of the

---

[44] A synod that met in Seville around 628/9 deposed the bishop of *Astigi* (Ecija): L. A. García Moreno, *Prosopografía del reino visigodo de Toledo* (Salamanca, 1974): no. 193, Martianus, pp. 99-100.

[45] Gonzalo Martínez Díez, *La Colección canónica Hispana*, vol. 1 (Madrid, 1966), pp. 257-70.

[46] Pierre Cazier, *Isidore de Séville et la naissance de l'Espagne catholique* (Paris, 1994), pp. 61-8.

Goths," with a solemn and lengthy condemnation of those who might conspire against the king, despite their oaths of loyalty to him.[47] What particular event may have prompted this is not known, though if the short-lived revolt of Iudila in Baetica is not to be dated to 631, it could have taken place in 633.

Whatever its causes, this canon represented the first of a series of attempts made by the Visigothic bishops to use the threat of spiritual sanctions, in the form of excommunication, as a means of protecting the legitimate kings from attempted usurpations, revolts, and noble coups. More detailed and extensive consideration was given to this issue at the Fifth Council of Toledo, called soon after the death of Isidore on April 4, 636.[48] This council also took place under a new reign. At some date before the bishops gathered for the council on June 30, 636, Sisenand had been replaced by a king called Chintila. As to why and how this took place, we are not informed by any source.

What is clear, though, is that Chintila was mightily worried about the security of his throne. Virtually all of the canons of the Fifth Council of Toledo were devoted to the protection of the king and of his family and followers. The rulings of the Fourth Council on this subject were reiterated and ordered to be made known to all throughout the kingdom. Chintila and his heirs were proclaimed to be inviolable in their tenure of the throne, and in the enjoyment of all the property they justly acquired. Anathemas were proclaimed against those who might attempt to put a curse on the ruler, or to harbor any hope of succeeding to his office while he was still alive. His eventual successors were forbidden from unjustly depriving the present monarch's supporters of the property he had given them. A new three-day penitential litany was also instituted, to be observed from December 13 each year, as a way of seeking divine forgiveness for the "abundance of iniquity and absence of charity" seen to be afflicting the kingdom.[49]

This council was presided over by the bishop of Toledo, Eugenius I (636-47), but was sparsely attended by only 22 other bishops and one deputy for an absentee; very possibly it had been called at short notice. Probably in consequence, another larger council was convened

---

[47] IV Toledo, canon lxxv, ed. González and Rodríguez, pp. 248-60.
[48] V Toledo, ed. González and Rodríguez, pp. 275-91.
[49] Ibid. pp. 277-8.

in January 638, at which 48 bishops were present, and which repeated most of the canons of the previous council, though reiterating their contents at greater length, as well as adding a number of new ones of a more purely ecclesiastical character.[50]

If Chintila thought he and his dynasty were well protected by the supernatural sanctions that this succession of councils had instituted to guard the person of the monarch and his heirs, he would have been posthumously disappointed. He died, most probably in 639, and was succeeded by his son Tulga, who is said by Fredegar still to have been a youth. This is sometimes taken to imply Tulga was a child, but Fredegar qualifies his vaguer initial mention of this subject by referring to the king's *aduliscencia* (*sic*).[51] Roman terminology on the ages of childhood is quite precise, as can be seen from Isidore's treatment of the subject in his *Etymologiae* (XI. ii. 4), and adolescence was taken as lasting from 14 to 28.[52] So Tulga was formally not a minor, and could rule in his own name. He could even, like Liuva II, have been in his early twenties. In practice, however, he seems to have been unable to impose effective authority on the kingdom and was deposed by a gathering of Gothic nobles. He was tonsured as a monk, thus making him ineligible for secular authority at any future point, and the kingdom was given to one of the Gothic lords, by the name of Chindasuinth.

Kings and the Political Elite, 642–672

Fredegar, with Gallic disdain, presented Chindasuinth's overthrow of Tulga as no more than another typical example of the Visigothic fondness for conspiring against their kings, but it may be seen instead as the operation of a mechanism for dealing with the problem of an ineffective monarch. Whether Tulga was personally incompetent to rule or whether the tensions within the ruling elite had become too severe to be tolerated cannot be judged with certainty. However, the reiterated injunctions of the Fifth and Sixth Councils of Toledo that

---

[50] Ibid. pp. 293-336.
[51] *Fredegar* IV. 82, ed. Wallace-Hadrill, pp. 69-70.
[52] Isidore, *Etymologiae* XI. ii. 4, ed. W. M. Lindsay, *Isidori Hispalensis Etymologiarum sive Originum Libri XX* (2 vols., Oxford, 1911), unpaginated.

the king's supporters, his *fideles*, should not be deprived of their property by his eventual successors would suggest that some elements in the ruling class in the kingdom had been benefiting disproportionately from royal favor and that they were afraid that under a new king their gains, ill-gotten or otherwise, might be taken from them.

This may well be just what happened early in the reign of Chindasuinth (642-53). According to Fredegar, the new monarch, said to be aged about 90 at the time of his death in 653, rapidly eliminated many of the leading men of the kingdom. Over 200 of those of the first rank and 500 of lesser standing are reported as being executed, while many others were exiled. Their property, widows, and daughters were then redistributed amongst the king's own supporters.[53] Whether or not Fredegar's figures be reliable, this sounds like a major redistribution of political power and wealth among the Visigothic aristocracy. As Chindasuinth's *fideles* were the main beneficiaries, it seems certain that it was those of Chintila and his family who were the principal losers by this process, which produced amongst other things a period of much greater stability in the royal succession and in king-making processes, that lasted up till 710. This may have been, therefore, another major turning point in the political history of the Visigothic kingdom.

One consequence of this was Chindasuinth's co-opting of his own son Reccesuinth to serve as joint ruler in 649. Fredegar refers to this, and to Chindasuinth's own death, which occurred in 653, and this serves as part of the evidence to show that he was writing his chronicle after the latter date, and probably not before ca.660, but his text otherwise breaks off with the account of events in Spain and in Francia around 642, and we lack his testimony on subsequent developments in the peninsula.

The elevation of Reccesuinth by his father, which is also affirmed by the existence of a joint coinage in both their names and bearing images of both kings, is the subject of a petition preserved in the small collection of 44 letters to or from bishop Braulio of Zaragoza (631-ca.651).[54] In this Braulio, together with a bishop Eutropius,

---

[53] See note 51.

[54] Miles, *Coinage of the Visigoths of Spain*, pp. 348-50. There are surprisingly few of these coins known, and it may be that the majority of issues continued to be just in the name of Chindasuinth. Braulio of Zaragoza, *ep*. XXXVII, ed. Luís Riesco Terrero, *Epistolario de San Braulio. Introducción, edición crítica y traducción* (Seville, 1975), p. 148.

whose see is not known, and a count called Celsus, requested Chindasuinth in the most diplomatic language to make Reccesuinth his co-ruler. As it is highly unlikely that the decision to do so was just the result of a petition from two bishops and a count in the Ebro valley, the more sensible assumption would be that this process was orchestrated from Toledo, and that such leading ecclesiastical and civil office-holders throughout the kingdom were encouraged to write in supporting or proposing just such a decision. Why this was necessary will emerge shortly.

Chindasuinth may have been the first of the kings for over half a century to commission a new codification of the laws of the kingdom, as a possible code of his creation has been detected by some scholars as forming a major component of that certainly promulgated by Reccesuinth in 654, the year after his father's death.[55] This certainly makes sense. If so, Chindasuinth seems to have been much less interested in the processes of the making of canon law, in that after the relative flurry of conciliar activity in the 630s, his reign saw only one church council being called in Toledo. This was the Seventh Council, held in October 646, which was attended by only 30 bishops and which promulgated just six canons. Five of these related primarily or exclusively to ecclesiastical matters, and included the requirement that the bishops of the sees in the vicinity of (a term not here defined) the "royal city" or *urbs regia* should spend one month of each year resident in Toledo.[56] This can be seen as a stage in the gradual elevation of Toledo as the primatial see of the whole church of the Visigothic kingdom.

Continuing the tradition of the more political legislation of previous councils was the first of the canons here promulgated, which excommunicated all members of the clergy and of the laity who fled the kingdom, conspired against the king, or gave aid to those engaged in so doing. The sentence of excommunication on such traitors was not even to be lifted on the deathbed of anyone thus sentenced, and any bishop who gave them communion, even if acting on the king's own orders, would himself be liable to the same

---

[55] P. D. King, "King Chindasvind and the First Territorial Law-Code of the Visigothic Kingdom," in Edward James (ed.), *Visigothic Spain: New Approaches* (Oxford, 1980), pp. 131-58.
[56] VII Toledo canon vi, ed. González and Rodríguez, pp. 356-7.

penalty. The council also earnestly begged all present and future monarchs by "the ineffable sacrament of the divine name" not at any point to consider lifting any such sentence passed on members of the clergy or the laity.[57]

The tenor of this conciliar enactment is rather different to those of the preceding councils, in which well-meaning but ineffectual attempts were made to protect the monarch against conspirators working within the kingdom. Here the emphasis is more on the punishment by supernatural means of those who might engage in plots from outside the kingdom. This probably needs to be seen in the light of Fredegar's words about Chindasuinth's executing and exiling of members of the nobility. Apart from those actually killed, it is likely that others must have fled, and members of the families of those executed may also have found it necessary to leave the kingdom. So, in the years between 642 and 646 it is likely that relatively large numbers of those who had prospered under the preceding royal regimes were either sent or took themselves off into exile, and that communities of such émigrés formed in southern Francia or in the Byzantine territories in North Africa, looking for an opportunity to return to Spain, and began fomenting plots that might bring about the political changes that would make it possible for them so to do.

The co-opting of Reccesuinth onto the throne by his father four years prior to his death did not in practice make the succession any easier. The death of the old king in 653 was followed by a regional revolt in the Ebro valley, where a man called Froia made a bid for power. It is likely that he was a count and had some following in the region, but he does not seem to have had the support of the leading local bishops. We know of this revolt only because it is referred to in a letter from Taio, bishop of Zaragoza (ca.651-pre 683) to his colleague Quiricus, then bishop of Barcelona and later of Toledo (667-80).[58] This prefaced a collection of extracts from the writings of Gregory the Great in five books, which Taio had made at Quiricus's request, and in it he referred to the recent disturbances as a reason for the delay in completing his task. He claimed that Froia had called in the Basques to assist him, and that they had

---

[57] Ibid. canon i, pp. 346-7.
[58] *Tajonis Caesaraugustani Episcopi Sententiarum Libri V, praefatio*, ed. Manuel Risco, *España Sagrada* vol. XXXI (2nd edn., Madrid, 1859), pp. 170-4.

been subjecting Zaragoza to a siege. Whether this was strictly true or whether they were just taking advantage of the disturbed conditions in the kingdom to raid the middle Ebro valley cannot be known for sure. However, a military expedition led by Reccesuinth led to the crushing of Froia's revolt and the withdrawal back into the mountains of the Basques.

An anonymous author writing in Toledo sometime after 754 said of Reccesuinth that he was "generous but loose-living."[59] The basis for this verdict is not known and the chronicler had no other information at his disposal on the events of the reign. Virtually his only source would seem to have been a copy of the collected acts of the church councils of the Visigothic kingdom, and our situation today is almost identical. While Reccesuinth's reign was the longest of any of the Spanish Visigothic kings, it is one of the obscurest in respect of our knowledge of the events that took place in it. As just mentioned, the suppression of Froia's revolt in 653 is one of the few exceptions. A few details on the king's death in September 672 have also been preserved, as these provide the opening of the account of the first year of the reign of his successor written by Julian of Toledo, but the 20-year period in between is an almost complete blank.[60]

While it is not always sensible, when faced with small and disparate pieces of evidence that have survived largely thanks to chance, to assume that they must be somehow linked and capable of being united to tell a single and coherent tale, in the case of the materials relating to the opening years of Reccesuinth's sole reign there may be some merit in such an approach. It could be suggested that Froia's revolt served as a catalyst for the political changes that took place later the same year. For one thing, such regional revolts served as a test of support for the reigning monarch, who relied upon the military contributions of the nobility for the army required to suppress such challenges to his authority. If he could no longer count on that backing or if the rebel seemed a more attractive choice as king, a change of ruler and of dynasty could take place. This had been what occurred in 631, when the aristocracy failed to back Suinthila against Sisenand.

---

[59] *Chronicle of 754* 25, ed. López Pereira, p. 46.
[60] *Historia Wambae* 3-4, ed. Mommsen, pp. 502-4 (*MGH* edition) or pp. 219-20 (*CCSL* edition).

In 653 Reccesuinth was clearly able to mobilize the support needed to eliminate Froia, but his position was clearly not a strong one, and the concessions that he made at the ensuing Eighth Council of Toledo, which opened on December 16 that year, may represent the price of the support he had needed earlier in the year. At the meeting of the Council, magnate representation was more overt than on any previous such occasion, although in the conciliar *acta* this was made out to be normal procedure. In the signatures to the acts 18 palatine office-holders are listed, the first time that such men had been called on to confirm the deliberations of an ecclesiastical council.[61] It must be assumed too that the bishops supported such a change in procedure and in the balance of power that it represented.[62]

The decisions of the council involved the making of significant changes to the settlement that had resulted from Chindasuinth's seizure of power in 642. The second canon of the council, after a very lengthy elaboration of the theological arguments behind it, removed the obligation under oath that had been placed on succeeding kings not to lift the penalties on those convicted of treason who had fled the realm, which had been laid down by the Seventh Council of 646.[63] That had itself been an extraordinarily solemn declaration, and now required an even weightier one to reverse it. The practical purpose behind this can only have been the effecting of some degree of reconciliation with those who had suffered loss of property and exile in the aftermath of Chindasuinth's coup d'état against Tulga.

While there might have been pressure to make it easier for some of the émigrés to return and thus reduce the perceived threat that they represented, it seems surprising that this was so significant an issue. It probably makes more sense when seen in the light of other issues raised at the Eighth Council. In particular, the assembled bishops stated that previous kings had been treating property confiscated from those condemned for treasonable activities as if it were their

---

[61] For the office and role of the palatine nobility see Amancio Isla Frez. "El *Officium Palatinum* visigodo. Entorno regio y poder aristocrático," *Hispania* 62 pt. 3 (2002), 823–47.

[62] VIII Toledo, ed. González and Rodríguez, pp. 447–8. On this council see Jeremy du Quesnay Adams, "The Eighth Council of Toledo (653): Precursor of Medieval Parliaments?" in Thomas F. X. Noble and John J. Contreni (eds.), *Religion, Culture and Society in the Early Middle Ages* (Kalamazoo MI, 1987), pp. 41–54.

[63] VIII Toledo canon ii, ed. González and Rodríguez, pp. 386–412.

own. A distinction was here being made very clearly between the property that a monarch owned privately, by virtue of inheritance from his family, and that which he administered by right of his office. The former was his own in an absolute sense, and which he could freely dispose of and transmit to his heirs. The property, both lands and goods, that he controlled by virtue of being king could only be passed on to his successor on the throne.

Such a distinction, which was a fundamental and distinguishing feature of Visigothic law, made sense in a political system in which the monarchy was elective, and hardly ever remained in the hands of one family for longer than two generations.[64] In fact, in the whole of the period from 531 to 711, only the dynasty of Liuva I and Leovigild was able to retain the throne for three generations, and the third of these did so for only two years. Built into the expectations of Visigothic monarchy in the two centuries after the extinction of the "Balt" dynasty of Alaric I in 531 was the presumption of dynastic impermanence. In consequence, it became very important for such a distinction to be made between the monarch's personal, family property and that which he held in trust. This latter will have included the royal treasures, which served as tangible symbols of the shared history of the people over whom the kings reigned. Sisenand had been prevented from alienating such an item in 631 by the Gothic nobility that had backed his coup against Suinthila.

While there may not have existed the same kind of ideological significance in respect of royal estates as opposed to treasures, a blurring of the distinction between a monarch's personal property and that of the fisc was equally threatening. A king could use the royal estates to enrich his own family and to alienate the resources needed to maintain the monarchy. As dynastic continuity was so short-lived as to be almost nonexistent, this could mean that royal property would be permanently lost if treated as the private possession of the family that currently held the kingship. Even if a son succeeded his father on the throne, grants of estates to brothers and other family members similarly removed them from royal control, and built up the wealth of the noble house concerned while depleting that of the monarchy. Thus, it is not surprising to find that one of

---

[64] On this see P. D. King, *Law and Society in the Visigothic Kingdom* (Cambridge, 1972), pp. 62-4 with references.

the specific complaints voiced by the bishops in 653 seems to have been gifts of property made by Chindasuinth to Reccesuinth's unnamed brothers.[65]

At the heart of the matter, however, seems to have been the more general unease over the fact that Chindasuinth in particular had taken over as his personal property much of what had been confiscated from those whom he had purged in 642 and thereafter. In other words, he had enriched his own family and not the monarchy. The bishops requested that this be rectified, and in particular that such properties confiscated from the supporters of previous kings be redistributed to the *fideles* of the present monarch.[66] In this, therefore, the bishops were acting as the mouthpiece of the court aristocracy, not least the 18 named office-holders who would sign the acts of the council, and whose position they so obviously supported.

So it seems that the nobles who had backed Chindasuinth in the early 640s, and who had come out in support of his son in 653, felt that the old king had kept far too many of the spoils of the victory for himself and had used them to strengthen the economic position of his own family rather than that of his office or to reward his followers. They used the council as a means of demanding redress. There also seems to have been a feeling that some of the confiscations carried out under Chindasuinth had been unjust or had been improperly handled. These were now to be investigated, with the bishops requesting that those who had wrongly been deprived of their property should recover it. In general, there was a reaction against what were seen as the excesses of royal power under the previous king, and some of the feeling about him may have been encapsulated in a very bitter epitaph that was written by bishop Eugenius II of Toledo at some date between 653 and his own death in 657.[67]

Another decision taken at the council and contained in one of its acts related to the processes of king-making. It was stipulated in the tenth canon that the election of a new king should henceforth take place only in the *urbs regia* or in the place where the previous king

---

[65] VIII Toledo *decretum*, ed. González and Rodríguez, pp. 448-57.
[66] Ibid.
[67] Eugenius II, *Epitaphion Chindasuintho regi conscriptum* (= *Carmina*, 25), ed. F. Vollmer (*MGH AA* vol. XIV), pp. 25-251.

should die. It was made clear that the election of a new monarch should be made specifically by "the bishops and the *maiores palatii*," by the latter meaning the principal office-holders and military commanders of the royal court.[68] As it took months to call together the episcopal body for the holding of a church council, in practice this requirement meant that the choice of king would be made by the palatine nobility usually attendant on the previous monarch, together with those bishops who were then at court or who could quickly be summoned to it. In reality this meant the metropolitan bishop of Toledo and some of his suffragans. Ecclesiastical representation was thus notional, but focused on the person of the bishop of Toledo, who also came to play a unique role in the ceremonial of kingmaking.[69] The real power in choosing the monarch was given to the nobles of the court, again represented in 653 by the 18 office-holders who signed the acts of this council, and in whose interests the bishops again seem to have been speaking. The procedure thus outlined was that which would be followed when Reccesuinth died in 672.[70]

What the bishops may have gained from their alliance with the court nobility was a period of more regular conciliar activity. This was something that had been an ideal, and not just in the church in Spain, for several centuries. But even under the Roman empire councils had been held very occasionally, and plans for a more frequent and regular pattern, such as one being called every two years, had never been realized in practice. In Spain, while such a program of holding councils had been proposed at the Third Council of Toledo in 589, in practice they had met only sporadically in the decades that followed. However, the Eighth Council of 653 was followed by the Ninth in 655 and the Tenth in 656.

Reccesuinth was clearly forced to concede much of what was demanded of him in December 653. He issued an edict taking back into royal possession lands that had been obtained by all of his predecessors since Suinthila, which had been turned into the personal property of the monarchs and their families. But he excluded from

---

[68] VIII Toledo, canon x, ed. González and Rodríguez, pp. 427-31.
[69] See below p. 98.
[70] *Historia Wambae* 3-4, ed. Mommsen, pp. 502-4 (*MGH* edition) or pp. 219-20 (*CCSL* edition).

this any such estates that had been legally bequeathed by the previous kings to their heirs.[71] This recognized the principle but limited its application in practice. He also recognized the force of what was being demanded of him in respect of the principle of royal property being of two types: the family property of the king and that which was his to administer while he held office. Here again he made a reservation, in that the latter had to be available to the monarch to dispose of as was politically or otherwise necessary. In practice, though, there must have been a recognition that it would be unwise of him to do so in favor of his own family, at least without a prior acceptance of this on the part of the leading nobles of the court.

The distinction between the two types of royal property was also enshrined in the civil legislation of Reccesuinth, in the code of laws that he promulgated in 654, known as the *Leges Visigothorum* or *Forum Iudicum*. This may have been revised and corrected by bishop Braulio of Zaragoza on the basis of an earlier draft and was put before the bishops for their approval, probably at the Eighth Council.[72] Its being issued at this point is again probably not coincidental, and represents part of the process of constraining and redirecting royal authority that seems to have been taking place in 653 and 654.

One feeling that emerges from the events of this period, seen also in the wider context of the history of royal successions throughout the seventh century, is that there existed a strong presupposition that long-term royal dynasties should not be allowed to come into existence. Kings were generally chosen by the court nobility from among their own number. The men thus elected rose from the ranks of the electors, who no doubt regarded them as the best choices in the particular circumstances, but who would not thereby wish to concede a permanent royal status to their descendants. Other evidence of this will emerge.

In the case of Reccesuinth it is likely that in 653 his aristocratic supporters were not anticipating the long-term survival of his dynasty. When he died in 672 he seems to have had no direct heir. No mention is made at any stage of his having children, and his only known wife, queen Recciberga, is said to have died some time before 657,

---

[71] VIII Toledo, *Lex edita in eodem concilio*, ed. González and Rodríguez, pp. 457-64.
[72] Braulio, *ep*. XL, ed. Riesco Terrero, p. 152.

aged 22 years and eight months, and after seven years of marriage.[73] She is one of the very few Visigothic royal wives whose name has been preserved, in her case thanks to a verse epitaph composed in her honor by bishop Eugenius II of Toledo (647-57). If Reccesuinth married again, we have no record of it. So, it must have become clear that a change of dynasty would follow his death, especially as there seems to have been no significant support for his brothers and their families.

---

[73] Eugenius II, *Epithaphion in sepulchro Reccibergae Reginae* (= *Carmina* 26), ed. Vollmer, p. 251.

4

The Visigothic Twilight, 672-710

Court Conspiracies, 672-681

We are unusually well informed about the events following Reccesuinth's death, which took place at his villa of Gerticos in the *Campos Góticos* west of Salamanca in September 672, as they form the opening section of the short historical work by Julian, bishop of Toledo (680-90), known as the *Historia Wambae* or "History of Wamba." To this were attached two rhetorical speeches denouncing what was described as the treacherous and disloyal conduct of Gaul, here meaning the province of Narbonensis.[1] These may have been written at an earlier date than the *Historia*, possibly in the immediate aftermath of the events themselves. While generally thought to have been composed while he was still a deacon, prior to his elevation to the episcopate, it has also been argued that the *Historia* was not written until after Julian was made bishop.[2] Like the two shorter pieces, the *History* was probably intended as a model composition, written for instructional purposes in the episcopal school of Toledo. But it may have also served to reinforce the view espoused by the church of Toledo that royal legitimacy was guaranteed only by a new king receiving unction at the hands of the bishop of the "royal city."[3] It thus had a predetermined ideological intent. While its origin and

---

[1] *Insultatio Vilis Storici in Tyrannidem Galliae* and *Iudicium in Tyrannorum Perfidia Promulgatum*, ed. W. Levison (*MGH SRM* vol. V), pp. 526-35; reprinted in *Corpus Christianorum*, vol. CXV, pp. 245-55.
[2] Yolanda García López, "La Cronología de la 'Historia Wambae'", *Anuario de Estudios Medievales* 23 (1994), pp. 121-39 for arguments on dating.
[3] Roger Collins, "Julian of Toledo and the Education of Kings in Late Seventh-century Spain," which is item III in idem, *Law, Culture and Regionalism in Early Medieval Spain* (Aldershot, 1992).

character mean that it should not be trusted implicitly, there are no grounds for doubting the reality of the events it describes, nor the reliability of many of its details.

Wamba was elected at Gerticos by the court nobles present when Reccesuinth died, according to the procedure laid down in the tenth canon of the Eighth Council of Toledo. That he was a member of that group himself is confirmed by a probable reference to him as the *vir illustris* who presented the testament of bishop Martin of Dumio to the Tenth Council of Toledo in 656, as well as by his presence at his predecessor's deathbed.[4] According to Julian, his legitimacy was ensured both by the procedures followed in his election and by his proceeding to Toledo to receive anointing at the hands of the bishop of the *urbs regia*, who at this time was Quiricus (667-80), formerly of Barcelona.[5]

Despite conciliar pronouncements, this correct following of the rules for the making of kings did not ensure Wamba a trouble-free succession. There were immediate problems in the province of Narbonensis, where count Ilderic of Nîmes and bishop Gumild of Maguelonne, together with an abbot Ranimir, were found engaged in a conspiracy. This may not have been so much an attempted usurpation, as Ilderic is never attributed with the title of king, as a plot to hand over these important border regions on the western edge of Narbonensis to Frankish control.[6] This was the kind of thing that Gregory of Tours reports as frequently happening in the case of the rival Frankish kingdoms in the later sixth century, with local magnates transferring their allegiances in return for better rewards and opportunities.[7] At the same time, as in 653, the succession of a new king and the outbreak of a regional revolt were also accompanied by Basque raids into the upper Ebro valley, and it was against these that Wamba seems to have directed his own efforts, while sending one of his electors, a duke of the name of Paul, to put down

---

[4] X Toledo, *decretum*, ed. José Vives, *Concilio visigóticos e hispano-romanos* (Barcelona and Madrid, 1963), p. 322. *Historia Wambae* 2, ed. Levison, pp. 501-2 (*MGH*) or 218-19 (*CCSL*).

[5] *Historia Wambae* 4, ed. Levison, pp. 503-4 (*MGH*), or 220 (*CCSL*). Luís García Moreno, *Prosopografía del reino visigodo de Toledo* (Salamanca, 1974), no. 250, p. 119, and no. 584, pp. 203-4.

[6] *Historia Wambae* 5-7, ed. Levison, pp. 504-7 (*MGH*), or 221-3 (*CCSL*).

[7] Ian Wood, *The Merovingian Kingdoms 450-751* (London, 1994), pp. 88-101.

the rebels in Narbonensis. They by this time had replaced the bishop of Nîmes, who had remained loyal to Wamba, by abbot Ranimir.[8]

Paul is almost certainly the "Paul Count of the Notaries," who was one of the 18 court office-holders who signed the acts of the Eighth Council of Toledo in 653, and under the same title was one of the four magnates who attested the acts of the Ninth Council in 655.[9] If so, he was one of the inner circle of the court, and probably longer established as such than Wamba, whose name does not appear in either list. Whatever the reasons that made Wamba seem the best choice for the kingship in 672, not all of his erstwhile colleagues may have been equally enthusiastic about his selection.

Paul certainly does not have seemed to have been. Instead of suppressing the rebels in Nîmes, he recruited them himself, and also obtained the backing of other local office-holders in the northeast. These included the powerful duke of the province of Tarraconensis, Ranosind, at whose suggestion Paul claimed the throne for himself.[10] An appeal for military support was also sent to the Franks. Paul received unction in Barcelona, as the metropolitan bishop of Narbonne refused to accept him as king, and apparently had to be crowned using a liturgical *corona* borrowed from a saint's shrine. Paul wrote a letter to Wamba, which prefaces the *Historia*, proclaiming himself a properly anointed king. He also referred to himself as king of the east, while referring to Wamba as king of the south.[11] This would suggest that he was not trying to challenge Wamba's legitimacy so much as proposing a division of the kingdom, along the lines of that made between Liuva I and Leovigild in 569. Such a solution was clearly rejected in Toledo, and the illegitimate foundations of Paul's claim to royal authority were a major feature of Julian's diatribe against him and his supporters.

Early in 673, following his action against the Basques, Wamba came down through the Rioja and the Ebro valley, apparently taking Barcelona and Gerona with little resistance. He then crossed the Pyrenees, drove Paul out of Narbonne and finally forced him to surrender after besieging him in the amphitheater at Nîmes. This is

---

[8] *Historia Wambae* 6–8, ed. Levison, pp. 504–7 (*MGH*), or 221–4 (*CCSL*).
[9] *Concilios*, ed. Vives, pp. 289 and 307.
[10] *Historia Wambae* 7–8, ed. Levison, pp. 506–7 (*MGH*), or 222–4 (*CCSL*).
[11] Ibid. *Epistola Pauli*, p. 500 (*MGH*), or 217 (*CCSL*).

useful literary evidence to support other indications that former Roman theaters and amphitheaters were turned into fortresses, and in some cases even into densely packed fortified settlements in the early medieval centuries. Paul was sent to Toledo for ritual humiliation and scalping in the course of Wamba's victory parade, before being sent into exile.[12]

As in 653, the ruling elite does not seem to have wanted to see a permanent political and economic degrading of those of their number who had supported Paul in 672-3, many of whom are named in the *Iudicium* or "Judgment," one of the two short texts Julian appended to his *Historia*.[13] At the Thirteenth Council of Toledo in 683 the next king, Ervig (680-7) readmitted the rebels of 672/3 to royal favor and restored their confiscated property.[14] They also recovered the right to give legal testimony, lost through the taint of treason.[15] It is just possible that this restitution extended to Paul himself and that he might even have been the count of that name who signed the acts of Sixteen Toledo of 693, but that would require him to have had an extraordinarily long, as well as varied, career.[16]

As in 653, the restoration of the property of the rebels of 672 through the acts of the council of 683 also involved suggestions that there had been improper force used against them and that coercion had been employed in securing confessions, resulting in unjust sentences of deprivation. It is remarkable to find such consistent patterns in the political life of the kingdom. What is not clear in either case is whether the reinstatement of those who had suffered in the course of a disputed succession involved the weakening or overthrow of those who at the time had been the principal beneficiaries of their disgrace. In other words, were the losers of 642 and 672 readmitted to a share in wealth and office because at least some of the victors in those episodes had now suffered a similar fate? That certainly would seem to be the case with the rehabilitation of the supporters of Paul, as may be seen from the events surrounding the ending of the reign of Wamba.

---

[12] Ibid. 12-30, pp. 512-26 (*MGH*), or 228-44 (*CCSL*).
[13] *Iudicium* 3-4, ed. Levison, pp. 531-3 (*MGH*), or 252-3 (*CCSL*).
[14] *Concilios*, ed. Vives, p. 412.
[15] Ibid. pp. 415-16.
[16] Ibid. p. 521.

It is striking that when the Twelfth Council of Toledo met in January 681 the bishops and leading nobles of the court seem to have combined once again, as they had in 653, to try and restrain the authority of the kings, and to suggest that the latter might have misused their power in the treatment of their political opponents. This was an alliance that had been brought into the open by the events of October 680, in the course of which the reign of Wamba was brought to an end. Unlike its opening stages eight years before, its conclusion is not well documented. The catalyst for what occurred may have been that the king fell seriously ill, to such an extent that it was assumed that he was going to die, in consequence of which he took on the state of penitence.

This was something that could be done only once in a lifetime, in that it was held to wash away all traces of sin, but at the same time, because it could not be repeated, a penitent had thereafter to lead a blameless and exemplary life, removed from temptations and worldly cares, if he were to avoid eternal damnation.[17] In the course of the next two to three centuries this procedure and the ideas that underlay it would give way to a new doctrine of penance, which transformed it into a repeatable sacrament which wiped out only the effects of those sins that had been confessed. Under the earlier view it was best to delay taking on the penitential state until close to death, even though there was a risk of leaving it too late, as the penitent would thereafter have to lead a severely restricted lifestyle, withdrawn from the world.

In the case of Wamba, apparent proximity to death would have made entering into the state of penance an obvious step. However, against all expectations he survived. In consequence, because of his penitential state, he was obliged to give up his royal office and enter into monastic life, where he passed the few remaining years of his life. In the context of contemporary theological ideas this makes perfect sense, but it cannot but be wondered if some other way around the problem might not have been found had there been sufficient support among the lay and clerical elite of the royal court for his continuing as king.

By the late ninth or early tenth centuries, when the brief chronicles of the Asturian kingdom were first being compiled, this episode had

---

[17] A. H. M. Jones, *The Later Roman Empire 284-602* (3 vols., Oxford, 1964), pp. 981-98.

come to be seen as a plot. The villain of the piece in this view was Wamba's successor Ervig (680-7), who is here said to have given him a potion that deprived him of his memory and left him prostrated and seemingly on the point of death. In all good faith, other courtiers not involved in the conspiracy put Wamba into the penitential state, and when the effects of the drug had worked off, he himself, recognizing his new status, willingly abdicated and retired into a monastery, where he lived for another seven years and three months.[18] It is generally recognized that there are a number of improbabilities about this Asturian version of these events, and that it should not be taken too literally, but the suspicion of foul play being involved in Wamba's abdication has always lingered.

The *Chronicle of 754* makes no mention of this episode at all, and passes over the succession of Ervig to Wamba without comment. The only contemporary evidence comes in an account of what had occurred that was included in the acts of the Twelfth Council of Toledo, which opened on January 9, 681. It is clear that some description of what had taken place only two months earlier, on October 31, 680, had to be given to the 38 assembled bishops (or their deputies), four abbots, and 15 court office-holders. This was the first item of business after they had recited a Trinitarian creed.[19]

Documents were presented in support of the report that was made, which stated that Wamba had received penance and "the venerable sign of the holy tonsure," and soon afterwards had signed a document ordering that Ervig should be his successor and should receive "the blessing of sacerdotal unction." In the records of the council the bishops confirmed that they had personally seen and inspected each of the documents concerned in turn. These consisted first of the statement by the nobles of the court (*seniores palatii*) about how the former king had received the tonsure and had entered into the religious life. The second text was Wamba's letter stating that he wished Ervig to succeed him as king, and the third was the instruction he wrote to bishop Julian, urging him to proceed to the unction of the new monarch with all possible speed. The bishops recorded that they recognized the signature of

---

[18] *Chronicle of Alfonso III* 2, in Juan Gil Fernández, José L. Moralejo, and Juan I. Ruiz de la Peña, *Crónicas asturianas* (Oviedo, 1985), p. 116.
[19] *Concilios*, ed. Vives, pp. 385-6.

Wamba on both of the latter two documents and confirmed their authenticity.[20]

There are a number of surprising features about this record and the documents to which it relates. First, receiving the sacrament of penance and being tonsured as a monk are not one and the same thing, but this is skirted over. What the magnates attested to was that the former king had taken the monastic habit. This, by the ruling made in canon 17 of the sixth council of Toledo of 638, made him ineligible for the royal office.[21] In other words, it prevented him from resuming the kingship. Secondly, in all of the previous conciliar legislation, designation of his successor by the reigning monarch had no part to play in the processes of king-making, but here it is made the key element in the choice of Ervig. Thirdly, while Julian had emphasized in his *Historia Wambae* the crucial constitutive role played by anointing, which had to be performed in the *urbs regia* and thus by the bishop of Toledo, there are no grounds for his doing so in the case of Ervig merely at the request of Wamba.[22] Election by the bishops and the magnates, which was presented as the key constitutive element in the choosing of a king in the acts of the Eighth Council of Toledo of 653, apparently plays no part at all in the succession of Ervig in October 680.[23] While the united testimony of the bishops gives no grounds for the suspicion that Wamba's two documents were forgeries, most other features of these events, as recorded in the conciliar *acta*, support the impression that the elevation of Ervig was the result of some kind of palace coup.

This is confirmed by the evidence on timing provided by another source. A detailed regnal list of late seventh-century date, which its editor called the *Chronica regum Visigothorum*, records that Wamba received the sacrament of penance in the first hour of the night on October 14, and that Ervig was proclaimed king the very next day, the 15th, while his anointing was briefly delayed until the 21st, which was the first Sunday after his accession.[24] All in all this was a very rapid chain of events. These details certainly undermine the story given out by the author of the *Chronicle of Alfonso III*, that Wamba

[20] Ibid. pp. 386-7.
[21] VI Toledo canon xvii, ed. Vives, pp. 244-5.
[22] *Historia Wambae* 3-4, ed. Levison, pp. 502-4 (*MGH*), or 219-20 (*CCSL*).
[23] VIII Toledo canon x, ed. Vives, pp. 282-4.
[24] *Chronica Regum Visigothorum*, ed. Karl Zeumer (*MGH LL* vol. 1), p. 461.

had been poisoned, and that when he recovered from what seemed a fatal illness he found himself a penitent and therefore, willingly or otherwise, stepped down from the throne. The regnal list makes it clear that Wamba's receiving penance preceded the proclamation of Ervig as king by a matter of only a few hours.

Furthermore, the testimony of the bishops indicates that Wamba must have been sufficiently sound in both mind and body to have signed the two documents that they recorded they had inspected and authenticated. So the evidence of contemporary sources confirms that the poison story is completely nonsensical. But also, more significantly, it establishes that Wamba was well enough to take the formal steps needed to designate his successor, while at the same time submitting himself to an act that involved his abdication.

If, as seems to be the case, these events represent the playing out of a coup on the part of the leading members of the court, it has often been suggested that the conspirators would have had one or more ecclesiastical accomplices in their ranks. Suspicion inevitably falls on Julian of Toledo, who succeeded to the bishopric earlier in 680, and who is known previously to have been friendly with Ervig, to whom he dedicated one of his lost works.[25] There were also reasons why the removal of Wamba would have been acceptable, even desirable, from Julian's point of view. Since the holding of the Tenth Council of Toledo in 656 there had been no large-scale or plenary council of the Spanish church. Reccesuinth had avoided calling another council during the remaining 15 years of his reign, though a council of the bishops of the province of Lusitania had been held in Mérida in 666. Under Wamba only provincial councils had been held, including one for the province of Carthaginiensis (known as the Eleventh Council of Toledo), that had met in the capital in 675.[26] It has long been suspected that after the highly critical line taken at the Eighth Council of Toledo, and the holding of the Ninth and Tenth in quick succession thereafter, the kings had intentionally prevented the convoking of any more plenary councils.

The death of bishop Eugenius II of Toledo in 657 may also have helped break the pattern established by the three councils of the

---

[25] The issue is fully discussed in F. X. Murphy, "Julian of Toledo and the Fall of the Visigothic Kingdom in Spain," *Speculum* 27 (1952), pp. 1-21.
[26] *Concilios*, ed. Vives, pp. 325-43 (Council of Mérida), and 344-69 (XI Toledo).

opening years of Reccesuinth's reign, but there are no reasons for suspecting that his successor, Ildefonsus (657-67), former abbot of Agali, was necessarily more compliant. He was the only significant bishop of the royal see who never presided over any council at all (even though the author of the *Chronicle of 754* mistakenly implied that he dominated the Eleventh Council of 675).[27] The next bishop, Quiricus (667-80) is probably the man of the same name who was previously bishop of Barcelona and dedicatee of Taio of Zaragoza's book of excerpts from the writings of Gregory the Great. If so, his translation from Barcelona, which was in defiance of canons of early church councils forbidding such a practice, is further testimony to the special status now being afforded to the bishopric of Toledo, which was gradually emerging as more than just one of the six metropolitan dioceses of the kingdom and was attaining primatial standing over the whole kingdom in theory as well as practice.

Under Wamba, whose legitimacy Julian had so eloquently argued in his *Historia*, the position of the see of Toledo was weakened by the king's decision to create new dioceses. One of these was established in Lusitania, centered on the monastery of Aquis (modern Chaves), the place of burial of an otherwise unknown martyr called Pimenius. The other new see, far more extraordinarily, was created in the *urbs regia* of Toledo itself, where the "Praetorian Church of Saints Peter and Paul in the suburb of the city" was placed in the hands of a new bishop. We know of these creations only from the acts of the Twelfth Council of Toledo of January 681, which abolished both of them.[28] Wamba was here blamed by name for these "foolish and unjust" creations, and was accused of violence in forcing them through against strong objections. As this was the king whose removal from the throne had just been so closely scrutinized by the bishops, it is clear that some of them at least were mightily relieved to see the back of him, and moved at once to suppress what they regarded as his illicit acts.

In the case of Toledo, the creation of a second see in the suburb and the giving of one of the three principal churches of the city to the new bishop can only have been intended to curb the authority of

---

[27] *Chronicle of 754* 36, ed. José E. López Pereira, *Crónica mozarabe de 754. Edición crítica y traducción* (Zaragoza, 1980), pp. 54-7.
[28] XII Toledo canon iv, ed. Vives, pp. 389-92.

the metropolitan. Particularly significant must be the fact that it was in this church that Wamba himself had been anointed king in 672, and would therefore be the likely site for future royal inaugurations. It was also here that the Eighth Council of Toledo had sat in 653, and it was from this church that the kings departed for war, following elaborate liturgical ceremonies in which they were presented with a large cross reliquary containing a fragment of the True Cross, which was carried before them during the ensuing campaign.[29] In other words this church, more than those of Saint Leocadia and of Saint Mary, was associated with the very elaborate ceremonial of kingship, which had become uniquely focused on Toledo in the course of the seventh century. This, it would seem, was to be taken out of the hands of the metropolitan bishops of the city and invested instead in those of a new bishop ruling over its suburb.

Not only was this immediately reversed once Wamba had been removed from power, but the council that carried it out itself met in the Praetorian Church of Saints Peter and Paul in order to do so.[30] This also makes sense of the fact that the acts of the Twelfth Council contain, by way of an appendix, those of a synod held in Toledo in 610 under king Gundemar, which had first established the metropolitan status of the city within the province of Carthaginiensis.[31] This was clearly intended to write the acts of that provincial synod into the record of the plenary councils of the kingdom, and to stress again the special significance of the bishopric of Toledo within its ecclesiastical province.

If the bishop of Toledo had reason to oppose Wamba, so too might some of the members of the aristocratic elite. The causes of their hostility are not so easily discerned, but it is noteworthy that of the few laws preserved that are ascribed to Wamba, one deals with the problem of getting the landowners to contribute military levies to the royal army when the king went on campaign.[32] While this has

---

[29] Roger Collins, "Continuity and Loss in Medieval Spanish Culture: the Evidence of MS Silos, Archivo Monástico 4," in Roger Collins and Anthony Goodman (eds.), *Medieval Spain: Culture, Conflict and Coexistence* (London, 2002), pp. 1–22; the text is to be found in Marius Férotin, *Le Liber Ordinum en usage dans l'Eglise Wisigothique et Mozarabe d'Espagne* (Paris, 1904), pp. 149–53.
[30] Vives, *Concilios*, p. 260.
[31] Ibid. pp. 403–7.
[32] *Leges Visigothorum* IX. ii. 8, ed. Zeumer, pp. 370–3.

sometimes been taken as a sign of general malaise and lack of public spirit in the late Visigothic period, in its context it is more indicative of a lack of willingness to support this particular king, and thus perhaps an early symptom of the possibility that he could not expect widespread backing should he be faced with the kind of regional revolt that led to the fall of Suinthila in 631. In such circumstances, for the court aristocracy to act to remove him before such a challenge emerged, which was something that could threaten them all, is perhaps not surprising. Wamba himself seems to have remained under something of a cloud, even after his death, as when in 693 king Egica referred back to the legislative activity of earlier kings, he spoke of "our predecessor of holy memory the lord Chindasuinth," while merely referring to Wamba as "the lord Wamba."[33]

The Uneasy Throne, 681–710

Why Ervig should have been the chosen beneficiary of the murky events surrounding the removal of Wamba is not made clear in any contemporary source. That he was the choice of the palatine aristocracy seems unquestionable, whether or not he was also that of his deposed predecessor. The Asturian *Chronicle of Alfonso III* offers more detail than is found in any earlier account, claiming that Ervig's father was called Ardabast and had come to Spain from Byzantium in the time of Chindasuinth, who had received him well and given him his own niece to marry.[34] This therefore made Ervig the great-nephew of Chindasuinth and cousin to Reccesuinth.

Whether there is any truth in this at all is unknown, as it is impossible to discover the source of this information. Much else that may be found in the chronicle's account of the late Visigothic period comes, like much of our own knowledge of it, from the acts of the councils. So, if genuine, it is not easy to know how and why this particular account of Ervig's family and origins was preserved uniquely in this Asturian text. It also has to be recognized that the Asturian monarchy, unlike that of the Visigoths, was transmitted through dynastic continuity. So Asturian chroniclers would have expected to

---

[33] XVI Toledo, "Tome" of Egica, ed. Vives, p. 487.
[34] *Chronicle of Alfonso III* 2, ed. Gil, p. 116.

find family links explaining royal succession in the Visigothic period, while those living at that time would not necessarily have done so. Thus, it is theoretically possible that Ervig was a member of the house of Chindasuinth through his mother, but this is more likely to be just the rationalization of an early tenth-century chronicler.

At the very least, what is known of actual succession practices in the Visigothic kingdom would imply that by itself such a family relationship would not have been sufficient grounds for his being elected king. It is perhaps also significant that no mention was made of this possible membership of the family of Chindasuinth in the detailed report on the events of 680 included in the acts of Twelve Toledo. Nor is it hinted at in any other contemporary text.

As in 653/4, the succession of a king in a position of some political weakness was rapidly followed by the issue of a revised version of the *Leges Visigothorum*. This contained a substantial body of new laws and revisions of existing ones.[35] Among the former were 28 measures directed against the Jews, which were ready in time for the Twelfth Council of Toledo of January 9, where they were approved by the bishops, led by Julian. Himself of Jewish origin, he was the most fervent or fanatical of all the churchmen of the Visigothic period in his anti-Jewish writings and activities.[36] The new laws were read out to the Jewish inhabitants of the city (or at least the leading men of the community) assembled in the church of Saint Mary on the 27th of that month, three days after the end of the council. The speed of this legislative activity is remarkable, and may suggest that some of it was already prepared, perhaps by Julian, in advance of the political events that permitted its being put into practice.

As in 654, so in 681 the issuing of a law code may be seen as a sign of unease on the part of the king, and/or of strength on the part of those members of the elite who wished to curb royal authority. So too may be the calling of plenary councils of the church of the kingdom; this was certainly associated with periods of monarchical weakness in the 630s and the early 650s. The Twelfth Council of January 681 was followed by the Thirteenth in November 683, the

---

[35] On this version of the code see P. D. King, *Law and Society in the Visigothic Kingdom* (Cambridge, 1972), pp. 19-22.
[36] *Chronicle of 754* 38, ed. López Pereira, p. 56, refers to Julian as being *ex traduce Iudeorum ut flores rosarum de inter vepres spinarum*.

Fourteenth in November 684, and the Fifteenth in May 688, matching something of the regularity in the holding of such assemblies of the early years of the sole reign of Reccesuinth.

As in the 630s, some of the conciliar legislation of the 680s shows a marked concern for the security of the monarch, his family, and supporters. As previously seen, those who had suffered under Wamba were rehabilitated and had their confiscated property restored in 683. The acts of the Twelfth Council, which had formally recognized the legitimacy of Ervig's coming to power, were officially reconfirmed by the Thirteenth, a unique occurrence.[37] The same council in 683 also addressed at length the question of the protection of the royal family after the king's death, naming specifically his wife, queen Liuvigoto, and referring also to those who were married to her sons and daughters. The bishops demanded that no one should openly or secretly seek to kill them or exile them, tonsure them, or deprive them of their property. The queen, her daughters, and daughters-in-law were not to be forced into monastic life following the king's death. All such acts or intentions were here forbidden by the bishops on pain of eternal anathema and judicial condemnation in the afterlife.[38]

In its very detail this canon seems to bespeak an air of desperation. A similar but far less specific ruling for the protection of the king's family and descendants had been issued by the Fifth Council of 636, clearly to no avail.[39] The inclusion of the queen by name in this one indicates that its purposes were very immediate, and that Ervig's heirs and relatives were looking to the future with little optimism. It is notable too that the canon implies the existence of sons of his already of marriageable age, but there is no suggestion that they were likely to succeed him on the throne. Quite the opposite would seem to have been expected.

The royal family certainly had reason to be worried, but it would not have expected that the real threat came from within its own ranks. Almost exactly seven years after the deposition or abdication of Wamba, Ervig was close to death, and a similar process of arranging the transfer of the throne took place, but with some significant

---

[37] XIII Toledo canon ix, ed. Vives, pp. 425-6.
[38] Ibid. canons iv-v, pp. 419-22.
[39] V Toledo canon ii, ed. Vives, pp. 227-8.

differences. On November 14, 687, Ervig proclaimed Egica as his chosen successor, and on the 15th he entered into the penitential state, and allowed the nobles gathered round his deathbed to depart to accompany the new king to Toledo. There Egica was anointed in the praetorian church of Saints Peter and Paul on November 24.[40] Among other things, these details would suggest that Ervig handed over the crown away from the capital, probably in a royal villa a few days' journey from Toledo.

His actual date of death is not recorded, any more than is his place of burial. The latter is true of all of the Visigothic kings. We do not know where they were buried, and among the survivals in the liturgical texts relating to kingship in the Visigothic period there are no items concerned with royal funerals or even the subsequent commemoration of the deaths of previous kings. These might have been expected to be standard features of the monarchical ceremonial of dynastic kingship, in which family relationships and continuity were emphasized, as in the case of the Merovingian Frankish royal house. But the Visigothic kingdom was in this as in other ways markedly anti-dynastic. It must be assumed that dead kings were buried by their families, and remembered primarily by them and not by subsequent rulers, to whom they had no links of blood.

While the *Chronica Regum Visigothorum* records the dates of the various stages in the transfer of power from Ervig to Egica in great detail, it gives no hint as to what lay behind this process. Information on this emerges from the acts of the ensuing Fifteenth Council of Toledo, which opened on May 11, 688, just about six months after the change of ruler. Much of this was taken up with a Christological controversy, over which bishop Julian had become embroiled with the papacy, which had queried the orthodoxy of some of his views on the nature of Christ. This had also been the primary focus of the Fourteenth Council of 684, but as this had been attended by only 16 bishops, it was reiterated at greater length in the Fifteenth, at which 80 bishops, deputies, and abbots were present, along with 17 counts.[41]

The principal political business of this gathering was the lifting of the anathema threatened by the Thirteenth Council against any

---

[40] *Chronica Regum Visigothorum*, ed. Zeumer, p. 461.
[41] On this see F. X. Murphy "Julian of Toledo and the Condemnation of Monotheletism in Spain," in *Mélanges J. de Ghellinck* (Gembloux, 1951), pp. 361–73.

who sought to harm the persons and property of the family of the previous king. In what may seem like a stunningly cynical act, the bishops agreed to the reversal of the ruling that had been made only five years before, not least by many of those present on this occasion. More specifically, they also justified the new monarch, Egica (687-702), in repudiating his predecessor's daughter, whom he had married as part of the arrangements made to secure his own succession. The former queen Liuvigoto was sent into monastic seclusion along with her daughters, and her family were deprived of their "unjustly acquired" possessions.[42]

Egica himself was most probably the count of that name who signed the acts of the Thirteenth Council. He could also have been related to a count Wittiza, who attended the Twelfth Council in 681.[43] He was thus a member of the inner circle of the court nobility, and leaving all other considerations aside, it may have been with the intention of attaching him firmly to the new royal family and its future protection that Ervig married him to one of his daughters at some stage during his reign, and then designated him as his successor. If so, this was a fatal miscalculation, as once he had become king Egica clearly felt it more expedient to rid himself of the connection, plunder the resources of Ervig's family and their allies, and free himself to marry again.

After this ruthless and profitable start Egica may have felt secure. He certainly did not encourage the calling of further plenary councils for a while. When the next one, the Sixteenth, did convene in Toledo in May 693, it was in the aftermath of yet more dramatic events. A key factor in its deliberations was a recent change in episcopal personnel. Sisebert, who had succeeded Julian as bishop of Toledo in 690, had been accused of involvement in a plot to dethrone and kill Egica. His co-conspirators were named as Liuvigoto, Frogellus, Theodemir, Luvilana, and Thecla. The bishops, in appropriately shocked tones, confirmed his deposition from his office, the confiscation of all his goods, and the sentence of perpetual exile passed upon him.[44]

In practice he must have been tried and condemned well before the holding of the council, as it was presided over by his successor

---

[42] XVI Toledo canon ix, ed. Vives, pp. 507-9.
[43] Vives, *Concilios*, pp. 434 and 402.
[44] XVI Toledo canon ix, ed. Vives, pp. 507-9.

Felix (693–c.700), who had been translated from the see of Seville (to which he had been promoted only after May 688).[45] Sisebert's fate had been decided long before the bishops proclaimed their acceptance of it. His fellow conspirators, if that is what they were, included the widow of Ervig, and it is a reasonable assumption that the other two women and the two men named were somehow related to her and the former king. This could be no more than the final elimination of the family of Egica's predecessor.

If so, he may have faced a far more serious threat at around the same period. A single coin that is related stylistically to those of the sole reign of Egica indicates that a king of the name of Suniefred seized power in Toledo at some point in these years, and for long enough to have the mint start issuing in his name. The name itself is also that of a *comes sanciarum et dux*, who signed the acts of the Thirteenth Council of Toledo in 683.[46] Exactly the same titles were held by Egica, whose name appears six places higher in the same list. If, like the bishops, the office-holders signed in order of seniority, Egica and Suniefred were colleagues, though with the former being of slightly longer standing.

Because of the chronological evidence, it has been suggested that the brief seizure of the throne by Suniefred and the treason for which Sisebert was condemned were one and the same thing.[47] It might be objected that no mention was made of Suniefred in the acts of the Sixteenth Council, but there was no necessary reason why there should be. Had he survived, he would have been dealt with by secular justice, and there would no formal reason for the council to be called to pronounce on his fate. In the case of Sisebert, his deposition as bishop required proper ecclesiastical procedure, and if it is right to think that the others named along with him were the surviving members of the family of Ervig, their inclusion would be justified by the fact that they had once been promised protection under threat of anathema by an earlier council. Recognition of their condemnation for treason completed the work done at the Fifteenth Council of Toledo to reverse that previous ruling.

---

[45] García Moreno, *Prosopografía*, no. 253, p. 122.
[46] G. C. Miles, *The Coinage of the Visigoths of Spain: Leovigild to Achila II* (New York, 1952), p. 405; Vives, *Concilios*, p. 434.
[47] Miles, *Coinage*, pp. 37–8.

In any case, the family of Ervig, if it were backing a revolt against Egica, would have needed a royal candidate of its own. Such a king, to be recognized as legitimate, would have had to have received unction. This, as Julian's *Historia Wambae* made clear, could be performed only in Toledo and by the bishop of the *urbs regia*. So, if Suniefred was established for long enough to be issuing coins in Toledo, it is reasonable to assume that he had already been anointed there, and for that he would have required the cooperation of bishop Sisebert.

Assuming this to be correct, Suniefred's actions may have had little to do with any sentiments of loyalty toward the unfortunate wife and family of his former royal master. Jealousy toward an erstwhile equal might have played a much stronger part, but there may have been another motive as well. Egica, unlike his two predecessors, took steps to establish the succession to the throne in his own lifetime, and was clearly determined that it should remain in the hands of his own family. He proclaimed his son Wittiza as co-ruler.

This event is normally dated to the year 698, on the basis of an entry in the chronicle of 754.[48] However, much more reliable is the evidence of the dating clause of a fragmentary but contemporary charter, which shows that Wittiza was associated with his father in the seventh year of the latter's reign, which began in late November 693.[49] That this is the preferable chronology is confirmed by the evidence of the coinage. Taking the total number of coin types issued per regnal year produces a fairly uniform pattern across the seventh century. The only exception is the joint reign of Egica and Wittiza, which by the traditional dating of it to the years 608-702 produces an anomalous and substantial increase in the number of types to the year.[50] If, on the other hand, this period is extended back to include the years from 694 to 698, the blip disappears and the resulting pattern coheres with that of other reigns. In other words, Egica and Wittiza need a longer joint reign than the generally accepted chronology allows. Thus, it seems certain that Egica proclaimed his son as co-ruler in 694. There is no way of knowing, but the intention to do so could either have been a contributory cause or a consequence of

---

[48] *Chronicle of 754* 44, ed. López Pereira, p. 62.
[49] Angel Canellas López, *Diplomática Hispano-Visigoda* (Zaragoza, 1979), no. 192, p. 255.
[50] Miles, *Coinage* pp. 406-30: compare the number of types for a supposedly four-year period with any other equivalent series.

the revolt of Suniefred. If the former, the prospect of the king trying to monopolize the royal office for his own family and exclude other equally throne-worthy noble lines may have prompted the attempt to overthrow him.

According to the *Chronica Regum Visigothorum*, Wittiza was not anointed king until November 24 in the year 700.[51] As, since Julian of Toledo's day at least, so much emphasis had been placed upon unction as a vital constituent part of the king-making process, it must be asked why this was delayed in his case for anywhere between two to eight years after his being proclaimed co-ruler by his father. The likelihood must be that he was deemed too young to receive this sacrament prior to this date. It may well be that it was only in late 700 that he achieved *adolescentia*, the point at which he would be able to rule in his own right and not subject to tutelage or a regency should his father die. This would make him about 14 years old. This might also confirm the statement in the *Rotense* version of the *Chronicle of Alfonso III* that Wittiza was the son of Egica's short-lived marriage to Ervig's daughter Cixilo, which we know ended soon after her father's death in late 687.[52]

Of the years of the joint reign a little is known. According to the *Chronicle of 754*, a Byzantine fleet which was raiding the Spanish coast was defeated at this time.[53] It is likely that this should be associated with the dispatch of a fleet from Constantinople in 697 by the emperor Leontius (695-8) to try to recover Carthage and the imperial province of Africa, which had just been conquered by the Arabs. Although initially successful, the Byzantine forces were driven out early in the following year. The fleet returned home, rebelling and setting up a new emperor in Crete on the way.[54] It is quite likely that during these operations in the West a detachment of this imperial fleet visited the Byzantine enclave around Ceuta and Tangiers. If so, this could have been the force that raided the Spanish towns on the opposite coast, and which was apparently then defeated by the Visigothic count Theodemir.

---

[51] *Chronica Regum Visigothorum*, ed. Zeumer, p. 461.
[52] *Chronicle of Alfonso III* 4 (*Rotense* version only), ed. Gil, p. 118.
[53] *Chronicle of 754* 87, ed. López Pereira, p. 112.
[54] Theophanes, *Chronica* A. M. 6190; on this episode see Warren Treadgold, *A History of the Byzantine State and Society* (Stanford, CA, 1997), pp. 337-8.

The *Chronicle of 754* also records the presence of plague in Spain in these years. An outbreak is reported in Constantinople in 698, and it is likely that the plague moved westward across the Mediterranean from there. The Spanish chronicler noted that so severe were its effects in the Visigothic capital that Egica and Wittiza left Toledo in 701.[55] It is possible that bishop Felix, who died at around this time, was one of the victims. He was succeeded by Gunderic (ca.700/1– before 711), who was said by the chronicler to be so holy that he started performing miracles.[56] No writings of his are known. He would at least have presided at the last known of the great series of Toledan councils, probably held in 703.

The last Council of Toledo of which the records survive, the Seventeenth, had been held in November 694. Its calling so close in time to the Sixteenth, held the previous year, would make of this another instance of councils meeting in relatively quick succession in periods of political weakness or of conflict. Again typically, this minor flurry of conciliar activity was followed by several years in which no plenary council was called.

The Eighteenth Council of Toledo met soon after the death of Egica in 702/3, but its acts have not been preserved. Its very existence is known only from a brief reference to it in a manuscript containing a conciliar collection, the last extant folio of which was destroyed in 1936, in the opening stages of the Spanish Civil War.[57] It is usually assumed is that the proceedings of this last council were lost because they came too late to be included in the final edition of the *Hispana* conciliar collection, first put together by Isidore and then revised and augmented by Julian of Toledo and others. However, there are some grounds for suspecting that the *acta* of the Eighteenth Council were deliberately suppressed because of what subsequently came to be seen as the controversial and heterodox nature of some of the decisions that had been taken, particularly those relating to clerical marriage.[58]

---

[55] *Chronicle of 754* 47, ed. López Pereira, p. 64; Theophanes A. M. 6190. This may explain the otherwise nonsensical report in the *Chronicle of Alfonso III*, ch. 4 (ed. Gil, p. 118) that Egica made Wittiza live in Tuy in Galicia, so that he might rule over the *Regnum Suevorum*.

[56] *Chronicle of 754* 48, ed. López Pereira, p. 64; García Moreno, *Prosopografía*, no. 254, p. 123.

[57] Gonzalo Martínez Díez, *La Colección canónica Hispana*, vol. 1 (Madrid, 1966), pp. 166-7.

[58] For this interpretation of the council see Roger Collins, *The Arab Conquest of Spain 710-97* (Oxford, 1989), pp. 15-19.

That there was some difficulty with the church in the ensuing period of Wittiza's sole reign is probably also implied by what the author of the *Chronicle of 754* has to say about the metropolitan bishop of Toledo in the final years of the reign. This was Sindered, who succeeded Gunderic at some point between ca.701 and 710. Although he is praised for his desire to lead a holy life, he is also said to have put pressure on the worthy old men of the church that had been put in his care, "not out of knowledge or from the zeal of holiness, but out of instinct and by command of king Wittiza."[59]

The somewhat elliptical quality of the author's remarks are, unfortunately, all too typical of his style. His original readers may have understood what he was alluding to, but it is not so easy for us. We can only guess at the nature of the events to which he refers, even in some of the most important parts of his narrative. In this case it is not possible to be sure if the "aged and honorable in merit" men to whom he is here referring were members of the clergy of Toledo or if his words applied more widely to the senior bishops of the kingdom, who by this period were in most respects subordinate to the primatial authority of the metropolitan of the *urbs regia*. In either case, it would be fair to suspect that what Sindered is being accused of is attempting to impose the king's will on the church, perhaps trying to enforce the controversial decisions taken at the recent Eighteenth Council. In any case Sindered's tenure of his office must have been brief, as he fled to Rome soon after the Arab conquest of the Visigothic kingdom.

Without the text of the decrees of this council, our knowledge of the political events surrounding the death of Egica and the beginning of the sole reign of Wittiza is also limited. A law in the civil code, the *Lex Visigothorum*, is dated to the sixteenth year of Egica, and was issued in Córdoba.[60] As it is known that he was anointed king on November 24, 687, his sixteenth year would begin on the same day in the year 702. It is thus quite possible that his reign extended into the year 703, contrary to what is usually asserted. But even the *Chronica Regum Visigothorum* deserts us at this point, as the reference to the unction of Wittiza in 700 forms its final entry. Two brief

---

[59] *Chronicle of 754* 53, ed. López Pereira, pp. 68-70; García Moreno, *Prosopografía*, no. 255, p. 123.
[60] K. Zeumer (ed.), *Leges Visigothorum* IX. i. 21, *MGH Legum, sectio I* (Hanover, 1902), 365.

continuations of this text are known, containing significant variations, but they only record approximate regnal lengths.[61] However, the *Chronicle of 754* provides a short but telling summary, which makes more sense when seen in the light of the precedents from earlier periods.

According to the chronicler, Wittiza reinstated those who had suffered at the hands of his father, recalling those who had been exiled and returning confiscated property. He ordered the public burning of *cautiones*, which has been translated as "pledges," that his father had unjustly extorted. What exactly is meant by this term is not entirely clear, but seems to indicate forced grants or cessions extorted by the former king, probably through legal processes. Wittiza also transferred property that Egica had taken as his own personal possession back to the royal fisc, in other words recognizing once again the distinction between the family property of the king and that which he held in trust by virtue of his office.[62]

This is so reminiscent of the complaints made against Chindasuinth in 653 and the restitutions made by Reccesuinth as to seem like a repeat performance of the same score. Parallels can also be made with the recall of exiles and restoration of their property that followed the replacement of Wamba by Ervig in 680. Particularly notable is the reiterated emphasis on preserving the royal estates distinct from those of the current holder of the title of king – a key element in Visigothic legal doctrine relating to kingship. The existence of two laws of Wittiza in several of the manuscripts of the *Leges Visigothorum* shows that the code was again revised and augmented in this period.[63] A reissue of the code may be linked to the political weakness of the king following his father's death in 703.

No contemporary or even near contemporary source reports the fate of Wittiza. It is normally assumed that his reign ended with his death, though he was probably only still in his mid-twenties. The year in which this occurred is generally taken to be 710, on the basis of deductions from the regnal lists that conclude the *Chronica Regum Visigothorum*. However, the author of the *Chronicle of 754* places the accession of the next king whom he mentions in the year 711.

---

[61] *Chronica Regum Visigothorum*, ed. Zeumer, p. 461.
[62] *Chronicle of 754* 44, ed. López Pereira, pp. 62-4.
[63] *Leges Visigothorum* V. vii. 20, and VI. i, 3, ed. Zeumer, pp. 244-5, and 250-1.

The new ruler, called Ruderic, is said to have "tumultuously invaded the kingdom with the encouragement of the Senate" and ruled for a year.[64]

The "Senate" here may be taken to mean the leading members of the aristocracy, and perhaps also some of the bishops, in other words, the lay and ecclesiastical elite that had dominated virtually every change in monarch since the time of Reccared. The chronicler's description of the new king as "invading" should probably not be taken literally, as he used the same word *regnum* for both kingdom and royal office, and it was almost certainly to the latter that he was referring. Ruderic had clearly seized the monarchy violently, albeit with the support of a significant part of the noble elite. His taking the throne was, therefore, far from being the kind of discreet coup carried out within the ruling group, and leaving little evidence of itself, that had taken place in 680. Wittiza had almost certainly been forcibly overthrown, and most probably killed.

The confused events that followed Ruderic's coup can best be left for consideration later, when the part they had to play in bringing about the Arab conquest of Spain will be examined. With the ending of the reign and the probable death of Wittiza in 710 or 711, a discrete phase in the history of the Visigothic kingdom came to an end. The final year of its existence would be marked by civil war, treachery, and violent dissension within the ruling elite, letting loose elements in the political life of the realm that had been kept under control or had been more effectively channelled in the years since Chindasuinth's coup d'état in 642.

Looking over the whole history of the Visigothic monarchy, in so far as we are now able to see it, in the 120 years following the conversion of Reccared in 587 and the suppression of the last of the revolts that had followed it, what is most striking is the role played by a small aristocratic elite centered on the royal court. This group becomes more clearly delineated once the court office-holders begin signing the acts of the plenary ecclesiastical councils in 653, but their prior existence can be deduced from the evidence discussed above. That these lay signatories to the conciliar *acta* never exceeded 20 in number, and may have been closer to 15, hints at the relative

---

[64] *Chronicle of 754* 52, ed. López Pereira, p. 68.

smallness of their numbers. We may be looking at two dozen families at most. But this is not out of keeping with what may be known about similar court circles in other early medieval western monarchies.

The family relationships within this group, both in terms of inheritance and descent, and of intermarriage, are almost entirely hidden from us. Only a little may be glimpsed in the case of the family of Egica and its ties to that of Ervig. The lack of documentary evidence also prevents us from seeing the changing patterns of court attendance and influence that can be deduced from the numerous and well attested charters of the Christian kingdoms of Spain in later medieval centuries. But it may well be assumed that the families who made up this select body were, by the standards of the time, extremely well endowed with wealth, in the form of both land and treasure, with which they were able to build up a hierarchy of supporters, whose military potential created the real weight behind these great families.

Out of this group alone the kings were chosen, and a marked feature of the political life of the kingdom, as just discussed, is the way in which no king could expect to turn his own family into a long-term royal dynasty. With the exception of the house of Leovigild, two generations were the longest any of these families managed, and in many cases the second of those generations had their tenure of the throne forcibly terminated by the members of the group out of which they themselves had risen.

We do not know how geographically extensive or wide-ranging were the estates of the court nobility. To judge by later equivalents, they probably had particular regional strengths and followings. Thus alliances were needed among themselves, and also with the more localized provincial aristocracies, whose backing gave them weight. A simple example of this would be the way that Paul, when sent by Wamba against the disaffected local aristocracy in Narbonensis in 672, instead recruited them to support his own bid for the throne. Something similar could have occurred with the revolt of Froia in 653, but then the court nobility preferred to throw its collective weight behind Reccesuinth, probably in return for the concessions made at the Eighth Council of Toledo later that year.

What is also remarkable is the apparent pattern of recovery and restitution of lands and offices that marks the political history of the kingdom. Noble factions known to have suffered at the hands of Chindasuinth in the 640s were reintegrated into the elite in 653.

Those who had been out of favor under Wamba were restored at the beginning of the reign of Ervig, and those who had been exiled and had their property confiscated by Egica were rewarded after his death. In each case there also seem to have been demands made, and probably also met, that the king should make sure that the lands he had acquired from confiscations did not become part of his family property.

This pattern of political conduct seems to center upon a determination on the part of the leading aristocratic families that none of their number should be able to use the royal office to build up their own personal and familial wealth and power to a degree that would make them permanently superior. Thus, while there were clearly extensive royal estates and great resources of treasure, these had to be kept distinct from the private property of the all too transient holders of the kingship, whose relatives and descendants were not to be allowed to establish a monopoly on the monarchy or to manipulate its resources for their own political and economic ends.

Only three times in this period do there seems to have been serious dissensions within the ruling body, as opposed to generally well-managed replacements of no longer satisfactory kings. These took place in the aftermath of the conversion of Reccared, following Chindasuinth's coup against Tulga, and in the tumultuous overthrow of Wittiza by Ruderic. In the two former cases, there seem to have been major changes in the fortunes of various families who had either supported the old regime or who now profited from its replacement. Even in these instances, there would seem to have been moves made to redress the political balance. As already mentioned, some of those who suffered under Chindasuinth were brought back under Reccesuinth, and in the case of Reccared's removal of the Arian elite that had been the principal support for his father, the fact that Witteric, who had been involved in the conspiracies after the Third Council of Toledo, was able to lead a coup against Liuva II in 603 would argue that he, and probably others like him, had been allowed to rise again in court circles in the intervening years.

Turbulent as the all too short history of the Visigothic kingdom might seem, much of it looks like the story of an oligarchy of wealthy families, with ecclesiastical as well as lay offices at their command, trying to manipulate a monarchical system in such a way as to produce effective but non-hereditary kings, while maintaining a balance of power among their own membership. It was their great misfortune that they temporarily lost control of these processes at the very moment that, on the southern frontier of the kingdom, a deadly threat to the continued existence of the whole Visigothic political system was waiting and ready to strike.

5
The End of the Visigothic Kingdom

The Coming of the Arabs

In trying to understand the final stages of the history of the Visigothic kingdom in Spain, it would be helpful to form a view of the nature and extent of the military challenge that faced it and which led directly to its collapse. At the same time, it is equally important to look for any other factors that can help explain why that defeat proved to be so complete and irreversible, and to see what other elements may have been involved in the outcome. In this chapter attention will have to be paid to the first of these questions, that of the causes and character of the Arab and Berber invasion of the south, before it is possible to make an assessment of the second. While this will briefly take attention away from Spain itself, such a change of focus has to be justified by the fact that the western expansion of Islam has been relatively little studied and understood, and that current interpretations depend heavily upon late and ideologically slanted sources that present an image of the processes of the conquest of North Africa that may have been justified by conditions and perspectives of the thirteenth century and later, but which have little to do with the realities of the second half of the seventh century and the early eighth.[1] The military threat that led to the fall of the Visigothic kingdom was a far more complex and subtle one than is often appreciated, and understanding it requires first of all stepping back in time to the earlier part of the seventh century, as well as a shift in geographical location from the Iberian peninsula to the other end of the Mediterranean.

---

[1] 'Abdulwahid Dhanun Taha, *The Muslim Conquest and Settlement of North Africa and Spain* (London, 1989), pp. 55–83, provides a useful if short interpretative overview, but does not distinguish the different chronological strata in his sources.

Quite how the rise of a new religious movement in the Hejaz, in western Arabia, turned into a wave of conquests that embraced much of the eastern and all of the southern shores of the Mediterranean, as well as the former Sassanian empire of Iran, is not easy to understand, not least thanks to the limited or partisan nature of the surviving evidence relating to the earliest phases of the rise of Islam.[2] The causes, as opposed to the consequences of the Arab conquests, do not form a necessary part of the present enquiry, but it is only fair to warn those looking for an explanation that it is very hard to find, and that perhaps none of the theories that currently hold the field is fully satisfactory.

Whatever forces may have led the tribes of the Arabian peninsula into a series of largely unexpected attacks on their powerful settled neighbors to the north, the beginning of the process can be dated to the early 630s. By the traditional chronology, the Prophet Muhammad had died in 632, and it was under his first successor as leader of the Muslim community, the caliph Abu Bakr (632-4) that the raids began.[3] Their targets, the Byzantine and Sassanian empires, were greatly weakened by a long war they had fought between themselves, which had begun in 602 and ended only in 628, and which had seen virtually all of the eastern provinces of the Byzantine empire overrun by the Sassanians in the years 610 to 615. Jerusalem had fallen to the Persians in 614, as had Egypt in 616.[4]

These losses in the south had been exacerbated by renewed pressure on imperial territory in the Balkans on the part of the Avars and the Slavs.[5] The latter had by this time settled in much of the countryside of the northern Balkans, in practice removing it from the emperor's control, while the nomad Avars to the north of the Danube raided Byzantine territory at will, carrying off treasure and slaves. These two threats had nearly combined in 626, when an Avar and Slav army besieged Constantinople, while a Persian one waited on the other

---

[2] Patricia Crone and Michael Cook, *Hagarism: The Making of the Islamic World* (Cambridge, 1977) offers a somewhat extreme reinterpretation, but gives a powerful presentation of the problems of the evidence.
[3] W. E. Kaegi, *Byzantium and the Early Islamic Conquests* (Cambridge, 1992), pp. 66-87.
[4] A. N. Stratos, *Byzantium in the Seventh Century*, vol. 1: *602-634* (Amsterdam, 1968), pp. 107-14.
[5] Ibid. pp. 118-23.

side of the Bosphorus, ready to assist in what might have been the destruction of the empire. Only the effectiveness of the Byzantine fleet kept the two forces from combining, and by thus preventing the Sassanians from bringing their knowledge of siege warfare to the assistance of the technically deficient Slavs, saved the city.[6] The empire's military weakness in these years explains the failure of the emperor Heraclius (610-41) to reinforce the Byzantine enclave in Spain, and thus why it was that it was at this particular time that the imperial forces there were finally expelled by king Suinthila.

The great war in the east ended in 628, when Heraclius was able to maneuver his way behind the Persian forces in Armenia and make an unchecked descent upon the Sassanian capital of Ctesiphon in Mesopotamia. This threat led to the overthrow of the shah Khusro II (591-628) and the conclusion of a peace, in which the provinces overrun by the Persians were restored to Heraclius.[7] However, the destructive nature of the war, in terms of the damage done to city defenses and the loss of military manpower, may have left much of the Byzantine east vulnerable to the unanticipated attacks by the newly united Arabs that followed only about five years later. The preceding loss of these territories, which had in many cases uninterruptedly formed part of the Roman empire for 600 or 700 years, to the Persians may also have served to weaken their ideological allegiance to Constantinople, especially as there existed serious theological rifts between the Orthodox and the Monophysite communities in the empire. The former, dominant in Constantinople and Asia Minor, included the emperor and his civil and ecclesiastical advisors in its number, while the latter may have constituted the majority population of many of the eastern provinces. Whether this divide, which was reinforced by imperial policies that the Monophysites regarded as persecution, contributed materially to the lack of resistance to the Arab conquest cannot be established with certainty, but it is not improbable.[8]

What is clear is that the defeat of the emperor and his army by the Arabs at the battle of Yarmuk in 635 led to the abandonment of the

---

[6] Ibid. pp. 173-96.
[7] Ibid. pp. 204-56.
[8] W. H. C. Frend, *The Rise of the Monophysite Movement* (Cambridge, 1972), pp. 316-53; see also A. J. Butler, *The Arab Conquest of Egypt* (Oxford, 1978), pp. 168-93.

imperial attempt to retain control of Syria. Damascus fell in the aftermath of the battle and Jerusalem soon after.[9] In 640 the Arab armies invaded Egypt, which rapidly fell, with the initial exception of Alexandria, which could be reinforced by sea.[10] It is unlikely that Heraclius saw his withdrawal in 635 as more than temporary. This was almost a repeat of the loss of the same provinces to the Persians roughly 20 years before, and that had been reversed. However, the emperor's declining health in his last years delayed any military counter-stroke on his part, and on his death in 641 there followed a period of considerable political instability in Constantinople.[11] One effect of this was the failure of Heraclius's successors to retain the most important port in the eastern empire.

The surrender of Alexandria in 642 completed the Arab conquest of Egypt, which was immediately followed by raids into the Byzantine province of Cyrenaica, whose main cities lay on a fertile coastal strip over 300 miles west of the Nile delta. All too little is known of the Arab conquest of this region, which was completed by 645, but a significant role in it seems to have been played by naval resources provided by the Alexandrians. It has long seemed natural to assume, when considering the Arab conquest of the southern shores of the Mediterranean, from Alexandria to Tangiers, that this was the product of a rolling process of land-based campaigning carried out over a period extending from 642 to 711, and that the outcome was the conquest and occupation of all the territory included between these two terminal points. In practice, however, there were very different conditions to be encountered across this vast area that extends for over 3,000 miles of coastline. In some regions, as those between Egypt and Cyrenaica, and then again from the west of Cyrenaica to the southern edge of the Sahel, the desert can come right up to the shore of the Mediterranean. Similarly, most of the western half of this total area, from around the modern frontier between Tunisia and Algeria as far the large coastal promontory on which Tangiers is

---

[9] Kaegi, *Byzantium and the Early Islamic Conquests*, pp. 112-46.
[10] On the conquest of Egypt se the classic work of A. J. Butler, *The Arab Conquest of Egypt and the Last Thirty Years of the Roman Dominion* (Oxford, 1902; reprinted with additional bibliography and edited by P. M. Fraser, Oxford, 1978).
[11] A. N. Stratos, *Byzantium in the Seventh Century*, vol. 2: *634-641* (Amsterdam, 1972), pp. 134-52, 175-205.

situated, is heavily mountainous. In all of the areas just mentioned population levels were low, and natural resources limited. The terrain in these regions was generally difficult to cross, and settlements and harbors were very few in number.

Rather than regarding this enormous tract of land from Alexandria to Tangiers as a unity, awaiting conquest and occupation by the Arabs, it makes more sense to see it in terms of a small number of discrete areas of relatively dense settlement and population, separated one from another by much larger stretches of marginal land, difficult to traverse, hard to control, and offering only limited economic benefit to those who attempted so to do. The pockets of relatively urbanized and cultivated territory consisted of the lower Nile valley and its delta, Cyrenaica, the Tunisian Sahel, and the Tangiers peninsula. Simply put, these were the only areas worth conquering and trying to retain. The primary phases of the Arab conquest of northern Africa thus need to be seen as a continuing process of obtaining control over all of these areas in turn, and in securing communications between them.

Maps that represent the Arab conquest of this enormous area in the seventh and eighth centuries as a uniform occupation of all the land mass between the Nile valley and the Atlantic are completely misleading. It is infinitely more sensible to see the westward extension of Arab power in the period 642 to 711 in terms of the conquest and occupation of a small number of discrete areas, essentially the ones that were both coastal and highly urbanized in nature. The main concentrations of Arab military power and their centers of government were by the end of this period located in two regions: the Nile delta and the Sahel (the coastal plain of modern Tunisia). There were subsidiary areas of essentially military occupation in Cyrenaica, Tripolitania, and the Tangiers peninsula. Between all of these, communications, when not maritime, depended upon treaties or the threat of reprisals.

It follows that the acquisition in 642 of the naval resources of Alexandria, and the assistance of the local population in providing ships and crews trained to sail them, was the first and in some ways most crucial step in the westward expansion of Arab power. This was not the only direction in which the conquerors' horizons were able to expand, thanks to their acquisition of a navy. The Arab conquest of Cyprus in 649 depended not least upon ships and troops sent from Alexandria.[12] Naval raids on coastal settlements in Asia Minor followed, and a Byzantine fleet commanded by the emperor Constans II (642-68) was defeated by the Arab governor of Syria off the coast of Lycia in 654.[13] To what extent Egyptian vessels were involved in these latter episodes is not recorded, as it is likely that ships from the Syrian coastal towns were also being used by the Arabs. The first Arab naval raid on Sicily, which is probably to be dated to 664, was certainly sent from Egypt.[14] In general, it would be safe to say that the previously substantial dependence of Constantinople upon annual grain shipments from Egypt meant that, in the early seventh century, Alexandria was home to what was probably the largest concentration of shipping in the Mediterranean, and that this provided the Arabs with much of the means needed for their naval raids and expeditions.[15]

Much of the conquest of Cyrenaica was achieved in a single campaign in 643, and it was completed with the fall of the last imperial stronghold at Tokra (or Taucheira) in 645. Although very little at all is known of the subsequent history of the region, archaeological evidence of the restoration of buildings and some Arabic inscriptions indicate that the conquerors settled in the main Roman towns, Apollonia and Cyrene, and that these continued in occupation up to at least the eleventh century.[16] Following the conquest of 643, Apollonia, which had been the capital of the Byzantine province, was replaced in this role by the inland town of Barce or Barqa, which became the region's *misr* or garrison town and administrative center. How long Christianity, which was long-established in Cyrenaica, survived is unknown, though there are no reasons to assume that its demise was speedy.

About 500 miles along the coast to the west of Cyrenaica lay Tripolitania, an area whose prosperity depended primarily upon its being at the northern end of an important caravan route across the Sahara, and upon the intensive irrigation of the hinterland of its three

---

[12] Theophanes, *Chronica* a.m. 6140; Andre Palmer, *The Seventh Century in the West-Syrian Chronicles* (Liverpool, 1993), p. 173, reconstructing the text of the *Chronicle of Dionysius of Tel Mahre*.
[13] Theophanes, *Chronica* a.m. 6146.
[14] Ibid. a.m. 6155.
[15] Butler, *Arab Conquest of Egypt*, pp. 111-13.
[16] See David J. Mattingly, *Tripolitania* (London, 1995).

main settlements, Lepcis Magna, Oea, and Sabratha.[17] As the entrepôts for the trade coming form the south of the Sahara, these cities had flourished in the earlier Roman empire, especially under the rule of Septimius Severus (193-211), who had himself come from Lepcis. Their economic and material condition declined in various ways in Late Antiquity, but two of them, Lepcis and Sabratha, survived into the ninth century, before giving way to newer settlements. The third, Oea, became the center of Arab rule in the region, and under its new name of Tripoli remained in continuous occupation to the present; this has meant that, unlike the cases of Lepcis and Sabratha, relatively few archaeological traces of its past have been preserved.

When Tripolitania came fully under Arab rule is by no means certain.[18] While the garrisoning of Cyrenaica can be documented from 643 and 645 onward, a permanent Arab presence may not have been established in Tripolitania for several more years. Later Arab sources record that 'Amr, the conqueror of Egypt, captured Tripoli itself in 643, but if so this does not seem to have resulted in a permanent occupation. However, trans-Saharan trade, which seems primarily to have then flowed eastward from Tripolitania to Cyrenaica and Egypt, and thence on to Syria and Asia Minor, obviously predisposed this region to follow its eastern neighbors in its political alignment, and thus into accepting Arab rule, especially once they had secured a maritime ascendancy in the eastern Mediterranean.

In 646 Gregory, the governor of the Byzantine exarchate of Africa, whose capital was at Carthage, rebelled and proclaimed himself emperor in opposition to Constans II.[19] The potential significance of this can be gauged from the fact that the founder of the ruling imperial dynasty, Heraclius I (610-41) had used Africa, of which his father was then exarch, as the launching place for a successful bid to overthrow the then emperor Phocas (602-10).[20] Whether Gregory had similar ambitions is not known, as his revolt was cut short in 647 by an Arab raid.[21] The invaders defeated and killed Gregory in a battle

---

[17] A. Di Vita, G. Di Vita-Evrard, L. Bacchielli, and R. Polidori, *Libya: The Lost Cities of the Roman Empire* (Cologne, 1999), pp. 13-182.
[18] See how brief is the account of al-Baladhuri, 225-226, trans. Hitti, p. 355.
[19] Theophanes, *Chronica* a.m. 6138.
[20] Stratos, *Byzantium in the Seventh Century*, vol. 1, pp. 80-91.
[21] Theophanes, *Chronica* a.m. 6139.

near Sbeitla (Roman *Sufetula*) in the southern Sahel. Perhaps surprisingly, this was not a prelude to conquest. Arab sources suggest that, in the aftermath of the battle, the invaders were paid to withdraw and returned to their base in Cyrenaica.

What happened in Byzantine Africa in the aftermath of the exarch Gregory's revolt and fall is unclear. Arab expansion westward halted. This did not imply inactivity, though the internal tensions of the last years of the caliphate of 'Uthman (644-56) and all those of that of 'Ali (656-61) limited military activity on the frontiers of the Arab empire.[22] However, their ensuing conquest of both the Byzantine exarchate of Africa and of the Visigothic kingdom of Spain would depend very largely upon the Arabs' use of substantial bodies of Berber tribesmen from the semi-desert regions to the south of Cyrenaica and Tripolitania. In part this must have resulted from preceding military campaigns against Berber tribes such as the Luwata, leading to their submission and the making of treaties with them.[23] But it is also necessary to appreciate that such nomad confederacies also had complex economic ties with the settled regions, upon which they may have preyed but upon which they were also dependent for the great majority of commodities that they were unable to produce themselves.[24]

Whether primarily through war or at least partly through economic dependence and diplomacy, the Berber tribes of inland Libya were led to provide the Arabs with large numbers of slaves, a feature recalled in some of the earliest of the Arab accounts of the conquests. Such slaves, who were thereby incorporated into the tribes of their Arab masters, were obliged to become Muslims, especially as most of them were not previously "people of the book" or *dhimmis*.[25] These processes must be assumed to have been taking place between the start of the Arab conquest of Cyrenaica in 643 and the beginnings of the conquest of Byzantine Africa around 670. Their crucial effect was to provide the Arabs with the military manpower necessary to carry

---

[22] For the events of this period see Hugh Kennedy, *The Prophet and the Age of the Caliphates* (London, 1986), pp. 69-81.
[23] al-Baladhuri 225, trans. Hitti, pp. 353-4.
[24] For the model of nomad society used here see C. J. Wickham, "Pastoralism and Underdevelopment in the Early Middle Ages," *Settimane di studio del Centro italiano di studi sull'alto medioevo* 31 (1985), pp. 401-51.
[25] P. Crone, *Slaves on Horses* (Cambridge, 1980), pp. 18-26.

out their most dramatic and successful campaigns in the west since the fall of Egypt.

The events surrounding the conquest of Byzantine Africa are highly obscure and controversial, although they are much more fully described in the extant Arab sources than the campaigns of the preceding three decades.[26] To a large degree the problem is one of contradictions and confusion in the sources, resulting not least from the character of much of the Arab historiography of the western conquests. Thus the Arab historians writing in Egypt, North Africa, and Spain from the later ninth century onward often worked backward from contemporary conditions and practices and tried to find an explanation for their existence in terms of what had happened in the past.[27] In practice this could often mean inventing a past that was able to make sense of the present. The lack of early written sources made such a topsy-turvy approach to historical writing virtually inevitable.

Added to this must be added the natural if regrettable tendency to give a particular region, tribe, people, or settlement a longer and more distinguished Islamic past than it might actually have enjoyed. This is particularly true of the vast mountainous regions that constitute much of what is modern Algeria and Morocco, whose actual conquest by the Arabs would be a far longer and slower process than the sources imply, and in which Islam would be established much less rapidly and with less homogeneity than the piety of thirteenth-century and later Muslim historians writing in North Africa would find able to credit.[28]

Attacks on the south of the Byzantine exarchate of Africa may have resumed in the 660s, at which time there also occurred the first Arab naval raids on Sicily. While the details may be thin and the chronology vague, it seems that enough headway had been made for a governor of *Ifriquiya*, as the Arabs would call the area of the exarchate, to be named in or around 670, in the person of 'Uqba ibn Nafi, who is said to have been a veteran of both the conquest of Egypt and of the campaigns in Cyrenaica and Tripolitania in the 640s.[29]

---

[26] al-Baladhuri 226-30, trans. Hitti, pp. 356-62.
[27] R. Braunschweig, "Ibn 'Abdalh'akam et la conquête de l'Afrique du Nord par les Arabes," in idem, *Etudes sur l'Islam classique et l'Afrique du Nord* (London, 1986), item xi.
[28] Michael Brett and Elizabeth Fentress, *The Berbers* (Oxford, 1996), pp. 81-7.
[29] al-Baladhuri, 227-228, trans. Hitti, pp. 357-8.

Under his leadership the Arabs and their Berber freedmen or *mawali* made themselves masters of the Sahel, but the Byzantines retained control of Carthage and the north. By 675 a new *misr* had been founded at Quayrawan (modern Kairouan) to serve as the military and administrative capital of the newly conquered territory.[30]

In 675 a new *wali* or governor of Egypt was appointed by the caliph Mu'awiya (661-80), in the person of Maslama ibn Muhallad al-Ansari, and he in turn could appoint the governor of *Ifriquiya*, who was his subordinate. 'Uqba was thus recalled, and replaced by 'Abu'l-Mujahir, a freed slave of the new governor of Egypt. This marked not just a change in personnel, but probably also in policy, with the earlier generation of "conquistadors" such as 'Uqba giving way to more flexible and diplomatic bureaucrats such as 'Abu'l-Mujahir. The latter immediately began to seek alliances with the leaders of the indigenous population, who had apparently been treated with scant respect by 'Uqba. In particular, a new cooperation between the Arabs and Kasila (or Kusayla), the ruler of the Berber Awraba confederation in the mountains west of the Sahel, led to significant advances against the Byzantines, whose administrative center of Carthage was also besieged for the first time in 678.[31]

The precise extent of Byzantine-ruled territory in North Africa at this time is not easy to determine. A series of inscriptions recording the building or restoration of fortifications in the period 539-44 gives some impression of the limits of imperial control in the aftermath of the emperor Justinian's destruction of the Vandal kingdom in 533/4. However, it seems probable that the Byzantine frontier contracted later in the century. Even so, various towns and fortresses in the province of Numidia, the largely mountainous inland region to the west of the Sahel, still formed part of the exarchate when the Arab conquests began. These settlements are the most likely targets for the joint campaigns of Kasila and his Arab allies.

As was often the case, the succession of a new caliph led to widespread changes among the holders of major offices in the Arab empire. Under the caliph Yazid I (680-3), 'Uqba was reinstalled as governor of *Ifriquiya* in 681, and he immediately broke off the

---

[30] Ibid. 229-230, pp. 359-61.
[31] Brett and Fentress, *The Berbers*, pp. 84-5; E.-F. Gautier, *Le Passé de l'Afrique du Nord* (Paris, 1952), pp. 252-5.

hitherto profitable alliance with Kasila. It was at this time, according to later tradition, that 'Uqba made his famous march across the whole extent of North Africa, from Qayrawan to the Atlantic, where he is said to have declared that if the sea had not been in his way, he would, like Alexander the Great, have carried on conquering forever, upholding Islam and fighting unbelievers.[32] Although widely credited, this whole episode is almost certainly completely fictitious, and in the light of the sanctity later attributed to 'Uqba, represents little more than a later justification for Arab rule over the Berbers in North Africa.[33]

In reality, in or around 683 'Uqba was killed in battle, possibly with Byzantine assistance, by Kasila, who then went on to capture Quayrawan in 684. In the same period, a Byzantine fleet attacked Cyrenaica and besieged Barqa. Arab rule in *Ifriquiya* was thus temporarily at an end, and there was little chance of it being revived in the immediate future. In consequence, Kasila made himself master of most of their conquests in the region. It has been suggested that he may have been a Muslim, as otherwise it is hard to see how as an unbeliever (*kafir*) he could have been accepted as an ally by the Arabs.[34] This is perfectly reasonable, though in the light of the previous widespread extent of Christianity in all parts of North Africa, it would be equally possible for him to have been a Christian. This might explain 'Uqba's unwillingness to deal with him, despite the alliance made by 'Abu'l-Mujahir. In any event, his rule proved short-lived. A short period of political instability in the Umayyad caliphate came to an end under the rule of 'Abd al-Malik (685-705), who appointed his brother 'Abd al-Aziz as his new governor of Egypt. In 686 or 688 (both dates being found in the sources) the latter dispatched an expedition to Africa, which defeated and killed Kasila, and regained control of Quayrawan.[35]

Although this avenged 'Uqba, whose death was regarded as a martyrdom, it did not result in further expansion of Arab rule. In the later

---

[32] Taha, *Muslim Conquest and Settlement*, pp. 65-6, who takes no cognizance of the incredible distance that would have had to have been covered. See ibid. note 65 on p. 79 for the Arab sources referring to the supposed expedition.
[33] Brett and Fentress, *The Berbers*, pp. 86-7.
[34] Brett and Fentress, *The Berbers*, p. 84.
[35] Taha, *Muslim Conquest and Settlement*, p. 69 and note 83 on p. 80 for references to differing dates and other details.

Arabic sources stories are given of fierce opposition to the Muslims on the part of various unspecified Berber tribes, confederated under the leadership of someone known as the Kahina. Although often described as a queen, there is no certainty that Kahina is a female name or title. It has also been suggested that he or she was Jewish, though this is by no means certain. Indeed, his or her very existence is questionable, as most of the extant stories, to be found in the fourteenth-century *History of the Berbers* of Ibn Khaldun, can be interpreted as being yet more allegories of the history of Arab relations with the Berbers and vice versa. At most, the tales concerning the Kahina may hint at further Arab campaigns in the Berber-dominated province of Numidia, prior to their final onslaught on Carthage in the mid-690s.

Following the termination of a civil war in the heartlands of the Arab empire in 692, more vigorous action on the frontiers quickly followed. More securely grounded in reliable evidence than the existence of the Kahina is the appointment either in 693/4 or in 695 of Hasan ibn al-Nu'man as governor of *Ifriquiya*, with the clear purpose of putting an end to the dwindling Byzantine enclave in the north.[36] Carthage fell to the Arabs soon after his arrival. Although it was reoccupied in 697 by a naval expedition sent by the emperor Leontius (695–8), it was retaken by the Arabs the following year, after the arrival of reinforcements from Syria. This final loss of Carthage in 698 marked the end of over 800 years of a Roman presence in northern Africa. The defeated Byzantine expeditionary forces that had been expelled from Carthage by Hasan's army, fearing the consequences of their failure, rebelled on their way home and overthrew the emperor who had sent them.[37]

Not surprisingly, the Arab capture of Carthage, which like Alexandria had long been a major mercantile and shipping center, was followed by a period of considerable naval activity, this time primarily in the western Mediterranean. Arab raids on Sicily, Sardinia, and the Balearic islands followed very soon after. Although one unnamed town in Sicily is said to have been captured and looted in a raid in

---

[36] Ibn 'abd al-Hakam; Brett and Fentress, *The Berbers*, pp. 85–6; cf. Taha, *Muslim Conquest and Settlement*, pp. 69–72.
[37] Theophanes, *Chronica* a.m. 6190. See Warren Treadgold, *A History of the Byzantine State and Society* (Stanford, CA, 1997), pp. 338–9.

704, none of these resulted in permanent conquests.[38] Further west, however, Arab and Berber forces sent by sea took Tangiers at some unspecified date between c.705 and 710.[39]

By this time a new governor had been appointed to *Ifriquiya*. This was Musa ibn Nusayr. Various dates are given in the Arab sources for his taking up his new office, but the most likely one may be 705.[40] In that year 'Abd al-Aziz ibn Marwan, the long-serving governor of Egypt, died, as soon afterwards did his brother, the caliph 'Abd al-Malik. One of the latter's sons succeeded as Walid I (705-15), and a number of changes in administrative personnel inevitably followed. That Hasan ibn al-Nu'man, the appointee of 'Abd al-Aziz ibn Marwan, was replaced at such a time is thus not surprising. However, it must be admitted that the chronology remains uncertain.

Ceuta, on the northeastern tip of the promontory on which Tangier is also situated, had certainly been in Byzantine hands in 687, and there are no good reasons for doubting that it remained so up to its fall to the expedition sent by Musa ibn Nusayr around 706. In later Arab narratives the governor of the town is said to have been a certain Visigothic count of the name of "Ilyan" or Julian, in the service of king Ruderic. In these stories Julian is said to have wanted revenge on the king, who had raped his daughter, and in consequence conspired to provide the Muslims who had recently made themselves masters of Tangier with the ships they needed to cross over into Spain.

While virtually all commentators disregarded or distrust the story about his daughter (who in some later medieval Spanish versions was given the name of Florinda), a surprising number of scholars are still prepared to believe in the existence of Julian.[41] In reality both father and daughter are fictional creations, who belong to a set of moralizing traditions intended to make sense of the catastrophe that so rapidly overcame the Visigothic kingdom by means of a simple drama of human passions.

---

[38] Taha, *Muslim Conquest and Settlement*, p. 74, citing Ibn 'Idhari, vol. 1, p. 42; this is not confirmed by any Byzantine or western source.

[39] al-Baladhuri, 230; trans. Hitti, p. 362; Brett and Fentress, *The Berbers*, p. 85, quoting Ibn 'Idhari.

[40] Brett and Fentress, *The Berbers*, p. 86, supports 705.

[41] Taha, *Muslim Conquest and Settlement*, pp. 75, 84-5, who is prepared to believe that Julian was both the Byzantine governor of Mauritania Tingitania and a relative of Wittiza.

As for the Arabs needing Julian's ships to make the very short crossing to Spain, it has to be asked how, if they did not have any of their own, they had been able to raid so extensively virtually all of the islands in the western Mediterranean in the course of the same decade? Similarly, it might be wondered how otherwise they had made themselves masters of Tangiers, nearly a thousand miles west of their nearest military base, which would have been at Carthage. That Ceuta as well as Tangiers remained in Byzantine hands until the Arab conquest of the region at some point in the years between 705 and 710 would seem the most logical assumption. With these and other settlements captured, the Muslim forces led by Musa's Luwata Berber freedman Tariq bin Ziyad were poised for their first expeditions across the straits and into the territory of the Visigothic kingdom on the northern shore. There conditions had become exceedingly disturbed – just the kind of circumstances the Arabs liked when launching an attack on a new target.

The Last Kings, 710–713

The ending of Wittiza's reign, when he was probably still only in his mid-twenties, plunged the Visigothic kingdom into the crisis that ultimately proved fatal to its survival. The sequence of events is not easy to determine, and this has not been assisted by the tendency of historians to take all the information relating to this period from all of the available sources and combine it to produce a synthetic account of what happened. This usually depends upon treating all the sources as if they were of equal weight and reliability, which they patently are not. Combining bits and pieces from different texts in this way serves only to blur the distinctions in worth between them and to erode the need to recognize that each source provides a perspective from a particular chronological and often also geographical context. The difficulty is that with only a limited body of evidence available, historians are reluctant to relinquish any of it. However, it has to be recognized that sources that represent later perceptions of earlier events are not only of no practical help in reconstructing what actually happened, but can even be positively misleading. The interpretations of the final stages of the history of the Visigothic kingdom in Spain provide a case in point.

The literary and other evidence relating to these events comes from a variety of different periods, ranging from the immediately contemporary to ones several centuries later. The testimony of these sources thus differs greatly in value and usefulness. As a rule of thumb, reliability, and also brevity of narrative, are usually in direct proportion to chronological proximity. Thus, the fullest and most elaborate versions, which provide the most detailed accounts, tend to be those most removed in time from the events they are supposed to describe. The soundest methodological approach would be to take the earliest evidence first, and then proceed to the later sources in roughly chronological order, in so far as that can be established. This way it will be possible to see at what period the different elements first enter the story. In other words, the literary evidence can be treated in an almost archaeological fashion to establish the strata in which the various components of the narrative first appear.

The only strictly contemporary material relating to the events surrounding the end of the Visigothic kingdom comes in the form of coinage. There exist coins of two kings that from their design could be expected to belong to the same chronological context as those of the sole reign of Wittiza. The names on the coins are Ruderic and Achila.[42] Coins of Ruderic are known bearing the mint signatures of Toledo and *Egitania* (probably Idanha a Velha, northeast of Castel Branco in central Portugal) on their reverse. Achila's coins come from Narbonne, Gerona, Tarragona, and Zaragoza.[43] Small as the sample may be, especially of the coinage of Ruderic, the lack of geographical overlap between them would imply that one king ruled over Toledo and at least parts of Lusitania, while the other controlled the major settlements of the provinces of Tarraconensis and Narbonensis.[44] No clear view can be taken from coin evidence of the political situation in Baetica and Galicia.

---

[42] G. C. Miles, *The Coinage of the Visigoths of Spain: Leovigild to Achila II* (New York, 1952), pp. 442-6.

[43] Ibid. pp. 444-6; for the coins of the mint of Zaragoza, all of which come from the excavations of the site of El Bovalar and were therefore unknown to Miles, see Pere de Palol, *El Bovalar (Seròs; Segrià): Conjunt d'època paleocristiana i visigòtica* (Lérida, 1989), pp. 20-8.

[44] Miles, *Coinage*, pp. 442-3, records only 12 coins of Ruderic in total. The spelling Rvdericvus, rather than the more familiar Roderic, is common to both coins and manuscript sources.

The impression to be gained from the coins confirms that of the two versions of the continuations of the Visigothic regnal lists. One of these, preserved in two manuscripts, records a king Achila as the immediate successor of Wittiza, allotting him a three-year reign, while in the other tradition, preserved in a single manuscript, the reign of Wittiza is followed by that of "Ruderigus," who is assigned seven years and six months.[45] It should be noted that these regnal lists are contained in manuscripts of much later date, and there is no way of knowing for certain where or when they were first compiled. The two traditions do not agree in the length of reign they assign to the various kings from Ervig onward, and there always exists the possibility of a crucial scribal error, particularly in the recording of numbers. A single stroke of the pen could turn a one ("I") into a five ("V"), for example. However, the general point would seem to be established, that there is good evidence for thinking that Wittiza was succeeded, under whatever circumstances, by two kings, controlling different parts of the kingdom.

The literary source nearest in time to these events is the *Chronicle of 754*, written about 40 years later, and most probably in Toledo.[46] Its author, rather surprisingly in the light of his usual practice, entirely fails to report the fate of Wittiza. What he says instead is that in the year 711 (Spanish era 749) Ruderic "tumultuously invaded the kingdom with the encouragement of the Senate" and ruled for a year.[47] By "Senate" is surely meant the leading members of the aristocracy, and perhaps also some of the bishops, in other words, the lay and ecclesiastical elite that had been involved in virtually every royal succession since the time of Reccared.

Quite how literally we should take the chronicler's reference to an invasion is an open question: was this a reprise of the events of 631 with a provincial military commander, or even an exile, rebelling against a king who had lost the support of the court nobility? Or did the events just unfold in the context of the royal court? The latter

---

[45] *Chronica Regum Visigothorum - Continuationes*, ed. K. Zeumer (*MGH LL*, vol. 1), p. 461.

[46] On this text see Roger Collins, *The Arab Conquest of Spain* (Oxford, 1989), pp. 57-63, and Carmen Cardelle de Hartmann, "The Textual Transmission of the Mozarabic Chronicle of 754," *Early Medieval Europe* 8 (1999), pp. 13-29.

[47] *Chronicle of 754*, 52, ed. J. E. López Pereira, *Chrónica Mozárabe de 754. Edición crítica y traducción* (Zaragoza, 1980), p. 68.

must be thought the more probable, but in either case, the reference to Ruderic taking power *tumultuose* must imply that this was far from being the kind of discreet coup carried out within the ruling group, leaving little evidence of itself, that had taken place in 680.

As already mentioned, no word is given here of the fate of Wittiza. Nor is there any mention of Achila. It would seem to be a reasonable assumption, if no more, that Wittiza had been overthrown violently. If he had just died of natural causes, and Ruderic had been chosen to succeed him with the backing of the political elite, it is hard to see why confusion or tumult should enter into the picture, especially as all royal successions since 642 had been made to seem peaceful and the result of consensus.

The chronicler, having mentioned Ruderic's length of reign, then goes on to record how the new king sent armies against the Arabs and *Mauri* (Berbers), who, led by "Taric Abuzara" and others, were raiding and destroying many towns. In one of these expeditions in 712 his forces deserted him and he was killed.[48] Unfortunately, the chronicler's words could hardly have been more obscure had he been trying to conceal the truth from his readers. There may be some problems with the textual transmission, but what at least seems clear from this all too brief and confusing narrative is that some kind of treachery was involved, and that some unnamed individuals had accompanied Ruderic "in rivalry and deceptively, out of ambition for the kingdom." Their presence seems to be linked to the flight of the army, but it also appears that they too perished in the disaster, though whether at the time or subsequently is not clear. This might imply that some of the court aristocracy had hoped to eliminate Ruderic by allowing him to be killed in battle, freeing the throne for another of their number, but that the plan in some way backfired, and many of them too fell in the course of the defeat or soon after.

An equally difficult and possibly corrupt passage records how the Arab and Berber forces under the command of Musa took Toledo in 711, and how this was followed by the execution of various "noble lords" who were still in the city, on the pretext of their being involved in the flight of Oppa, a son of king Egica.[49] The logic of the chronicler's chronology would be that the fall of Toledo occurred

---

[48] Ibid. 52, ed. López Pereira, p. 68.
[49] Ibid. 54, ed. López Pereira, p. 70.

before the battle in the south in which Ruderic was killed. However, the Arab capture of the city is placed after the defeat of the king, and as this is the more likely sequence of events, it is probably wiser to follow the ordering of the chronicler's narrative in preference to his stated chronology. Thus it may be that the death of Ruderic and the fall of Toledo both took place in 712.

It is also possible that the reference in the chronicle to the killing of Ruderic's rivals, which made little sense in its immediate context, may apply at least in part to these events in Toledo. The chronicler certainly refers to Spain being destroyed both by the attacks of the Arabs and by "internal fury." It is thus feasible that the ruling elite had split, and that not only did Ruderic have to contend with a rival king in the northeast, in the person of Achila, but he may also have lost control of Toledo to Oppa, son of Egica. At the very least it is certain that there were serious internal dissensions wracking the kingdom at the very time that the Arabs and Berbers were raiding and devastating a growing number of towns in the south.

To pass from this picture of events in Spain in the years 711/12, drawn from the only contemporary and near contemporary evidence, to that given by the next generation of sources is to enter a rather different world. Although there are many and serious problems to be faced (as they all too rarely are) in the text traditions, source criticism, and evaluation of the Arabic accounts of the conquest of Spain, it is safe enough to say that the earliest of these date from no earlier than the mid-ninth century, and were written in Egypt. They do not, it should also be stressed, derive from some immutable and reliable oral tradition that gives them greater authority.

Around 860, in the first such narrative of the conquest of al-Andalus, Ibn 'Abd al-Hakam (ca.803–71) wrote in his *Futuh Misr wa'l-Maghrib* ("Conquest of Egypt and of the Maghreb") that Tariq ibn Ziyad, who commanded the Arab and Berber garrison of Tangiers, made contact with "Ilyan," lord of Ceuta and Alchadra, who was subject to Roderic, the ruler of Spain. He went on to explain that "Ilyan" had a grudge against Roderic, who had had an affair with his daughter, while she was being educated at the court in Toledo, and to get his revenge offered to transport Tariq and his forces across the Straits to Spain. Once there the Muslims occupied Cartagena and headed for Córdoba, defeating an army that tried to block their advance. In response to the threat to Córdoba, Roderic and his army fought a battle with Tariq at a place called "Shedunya," in which the Visigoths were defeated and the king killed. Tariq then proceeded to Toledo, where among other treasures he found the table (or carpet) of King Solomon.[50]

Quite a lot of this brief narrative is devoted to explaining how various placenames in the south of Spain derived from those of the principal actors in this drama. Best known is *Jabal-Tariq* or "Tariq's Mountain," modern Gibraltar. Such toponym associations are about as reliable as those with Hengist and Horsa and other early Saxons that may be found in the opening sections of the *Anglo-Saxon Chronicle*, in defiance of all else that is known about the early history of Wessex. More complex ideological purposes behind Ibn 'Abd al-Hakam's narrative have also been uncovered, and these have little to do with the recording of the events of the conquest for their own sake.[51] Significantly, and despite variations in detail, all subsequent Arab accounts of the conquest are derived to a greater or lesser degree from those first elaborated by Ibn 'Abd al-Hakam in Egypt in the mid-ninth century, and they share common narrative features, notably the role of count "Ilyan" or Julian and his search for revenge, and a decisive battle in a location that is generally identified as the valley of the Guadelete, near Medina Sidonia.

Not long after Ibn 'Abd al-Hakam wrote, the first historical narratives of the conquest from the Christian kingdoms of northern Spain began to take shape. These came in the form of the *Chronicle of Albelda*, named after the monastery in the Rioja where a final extended version was completed around 976, and the *Chronicle of Alfonso III*.[52] The latter exists in two different versions with marked differences in parts of their narrative, which probably date from the early tenth century. They are known as the *Rotense* and the *Ad Sebastianum* versions, after a monastery in which the earliest manuscript of the former was found, and after the addressee of a prefatory letter unique to the latter. The *Rotense* version is generally fuller than the *Ad Sebastianum*. They are thought to derive from a common lost

---

[50] English trans. John Harris Jones, *Ibn 'Abd el-Hakem: History of the Conquest of Spain* (Göttingen, 1858), pp. 18-22.

[51] See Braunschweig (note 27 above).

[52] Both of these works, including the two versions of the *Chronicle of Alfonso III*, will be found edited, with Spanish translations and commentaries, in Juan Gil, José L. Moralejo, and Juan I. Ruiz de la Peña, *Crónicas Asturianas* (Oviedo, 1985).

original version of the work that may have been written by or for the Asturian king, Alfonso III (866-910), after whom it is named.[53]

The *Rotense* version of the Alfonsine chronicle, followed in part by the *Ad Sebastianum*, makes several highly critical remarks about Wittiza, who is accused of having many wives and mistresses and of trying to make his bishops marry, something that is seen as the reason for the ensuing "ruin of Spain." However, he is said to have died of natural causes in Toledo in 711, and Ruderic was elected king in his place "by the Goths."[54] An account is then provided of the new monarch's origins. He is described as being a son of Theodefred, himself a son of king Chindasuinth, who had been blinded by Egica out of fear that the Goths might try to make him king. Thus rendered incapable of ruling, Theodefred had retired to Córdoba, where he had married an aristocratic lady called Riccilo, thus fathering Ruderic.[55]

According to the Asturian chronicler, the Arabs came into Spain in the third year of Ruderic's reign "because of the treachery of the sons of Wittiza."[56] The king marched against the invaders, but because of their heavy burden of sin and thanks again to the treachery of the sons of Wittiza, the Gothic army was defeated. Nothing apparently was known of the fate of Ruderic, but in the resettlement of the town of Viseu an epitaph was found in a ruined church, recording the fact that "Here lies Ruderic the last king of the Goths."[57] As the chronicler refers to the repopulation of the town as being recent and being carried out under his orders, this is one of the passages used to confirm king Alfonso III's own authorship of this work.

Seen like this, there are very clearly three very different sets of stories here. There is evidence of a little cross-fertilization. The *Chronicle of Alfonso III* refers to the existence of a "Palace of Ruderic" in Córdoba, giving the Arab name for it.[58] This is reminiscent of the taste for associating places and buildings with famous people and events of the past, testified to in the works of Ibn 'Abd al-Hakam and other Arab historians, and it may be that knowledge of the supposed palace site reached Oviedo through Asturian diplomatic and other

---

[53] Ibid. pp. 60-5.
[54] *Chronicle of Alfonso III* chs. 5-6 (both versions, ibid.) pp. 118-21.
[55] Ibid. ch. 6, pp. 120-1.
[56] Ibid. ch. 7, pp. 120-3.
[57] Ibid. pp. 122-3.
[58] Ibid. ch. 6 (*Rotense* version only), p. 120.

contacts with the south. Similarly, the name Oppa appears in both the *Chronicle of Alfonso III* and the *Chronicle of 754*. In the latter he is the son of king Egica, who may have escaped from Toledo when the Arabs took the city, but in the former he is made out to be a son of Wittiza and bishop of Toledo (or of Seville in the *Ad Sebastianum* version of this chronicle), who accompanied the Arab armies into the Asturias when they came to crush the resistance being led by Pelayo, the founder of the Asturian royal line. Pelayo and Oppa engage in a long debate, by the standards of this chronicle, prior to the Asturians winning the battle of Covadonga.[59] That this is totally unhistorical has generally been recognized.

That Oppa cannot be both a son of Wittiza and a son of Egica, a lay lord and a possible royal claimant and also bishop of Toledo or Seville must also be accepted. There may have been a bishop of Seville of this name at about this time, as testified in an episcopal list preserved in a late tenth-century manuscript.[60] That Oppa could not be a son of Wittiza can also be shown.[61] In any case, priority has to be given to the account of the *Chronicle of 754* over the Alfonsine one, as it is so much closer in date. In fact it looks as if the Oppa of the *Chronicle of Alfonso III* derives from a garbled or poorly transmitted version of the events that are independently recorded in the 754 chronicle, but with some deliberate recasting and revision of them, intended to promote the ideological program of the Asturian monarchy.

It may seem remarkable that none of these three sets of later narratives makes any reference to king Achila, whose existence, testified by both coinage and king lists, is one of the few definite things that can be known about the final phase of the history of the Visigothic kingdom. An all too common but methodologically totally unjustifiable reaction is to assume that all these different pieces must somehow fit together, and in the case of Achila, for example, to claim that he should be identified with one of the characters from the literary narratives. So he is seen as being Oppa of the *Chronicle of 754* or one of the unnamed sons of Wittiza of the Asturian chronicles,

---

[59] Ibid. chs. 8-9, pp. 123-7.
[60] Juan Gil (ed.), *Corpus Scriptorum Muzarabicorum* (2 vols., Madrid, 1973), vol. 1, p. xviii, but it has to be recognized that this may be no more than a reflection of the story as found in the *Ad Sebastianum* version of the *Chronicle of Alfonso III*.
[61] See below p. 000.

without any further thought being given to the reliability of those texts.[62]

A good example of the kind of difficulties into which such an approach may lead comes with the story of the sons of Wittiza in the *Chronicle of Alfonso III*, whose undefined treachery is said to have been instrumental in the kingdom's downfall. However, it is this very chronicle that records that Wittiza was the son of Egica's marriage to Cixilo, daughter of Ervig.[63] As this marriage was planned as part of the arrangements for Egica's succession to Ervig, and if Wittiza was the offspring of it, he cannot have been born much before 688. If then he was only in his mid-twenties at the time of his death or deposition, he could not have had children old enough to betray anybody or anything; at best the oldest of them would still have been less than 10 years old in 711/12. The narrative is totally self-contradictory. As in the case of its account of the replacement of Wamba by Ervig, the *Chronicle of Alfonso III* is of no use whatsoever in trying to piece together the reality of the events surrounding the end of the Visigothic kingdom. As a view of how they were seen 200 years later, it is invaluable.

Similar problems exist with respect to the Arabic sources, most of which are even later in date, but which are by and large no more than elaborations on a core of legendary materials put together or devised in the middle of the ninth century. In general it has to be admitted that both these later levels, the Arab and the Asturian, add little or nothing to a proper understanding of what actually happened around 711, and if anything only get in the way of achieving one.

Pared down to the bare essentials, it looks as if Wittiza was overthrown in a coup, probably in the year 711 but possibly in 710. This was carried out by Ruderic with the support of some at least of the secular and ecclesiastical elite of the court, but it may have been violent and certainly did not achieve the level of consensus among the aristocracy secured by some earlier transfers of power. As in 653 and 672, an uneasy or unpopular royal succession led to a regional

---

[62] D. Claude, "Untersuchungen zum Untergang des Westgotenreiches," *Historisches Jahrbuch* 108 (1988), pp. 329–58; see also Miquel Coll i Alentorn, *Els successors de Vitiza en la zona nord-est del domini visigòtic* (Barcelona, 1971).

[63] *Chronicle of Alfonso III*, ch. 4 (*Rotense* version), ed. Gil, Moralejo, and Ruiz, p. 118.

attempt to challenge it, and as in those two previous cases, this was based in the northeast. This would seem the most reasonable explanation for the existence of Achila and for his power base being located in the provinces of Tarraconensis and Narbonensis. That he, unlike Paul, who had proclaimed himself king in this region, survived and, according to the king list, reigned for three years, may be due to the fact that he and Ruderic never came to fight it out between them. It is unlikely that this was due to any degree of mutual tolerance, let alone a formal division of the kingdom, of the kind offered to Wamba by Paul in 673. It is more probable that a more serious threat intervened, in the form of the Arab raids on the south, before they could come to blows.

The traditional account given by the Arabic sources implies a single expedition, led by Tariq, which resulted in one major battle, in which Ruderic was defeated. The *Chronicle of 754*, far closer in time to these events, indicates a rather different pattern of events, with the crucial battle being preceded by destructive raids, in which various towns were attacked. Once the nonsense of count Julian and his daughter is dismissed, and with it the idea that the Arabs and Berbers lacked shipping of their own, both to bring them to the Tangiers peninsula in the years around 705/6 and then to transport them across the Straits into Visigothic territory at will, it is easy to see how a series of sea-borne raids on southern Spain could have followed on from the subjugation of Tangiers and Ceuta.

What happened next is exceedingly obscure and will probably always remain so. It is just possible, from the words of the *Chronicle of 754*, that another son of Egica, called Oppa, had been set up as king in Toledo while Ruderic was away in the south, or this may have happened in the brief period between the latter's defeat and the Arab conquest of the capital. Ruderic's death almost certainly took place in the context of a battle against one of the Arab and Berber raiding forces, and may have been the result of treachery on the part of some of his supposed followers. If so, this was with an eye to effecting a change of ruler and not to betraying the kingdom to the invaders, who, however, were quick to take advantage of an unexpected opportunity to turn a raid into a conquest. In the northeast, the end of Achila's three-year regnal period would have coincided with the Arab conquest of the Ebro valley and Zaragoza, which the coinage shows to have been part of his kingdom. It is thus possible that his death was linked to the fall of this part of his realm. His successor Ardo is known only from a regnal list, and is given a reign length of seven years. This would take him to 721, in which year the Arab and Berber armies crossed the Pyrenees and conquered Narbonensis.[64] He, the last of all the Visigothic kings, may have gone down fighting, like his predecessor.

While the elimination of vengeful counts and treacherous children may help to clarify the all too uncertain pattern of events, there remains a fundamental question of how it was that an apparently powerful and hitherto peaceful kingdom should fall so quickly to a relatively small number of invaders. In the past, such questions gave rise to the idea that the kingdom must have been in a state of moral decline, decay, and demoralization.[65] Such an approach must now seem rather archaic, and in many ways it was conditioned by the reactions of the Spanish intelligentsia to the state of their country in the late nineteenth and early twentieth centuries, and in particular the humiliating defeat in the Spanish-American War of 1898, which had lost Spain most of her remaining overseas territories. Explanations found for the decay of Spain's once great empire were also thought to be applicable to earlier national disasters.

The decline in the credibility of such an approach to the problem of understanding why the Visigothic kingdom proved so fatally unready to deal with the Arab and Berber invasion has tended to sideline the question rather than provide an alternative answer. But the enquiry itself is still a valid one, all the more so if it be accepted that the conquest was in some senses little more than an accident that was skilfully exploited by the beneficiaries. As has been shown earlier in this chapter, the Arabs had extended themselves over an enormous stretch of territory, encompassing the whole southern shore of the Mediterranean, by conquering the main settlements along what was a very long and narrow coastal region. There was no large-scale conquest, let alone assimilation at this time, and each of the discrete regions conquered had to be garrisoned. Their numbers were small, even after they began recruiting indigenous tribesmen, and

---

[64] Collins, *Arab Conquest*, p. 45.
[65] Luis García Moreno, *El fin del reino visigodo de Toledo; decadencia y catastrofe* (Madrid, 1975); see also idem, "Los últimos tiempos del reino visigodo," *Boletín de la Real Academia de la Historia* 189 (1992), pp. 425-59 for his more recent views.

relatively small forces would have been used in each phase of the expansion.

It is almost impossible to know the size of the forces involved. Later Arab sources speak of an invading force of 7,000 to 12,000 men, but as this was supposed to encounter a Visigothic army over 100,000 men strong, no trust can be placed in the accuracy of the figures.[66] In any case, 7,500 is likely to be too high for the size of the Arab and Berber forces who entered Spain in 711/12. Something like a quarter of that number may be more realistic.

Reducing the scale of the invading army may seem to make the question of why it proved so devastatingly effective all the more significant. But it needs to be understood that the forces that confronted them were probably not much larger in number. The brief survey of the political history of the kingdom attempted in the preceding chapters should have suggested how very small the Visigothic elite really was. There were a tiny number of families, perhaps no more than a couple of dozen who controlled many of the economic assets of the kingdom, and who provided the personnel for the court aristocracy. Their immediate followings would also have constituted the principal constituents of the royal army, along with those troops the kings themselves would have raised from their own lands and those that formed the fiscal estates.

The size, maintenance, and armament of such forces cannot be known from the evidence available to us, but it is unlikely that numbers were large. For one thing, the military threats to be faced in and by the Visigothic kingdom were generally quite limited. Essentially, they consisted of the repression of banditry, defence against Basque raids, and securing the frontiers up in the northeast against the possibility of attack by the Franks, or in the late seventh century by the dukes of Aquitaine. The last of these was probably the most significant, and the fact that most of the serious military challenges to the kings in Toledo, as in 631, 672/3, and 711, came from this region may imply a greater concentration of forces in this area than elsewhere in the kingdom.

[66] Taha, *Muslim Conquest and Settlement*, p. 86 and references favors 12,000 for the invaders, in two groups; one of 7,000 and the other of 5,000, on the basis of the later Arab accounts, but even these numbers may be much too large. The figure of 100,000 for the Visigothic army is to be found in al-Maqqari.

There is no evidence that Visigothic Spain was a society organized for war, in the way that was true of their Frankish neighbors.[67] Among the latter it was the practice for annual assemblies to be held, in which the kings and their nobility would, among other things, decide upon the target for a military campaign in which they would all join later in the year. Although this practice may not have been followed consistently, especially after the mid-seventh century, it meant that the Frankish kingdoms were frequently aggressive and expansionary, as far as their neighbors were concerned, and the resulting spoils of war played an important part in enhancing the power of the most effective of the Merovingian kings.

The Iberian peninsula, unlike Francia, had geographically defined boundaries and provided far fewer opportunities for military expansion. After the disaster suffered by Theudis's forces in Ceuta in the mid-sixth century, no subsequent king seems to have tried to reestablish a Visigothic enclave across the Straits of Gibraltar, and warfare on the borders with the Franks and Aquitainians always seems to have been defensive in character. Thus there was hardly any need for large armies, especially after the decline of the Frankish threat in the 630s. Wamba had to use threats of severe punishment to try to force lay and ecclesiastical landowners to produce military contingents.[68] The Arab raids around 711 may not at the time have seemed more threatening than the frequent depredations of the Basques in the Ebro valley, and there is no reason to assume that unusually large forces could or would have been raised to counter them.

The disaster seems therefore to have resulted from the death of the king in battle, the first time this had happened since 507, and the related destruction of a significant proportion of the aristocratic elite. Some of these may have fallen in the battle, and others, according to the *Chronicle of 754*, were killed in Toledo soon after the Arabs took the city. The loss of king, capital, and palatine aristocracy would have had a paralyzing effect on a political system in which the transmission of royal authority depended entirely upon a process of selection by the court elite of one of their own number, with a formalizing of it that could be held only in the *urbs regia*.

---

[67] For Frankish military practices see F. L. Ganshof, *Frankish Institutions under Charlemagne* (New York, 1968), pp. 59-68.

[68] LV IX. ii. 8; dated the Kalends of November in the second year of Wamba's reign (November 1, 673).

There were of course regional nobilities, but these had been excluded from any part in the king-making processes from at least 653 onward. Nor were their individual resources sufficient to challenge the authority of the conquerors, who had replaced the former Visigothic elite. So it is not surprising that in the immediate aftermath of the defeat of Ruderic and the fall of Toledo, regional leaders, such as count Theodemir, who seems to have controlled seven small towns in the southeast, made treaties with the invaders that ensured their personal continuance in their offices, landholdings, and local authority.[69] Overall, it is hard to resist the impression that the Gothic ruling classes were at the end of the history of their kingdom, as at the beginning, a small military aristocracy perched on top of a large civilian subject population that, for all the best efforts of the church, did not greatly care whether they survived or not.

---

[69] Collins, *Arab Conquest*, pp. 39-42.

Part II
Society and Culture

6

Books and Readers

The Legacy of Africa

In the seventh century the Spanish church appears intellectually outstanding. It produced a succession of authors of theological, literary, and liturgical texts that were unparalleled, at least in the West, at this time.[1] Many of the writers were also leading figures in the political life of the period, especially the bishops of Seville and Toledo, and most of them were involved in the impressive series of ecclesiastical councils held in Spain during the course of the century. The works of several of them, most notably Isidore of Seville (died 636) and Julian of Toledo (died 690) subsequently circulated widely outside the Iberian peninsula, as would the *Hispana* collection of canon-law texts, in the compiling of versions of which both these bishops were probably involved.[2] Other authors of the Visigothic period, such as Ildefonsus of Toledo (died 667) and the monastic founder Fructuosus of Braga (died c.670) may have been less well known outside the Iberian peninsula, but within it their writings remained influential for centuries. The largely anonymous liturgical legacy of the Spanish church of the Visigothic period was outstanding for both its literary and theological qualities, and continued in use until finally suppressed in favor of Romano-Frankish traditions in the late eleventh century.[3]

The variety of texts produced in the century and a quarter between the conversion of Reccared and the Arab conquest included works of history, devotional and dogmatic theology, biblical studies, poetry,

---

[1] See M. C. Díaz y Díaz, "La cultura de la España visigótica del siglo VII," in his *De Isidoro al Siglo XI* (Barcelona, 1976), pp. 23-55, and idem, "La cultura literaria en la España visigótica," ibid. pp. 59-86.
[2] G. Martínez Díez, *La Colección Canónica Hispana* (Madrid, 1966), pp. 327-54.
[3] M. C. Díaz y Díaz, "Literary Aspects of the Visigothic Liturgy," in Edward James (ed.), *Visigothic Spain: New Approaches* (Oxford, 1980), pp. 61-76.

monastic rules, saints' lives, polemics, and educational texts, in addition to canon law and liturgy. Many of these items were not original, in that they consisted of rearranged excerpts from the works of earlier writers, thought to be particularly authoritative. But the compiling of them required the existence of libraries containing substantial collections of books. It would be wrong to assume that the often rare and early texts thus used by the authors of the Visigothic period would have been easily available to them, or would have survived in the peninsula from the later Roman period. The evidence for the marked lack of intellectual activity in Spain in the intervening centuries would argue against such a view. What has been called "the Isidoran Renaissance," from the central role played in it by Isidore of Seville, depended on the presence in Spain by the late sixth century of very specific literary resources.[4] How they came to be there requires an explanation, and it is one that involves looking outside the Iberian peninsula to some contemporary events in Byzantium and Africa.

Around 578/9 a young man from *Scallabis* (modern Santarém), called John but of Gothic origin, returned home after spending seven years in Constantinople. According to the brief account of him by Isidore of Seville, he had gone there to study.[5] It is noteworthy that despite the ongoing war between the Visigothic kings and the Byzantine forces in Spain, it was clearly possible for a Goth to travel to Constantinople without difficulty, and that Latin literary studies were still being cultivated there.

Isidore's words are not the only proof that Latin learning was still actively promoted in Byzantium. A Latin poet, Flavius Corippus, who had written a verse panegyric on one of the imperial viceroys of his native province of Africa, was encouraged by his literary success to move to Constantinople in search of patronage. There he wrote another panegyric on the accession of Justin II in 565, which tactfully omitted any hint of opposition to the new emperor's supposedly unanimous selection by senate, army, and people.[6] Whether this gained him the rewards he sought is not known.

---

[4] Jacques Fontaine, *Isidore de Séville et la culture classique dans l'Espagne wisigothique* (2 vols., Paris, 1959; 3 vols., rev. edn. Paris, 1983), vol. 2, pp. 735-62.

[5] Isidore, *De Viris Illustribus* 31, ed. Carmen Codoñer Merino, *El "De Viris Illustribus" de Isidoro de Sevilla* (Salamanca, 1964), pp. 151-2.

[6] Averil Cameron (ed.), *Flavius Cresconius Corippus, In laudem Iustini Augusti minoris Libri IV* (London, 1976), pp. 1-7.

Other Latin authors were also present in Constantinople for rather different reasons. These were bishops from Africa and Italy who were being detained there for opposing the emperor's theological policies. Several of them wrote works to send to their supporters in the West, urging continued resistance to the emperor's theology. They also recorded the ill-treatment they had received, which they saw as a modern counterpart to the imperial persecution of the early Christian confessors and martyrs.

One such work is the world chronicle of bishop Victor of Tunnuna (modern Tunis).[7] Its earlier sections came from Jerome's Latin translation and continuation of the chronicle of Eusebius of Caesarea, and from the further continuation to 443/4 by Prosper of Aquitaine, to which Victor added his own set of annals up to the succession of Justin II in 565. In this original section of his world chronicle, he provided a great deal of information on contemporary events, not least about the dispute over "the Three Chapters."

This had originated in an attempt by the emperor Justinian I to resolve the Monophysite controversy, a much wider theological debate over the Human and Divine Natures of Christ, that had divided the East since the early fifth century and had led to the establishment of rival churches. Successive emperors, even if not themselves Monophysites, had looked for ways to heal the rift.[8] In a fresh bid for reconciliation, Justinian had been persuaded by his theological advisor, bishop Theodore Ascida of Caesarea, to condemn the works of three later fifth-century authors whose views the Monophysites opposed. But far from resolving the problems in the East, Justinian's intervention only stirred up opposition in the West, as the condemnation of the three authors was seen as an attack on the Council of Chalcedon of 451, whose definition of the Natures of Christ was authoritative for the orthodox or anti-Monophysite party.

Victor of Tunnuna was one of six African bishops summoned to Constantinople in 564 for defying the emperor on this issue; they were then imprisoned in monasteries in the capital. Since his chronicle ends with Justinian's death the following year, he probably completed

---

[7] *Victoris Tunnunensis Chronicon*, edited by Carmen Cardelle de Hartmann in *Corpus Christianorum Series Latina*, vol. CLXXIIIA, pp. 3-55.
[8] W. H. C. Frend, *The Rise of the Monophysite Movement* (Cambridge, 1972), pp. 255-95.

his work in prison. His own fate is unknown, but it was in Constantinople that John acquired a copy of Victor's chronicle, following his arrival in the city in the early 570s. In consequence he became uniquely responsible for the preservation of Victor's chronicle, which he then continued up to the year 590, as it is only in this extended version that the work survives.[9]

A copy of Victor's work may not have been the only literary souvenir that John brought back from his seven years in Constantinople. He may also have obtained a copy of Corippus's eulogy on the accession of Justin II. This is one of very few such Late Antique verse panegyrics to survive. Like Victor's chronicle, this work enjoys a Spanish manuscript tradition, not easily explicable of an African author writing in Constantinople.[10] While a direct association with John is lacking in this case, it is likely that it was he or another such traveler who brought it to Spain. An alternative candidate might be Leander of Seville, who visited Constantinople in the early 580s. Whoever was responsible, the list of literary imports does not stop here.

The manuscript of the only complete text of Corippus's *In laudem Justini Minoris* also contains the verse *Carmen de Satisfactione Paenitentiae* of Verecundus of Junca.[11] Verecundus was another of the African bishops who had resisted Justinian over the Three Chapters.[12] He went to Constantinople in 551 to support pope Vigilius (537-55), and there took part in the excommunication of Justinian's theological adviser Theodore Ascida. In consequence he and the pope had to take sanctuary in a church in Chalcedon, where he died in 552. The only certain works by Verecundus are two poems; the one preserved with Corippus's *In laudem* in the Azagra codex (MS Madrid, BN 10,029), and another on the Resurrection, which is lost but whose existence is recorded in a mid-seventh-century Spanish source.[13] So it

---

[9] *Johannis Biclarensis Chronicon*, ed. Carmen Cardelle de Hartmann in *Corpus Christianorum Series Latina*, vol. CLXXIIIA, pp. 59-83.
[10] Corippus, ed. Cameron, pp. 20-4.
[11] Madrid Biblioteca Nacional MS 10,029, ff. 77-81.
[12] *Victoris Chron., post cos. Basilii anno xi* and *anno xii*, ed. Hartmann (*CCSL* vol. CLXXIIIA), pp. 47-8; see also A. Hudson Williams, "Notes on Verecundus," *Vigiliae Christianae* 6 (1952), pp. 47-51.
[13] The extended version of Isidore's *De Viris Illustribus*, on which see note 62 below. See H. Koeppler, "*De Viris Illustribus* and Isidore of Seville," *Journal of Theological Studies* 37 (1936), pp. 16-34.

may be that whoever brought Corippus's work to Spain also had Verecundus's verses in his luggage.

Yet another of the African bishops involved in the prolonged resistance to Justinian's religious policies was Facundus of Hermiane, who had been in Constantinople at the very beginning of the controversy. There he wrote his treatise *Pro defensione trium capitulorum* or "In Defence of the Three Chapters." While the only extant manuscript of this work is in Verona, a center of Italian resistance to efforts to condemn the three authors, there are good grounds for suspecting that it was known to and used by Julian of Toledo (680-90), and this would suggest the existence of a now lost Spanish transmission.[14] It is impossible to determine if Facundus's "Defence" reached Visigothic Spain via Africa or directly from Constantinople.

While it is possible to identify some of the Spanish travelers to the imperial capital in the 570s and early 580s, and some of the texts they may have acquired there, this route was secondary in terms of how African influences were making themselves felt in Spain in the later sixth century. Far more substantial and prolonged was the effect of the direct connections between the two. This flow of cultural influence seems to have been entirely one way, and was principally mediated through individuals and groups who migrated from Africa to the Iberian peninsula.

They came for various reasons, one of which was certainly the growing threat to the towns and country estates of the African provinces from the Berber tribes of the interior.[15] Wars were fought by the Vandals and then by a succession of imperial governors to defend the shrinking frontiers from Berber attacks. After Procopius's narrative, which ends in 545/6, the only sources for this are Corippus's probably flattering panegyric on John, Master of the Soldiers from 546 to 551/2, and a few entries in the chronicle of John of Biclarum, the Visigothic continuator of Victor of Tunnunna. John's chronology cannot be trusted, but what he says of the deaths of various imperial

---

[14] Jocelyn Hillgarth, "Las fuentes de San Julián de Toledo," *Anales Toledanos* 3 (1971), pp. 97-118, at 115 lists quotations from Cyril of Alexandria's *Scholia de incarnatione unigeniti*, which he believes Julian obtained primarily via Facundus; personal communication.

[15] Ildefonsus, *De Viris Illustribus* 3 on Donatus: "*Hic violentias barbararum gentium imminere conspiciens...*," ed. Carmen Codoñer Merino, *El "De Viris Illustribus" de Ildefonso de Toledo* (Salamanca, 1972), p. 120.

commanders in battles with the Berbers seems credible.[16] Little geographical information is given, so it is not possible to know where the fighting was concentrated, but there is explicit evidence that it was a major cause of a displacement of population from Africa into Spain.[17] Berber raids were not the only cause of this movement of African clerics and monks into Spain. Another factor was the attempts made by Justinian to force the African church into accepting his condemnation of the Three Chapters, and the punishments being inflicted on those who resisted.[18]

Why it was principally toward Spain, nearly a thousand miles to the west, that the resulting migration of men and books was mainly directed may be related to the troubled conditions in Italy in the aftermath of the Byzantine-Gothic wars and the invasion by the Lombards in 568. There also existed well-established trade routes by sea between Africa and the Iberian peninsula, which had grown in importance in the later Vandal period while those to Italy may have declined.[19]

Among the Africans found in the Spanish sources at this time are an abbot Nanctus, who together with his monks was given an estate in the vicinity of Mérida by king Leovigild (569-86), and the monk Donatus, who sought refuge in the peninsula in the same period, and who founded the monastery of *Servitanum* in the Levante. Donatus is said in the *De Viris Illustribus* of Ildefonsus of Toledo to have been accompanied by 70 monks and by a large collection of books. He is also described here as being the first to introduce a monastic rule of life into Spain.[20]

Taken literally, this must be an exaggeration, in that it ignores the strong influence exerted by Gallic monastic ideas and practices on the northeast of the peninsula from the fifth century onward. Nor does it take account of the specific references made to monks and

---

[16] Roger Collins, "An Historical Commentary on Iohannis Biclarensis *Chronicon*," in Hartmann (ed.), *Corpus Christianorum Series Latina*, vol. CLXXIIIA, pp. 110-48.
[17] See note 15 above.
[18] Robert Markus, "Reflections on Religious Dissent in North Africa in the Byzantine Period," *Studies in Church History* 3 (1966), pp. 140-50.
[19] Michael McCormick, *Origins of the European Economy: Communications and Commerce AD 300-900* (Cambridge, 2001), pp. 100-1 and references in note 71.
[20] *Vitas Patrum Emeretensium* III, ed. A. Maya Sánchez, *CCSL* vol. CXVI (1992), pp. 21-4; Ildefonsus, *De Viris Illustribus* 3, ed. Codoñer, p. 120.

monasteries in some of the sixth-century Spanish conciliar legislation.[21] However, all of the textual and other evidence for regular monasticism in Spain prior to the later sixth century relates exclusively to a limited geographical area: essentially the Mediterranean coastal region from Tarragona northward, together with the lower Ebro valley. Thus, references to monastic practices appear only in the acts of provincial ecclesiastical councils held in the province of Tarraconensis, notably those held at Tarragona in 516 and in Lérida in 546.[22] No mention can be found of monks or monasteries in the center, south, or west of the peninsula before the late sixth century.

What certainly did exist, and is attested in the acts of the Second Council of Toledo of 527 (or more probably 531) were features of an older tradition of individual or family asceticism, represented by voluntary celibacy and the setting up of private monastic households, similar to those that had been been known in Italy and North Africa since the late fourth century.[23] So the influx of African communities in the second half of the sixth century could represent the first establishment in the south and center of the Iberian peninsula of monastic communities following received rules. Ildefonsus's own monastery of Agali, which produced a number of the most prominent of the seventh-century bishops of Toledo, could have had such an origin at this time.[24]

Later in the late sixth century, it was Donatus's successor as abbot of *Servitanum*, Eutropius, who is recorded in John's chronicle as sharing the leading role with Leander of Seville at the Third Council of Toledo of 589, which formalized the conversion of the Visigoths from Arianism to Catholicism.[25] That he was one of the African monks who had accompanied Donatus is probable. He subsequently became bishop of Valencia, and was the author of two now lost epistolary treatises on infant baptism and on the monastic life.[26]

---

[21] References most easily found in José Vives, *Concilios visigóticos e hispano-Romanos* (Barcelona and Madrid, 1963), p. 546: Monasterio, Monje.
[22] Martínez Díez and Felix Rodríguez, *Colección Canónica Hispana*, vol. IV (Madrid, 1984), pp. 269-311.
[23] Ibid. pp. 345-66.
[24] Luís A. García Moreno, "Los monjes y monasterios en las ciudades de las Españas tardorromanas y visigodas," *Habis* 24 (1993), pp. 179-92. Helladius, who became bishop of Toledo in 615, had been its second abbot, so a foundation around 590/600 seems likely.
[25] *Iohannis Biclarensis Chronicon* 91, ed. Hartmann, p. 81.
[26] Isidore, *De Viris Illustribus* 32, ed. Codoñer, p. 152.

The other luminary of the Third Council of Toledo, Leander of Seville (died 599/600) is much better known. The eldest of three brothers, all of whom became bishops, and with at least one known sister, he was the son of Severianus. In his *De Institutione Virginum et Contemptu Mundi*, dedicated to his sister Florentina, Leander refers to the family's exile from its homeland as having occurred during his own lifetime.[27] This is usually interpreted in the light of the short account of him by his brother Isidore, who succeeded him as bishop of Seville.

Isidore mentions Leander's time in the province of Carthaginiensis, prior to becoming bishop of Seville (in the 570s).[28] Some of this province, particularly its Mediterranean coastal region and including the city of *Carthago Nova* or Cartagena from which it took its name, had been captured by imperial forces in 552. So it has been assumed that it was from Cartagena that Severianus and his family were either forcibly exiled or had fled.[29]

This is possible, but Isidore, who made a virtue of stylistic brevity, was actually making an elegant literary parallel. What he says of Leander is that "by profession a monk from the province of Spanish Carthaginiensis, he was made bishop of Seville in the province of Baetica."[30] In other words, he equated the change in status from monk to bishop to that made geographically from Carthaginiensis to Baetica. All that he is saying is that Leander had been a monk in the province of Carthaginiensis, not that he was born there, let alone had to flee from it. So it is not necessary to believe that the family originated in Spain at all, and as both Leander and Isidore had Greek names, it could be that their lost homeland lay outside the Iberian peninsula, possibly in Africa. The third of the brothers, Fulgentius, who became bishop of Ecija, has a name most of whose other associations are African.[31]

---

[27] Leander *De Institutione Virginum* 31, ed. Jaime Velázquez, *De la Instrucción de las Vírgines y Desprecio del Mundo* (Madrid, 1979), pp. 170-4.

[28] Isidore, *De Viris Illustribus* 28, ed. Codoñer, pp. 149-50.

[29] Jacques Fontaine, "Qui a chassé de Carthaginoise Severianus et les siens? Observations sur l'histoire familiale d'Isidore de Seville," in *Estudios en Hoenaje a Don Claudio Sánchez Albornoz en sus 90 annos*, vol. 1 (Buenos Aires, 1983), pp. 349-400, especially pp. 353-69 for the interpretation of ch. 31 of Leander's *De Institutione*.

[30] On *brevitas* see E. R. Curtius, *European Literature and the Latin Middle Ages*, trans. W. R. Trask (Princeton, NJ, 1973), pp. 487-94.

[31] e.g. Fulgentius 2 and Fulgentius 3 in J. R. Martindale (ed.) *Prosopography of the Later Roman Empire*, vol. 2 (Cambridge, 1980), pp. 487-8.

It could be objected that for fugitive African monks to be able to establish monasteries in Spain makes sense, but for first-generation immigrants to become bishops of major sees such as Seville and *Astigi* or Ecija is harder to understand. But in this period Mérida, the metropolitan bishopric of the province of Lusitania, was held by two successive bishops of Greek or eastern Mediterranean origin.[32] Their successor Masona, who was bishop at the time of the Third Council of Toledo of 589, is said in the same source to be of Gothic birth, but it is remarkable that his name is not of Gothic but of Berber origin. No name in the Gothic onomastic register is in any way close to it, and every other Masona, Massona, Massuna, that may be found in classical, Late Antique, and early medieval sources is an African.[33]

As well as being accompanied by his 70 monks, Donatus is said to have come to Spain "with a very large collection of books."[34] He was unlikely to have been the only African immigrant to bring books with him. They were also traded or used as gifts, as in earlier centuries. For example, foreign merchants coming to Mérida are described as always paying their first visit to the bishop, and books could easily have entered Spain from the east in this way, as well as by being carried there by fugitives and immigrants.[35] Whatever the routes taken and the intermediaries involved, it is certainly possible to detect the presence and influence of African books in Spain in the later sixth and seventh centuries.

Among the best examples is a collection of verse by the late fifth-century Roman African poet Dracontius. While imprisoned for treason, he wrote a poem on the first six days of Creation. This was certainly known to Isidore of Seville, who included Dracontius in his *De Viris Illustribus*.[36] Another copy of this *Hexameron* was to be found in the royal library in Toledo by the middle of the seventh century, when bishop Eugenius II (646-57) revised it, adding a new final part dealing with the seventh day of Creation at the request of king Chindasuinth.[37]

---

[32] *Vitas Patrum Emeretensium* IV. 1 and 3, ed. Maya Sánchez, pp. 25 and 31.
[33] *Vitas Patrum Emeretensium* V. 2, ed. Maya Sánchez, p. 48.
[34] Ildefonsus, *De Viris Illustribus* 3, ed. Codoñer, p. 120.
[35] *Vitas Patrum Emeretensium* IV. 3, ed. Maya Sánchez, p. 31.
[36] *De Viris Illustribus* 24, ed. Codoñer, p. 146.
[37] *Eugenii Toletani Episcopi Carmina*, ed. F. Vollmer (*Monumenta Germaniae Historica, Auctores Antiquissimi*, vol. XIV) (Berlin, 1905), pp. 23-129.

Eugenius also edited Dracontius's *Satisfactio*, a verse appeal to the Vandal ruler Gunthamund (484-96).

Other collections of shorter poems of African origin, principally miscellanies by named or anonymous authors, entered Spain around this time, and were formed into larger compilations, probably in Toledo around the middle of the seventh century.[38] Although some may already have been known in Spain in the Late Roman period, numerous African theological writings also arrived or were reintroduced in the late sixth century. These may have included such well-known works as the letters of Cyprian and treatises by Augustine, but also such rarities as some of the writings ascribed to the African bishop Vigilius of Thapsa (ca.484), and Lactantius's *De Mortibus Persecutorum*, the latter only subsequently transmitted via Spain.[39] The probably African anonymous *Altercatio Ecclesiae et Synagogae* (fifth century) may have arrived around this time in Spain, where it was used by Julian in his polemical anti-Jewish writings, and was transmitted thence to Francia and southern Italy.[40] Likewise making a similar journey was at least one collection of the acts of the Oecumenical Councils of the early church combined with those of the main African councils.[41] This became the basis for the even larger *Hispana* collection, incorporating Gallic and Spanish conciliar *acta*, of which the first edition may have been produced by Isidore of Seville.[42]

Roman Africa was famous for its grammarians in Late Antiquity, and the evidence for the presence of African grammatical treatises in seventh-century Spain is further testimony to the migration of texts. A good example is the late fifth- or sixth-century commentary of Pompeius on the *Ars Maior* of his fellow African, Aelius Donatus, which first appeared in Spain in the time of Isidore, and was transmitted

---

[38] A. Riese (ed.), *Anthologia Latina* (Leipzig, 1906), vol. 1/1, vi, and 1/2, iv; idem, "Zur lateinischen Anthologie, Nachträge und Beiträge," *Rheinisches Museum* 65 (1910), pp. 495-503.
[39] Díaz y Díaz, "Obra literaria," p. 111, and Louis Holtz, "Prose et poésie latines tardives transmises aux Carolingiens par l'intermédiaire de l'Espagne," in Jacques Fontaine and Christine Pellistrandi (eds.), *L'Europe héritière de l'Espagne wisigothique* (Madrid, 1992), pp. 213-22, at p. 222 with n. 47.
[40] *Altercatio Ecclesiae et Synagogae*, ed. J. N. Hillgarth (*Corpus Christianorum, Series Latina*, vol. LXIXA, 1999), pp. 3-53.
[41] Martínez Díez, *Colección Canónica Hispana* I, pp. 271-88.
[42] Ibid. pp. 206-18, 306-25.

thence to other parts of western Europe.[43] The same route was probably followed by some of Donatus's own works, as his *Ars Maior II* was the subject of an anonymous commentary written in Toledo in the reign of Egica (687-702/3).[44] The grammar written by Julian of Toledo (680-90) was also heavily indebted to African sources.[45]

Liturgical *libelli* or small service books certainly made the journey from Africa to Spain. One of these has been at least partly preserved in a unique manuscript written in the Riojan monastery of San Millán de la Cogolla in the mid-eleventh century. This *Liber Ordinum*, containing texts for special ceremonies, includes a number of items that must have been written in Toledo in the seventh century. Best known is the order of service for when the king sets out to war, but of older and more distant origin must be the service for the reconciling of Donatists found in the same section of the manuscript. As Donatism, a peculiarly African schismatic movement starting in the early fourth century, never affected Spain, this text is clearly derived from an African liturgical collection.[46] Other items may have come with it, and have been absorbed less conspicuously into the generally anonymous corpus of the service books of the Visigothic liturgy.

Another type of book that can even more clearly be shown to have traveled from Africa to the Iberian peninsula in this period is that of the anti-Arian treatise. Among the examples of such a work may be the anonymous early fifth-century *Contra Varimadum*, which now survives only through independent Gallic and Spanish manuscript transmission.[47] Less clearly preserved is the Hispanic tradition of the writings of Fulgentius of Ruspe (died ca.527), but that this was once very strong may be confirmed by the laudatory references to him in Julian of Toledo (680-90), and even more strikingly by the letter sent

---

[43] Louis Holtz, "Tradition et diffusion de l'oeuvre grammaticale de Pompée, commentateur de Donat," *Revue de Philologie* 45 (1971), pp. 48-83, and idem, "Prose et poésie latines tardives," p. 219.

[44] Louis Holtz, "Édition et tradition des manuels grammaticaux antiques et médiévaux," *Revue des Études Latines* 52 (1974), pp. 75-82, esp. p. 80 and n. 3.

[45] María A. H. Maestre Yenes, *Ars Iuliani Toletani Episcopi* (Toledo, 1973), pp. xxix-lx

[46] Roger Collins, "Continuity and Loss in Medieval Spanish Culture: the Evidence of MS Silos, Archivo Monástico 4," in Roger Collins and Anthony Goodman (eds.), *Medieval Spain: Culture, Conflict and Coexistence* (Basingstoke and New York, 2002), pp. 1-22, at pp. 7-9.

[47] Ed. B. Schwank, *Florilegia Biblica Africana Saec. V* (= *Corpus Christianorm, Series Latina*, vol. XC, 1961), pp. vii-xvi, 1-134.

to the Frankish bishops by their Spanish confrères at the height of the Adoptionist controversy in the 790s. In the latter, in support of their position, the Spanish bishops called upon the authority of a line of holy and orthodox Fathers of the Church, naming specifically Hilary, Ambrose, Augustine, Jerome, and Fulgentius.[48] Nowhere else in Latin Christendom would Fulgentius have been thought to enjoy equal membership of such a distinguished body.

The full impact on the Spanish church in the later sixth century of the anti-Arian treatises of Fulgentius and other African writers can now only dimly be appreciated, because of the loss of so much of the polemical literature of the period that was produced in Spain. Thus, we know from Isidore that his brother Leander composed a number of such works "during the pilgrimage of his exile"; probably referring to the period between the fall of Seville in 584 and the death of Leovigild in 586, when he may have been exiled for his support for Hermenegild. None of these writings have survived. The same is true of the treatise by his contemporary, bishop Severus of Málaga, directed against the apostate bishop of Vincent of Zaragoza, who had converted to Arianism.[49]

It is likely that such works subsequently ceased to be copied because the successful elimination of Arianism from the peninsula by 590 undermined their usefulness. But their importance in their own day should not be minimized, any more than their probable debt to earlier African equivalents. This needs stressing because the literary controversy with the Arians in the later part of the reign of Leovigild marks the beginning of a change in the intellectual strength of the Spanish church as a whole. Paradoxically, it was probably the Arian king who acted as the catalyst for this.

It is remarkable in the light of views held since at least the fourth century about the spiritual danger posed by contact with heretics and schismatics, that there is no mention in contemporary Spanish sources of the fifth and most of the sixth century that the ruling elite in the peninsula followed a form of Christianity regarded by most of their subjects as heretical. Modern scholarship has shown that there really was no such thing as Arianism in the fourth century. That is to

---

[48] Hillgarth, "Fuentes," 115 for Julian's use of Fulgentius; *Epistula episcoporum Hispaniae* 1, ed. Juan Gil, *Corpus Scriptorum Muzarabicorum* (2 vols., Madrid, 1973), vol. 1, p. 82.
[49] Isidore, *De Viris Illustribus* 28 and 30, ed. Codoñer, pp. 149-51.

say, while there were many and complex divisions within the church at that time over the nature and interrelationships of the Three Persons of the Trinity, none of the various theological factions regarded themselves as disciples of the Alexandrian deacon Arius, who died in 336, in circumstances that later writers liked to make out as particularly humiliating and disgusting.[50] It was only in the fifth century that western authors began producing handbooks classifying different kinds of heresy and presenting their salient features in an over-simplified fashion.[51] From these the Hispano-Roman clergy would have learned that their new Gothic rulers' views on the Trinity should be labelled as Arian, However, this important fact is never mentioned in any of the ecclesiastical councils or other contemporary texts relating to Spain in the period before about 579.

Why this was never discussed, and why Spain failed to produce bishops such as Fulgentius in Africa or Avitus in Burgundy, who tried to convert the Germanic rulers to the orthodox Christianity of the majority population, is hard to understand. It had nothing to do with persecution or the fear of it, and may again be a reflection of the intellectually and organizationally enfeebled state of the Spanish church for most of this time. The religious divide between Arians and Catholics seems to have been brought into the open only in the reign of Leovigild. The *Vitas Patrum Emeretensium* implies that it was he who initiated conflict by trying to secure Arian control over some of the major churches and relics of Mérida. Whether this was true elsewhere is not known, but it is notable that the Arian synod of Toledo of 580 was the first Spanish council in which the theological questions relating to the Trinity were ever discussed.

It used to be taken for granted that this was a response to the revolt of Hermenegild the previous year, and that the rebellion itself had been prompted by the latter's conversion to Catholicism. However, the evidence relating to this suggests that conversion and revolt were not simultaneous, and that he may not have become a Catholic until as late as 582. It is likely instead that the rebellion had received

---

[50] Rowan Williams, *Arius* (2nd edn., London, 2001), pp. 80-1. For fourth-century western "Arianism" see D. H. Williams, *Ambrose of Milan and the End of the Arian-Nicene Conflicts* (Oxford, 1995), pp. 38-103.
[51] Judith McClure, "Handbooks against Heresy in the West, from the late fourth to the late sixth centuries," *Journal of Theological Studies* 30 (1979), pp. 186-97.

at least some of its impetus from Leovigild's prior attempts to enhance the standing of the Arian church in his kingdom.[52] If this was the cause, the Catholic establishment proved far more resilient in its resistance in the 580s than its history over the preceding century and a half might have suggested, and for this the recent African input could have been responsible.

In the fourth century the church in Spain had been distinguished in a number of ways. It produced several of the more significant of the second-rank Christian authors of the period, such as Gregory of Elvira, Potamius of Lisbon, and Pacian of Barcelona, as well as a major ecclesiastical politician in the person of bishop Hossius of Córdoba, who was one of the emperor Constantine's chief ecclesiastical advisors. It also gave rise in the late fourth century to its own home-grown heresy in the form of Priscillianism, and had provided the venue for what was possibly the earliest series of western church councils, meeting in Elvira. Overall, Spain easily stands comparison with Gaul, Africa, and even Italy as a major contributor to the theological culture and the political life of the Christian church in the West throughout the fourth century. On the other hand, with the entry of the Vandals and Sueves into the peninsula in 409 and especially after the departure of Orosius in 417, a very different picture emerges. From then until the 570s, the intellectual landscape in Spain seems a very bleak one indeed, with the Galician chronicler Hydatius (died c.470) as its sole literary luminary.

The formation of a small collection of the decretals or authoritative letters of pope Hormisdas (514-23) may be the only evidence of intellectual activity in the south in this period.[53] The northeast was somewhat better served, thanks to a few provincial councils, but only between the years 516 and 549. The extension by pope Symmachus (498-514) of the legatine authority of the Gallic bishop Caesarius of Arles to include at least northeastern Spain should be seen against this background of the moribund ecclesiastical life of the peninsula.[54] However, this intention may never have been put into practice.

---

[52] For argument see Roger Collins, "Mérida and Toledo, 550-585," in James (ed.), *Visigothic Spain*, pp. 189-219.
[53] Martínez Diéz, *Colección Canónica Hispana*, vol. 1, pp. 271-4.
[54] A. Malnory, *Saint Césaire, Évêque d'Arles* (Paris, 1894), pp. 112-14.

There is hardly a feature of the history of the church in Spain in the fifth and the first three-quarters of the sixth centuries that would anticipate the revival that got under way by the 580s, let alone the ensuing period of the so-called "Isidoran Renaissance." The cultural resources upon which the latter was based may sometimes have been exaggerated, but for many of both the secular and the ecclesiastical texts that have been identified as existing in the episcopal library in Seville in Isidore's day, an African origin may be postulated or clearly established.[55]

The limited intellectual vitality of the Spanish church and the very serious problems of political instability, banditry, war, and destruction across the whole of the peninsula throughout the period from about 409 to 584 make it highly unlikely that classical and Patristic texts would have been widely disseminated or easily acquired at this time. At the same time, the loss of earlier works that once existed in Spanish church libraries is all too probable. So, it may well be that even some of the best-known and otherwise most widely read of Latin theological works, such as some of the writings of Augustine, first reached Spain under African aegis in the second half of the sixth century. At the very least, it has to be admitted that it is only after this time that many of them are first recorded in an Iberian context.

So there is at least a *prima facie* case for the idea that a migration of books, individuals, families, and whole monastic communities from Africa to Spain from the mid-550s onward gave something of a kick start to the revival of intellectual life in the Catholic church in the peninsula, and that this helps explain something of the vitality the latter then showed for much of the seventh century.

A Golden Age

If Leander was the leading figure in a newly revitalized Spanish church, few literary monuments to him remain. As well as his anti-Arian writings, a collection of his letters and what may have been a substantial body of liturgical texts and music have also failed to survive. As testimony to his skills as orator and writer there remain only the

---

[55] Jacques Fontaine, *Isidore de Séville et la culture classique*, vol. 2, pp. 854–9.

sermon that he addressed to the Third Council of Toledo in 589 and a treatise on monastic life for women that he wrote for his sister Florentina. While the sermon displays rhetorical skill, neither of these could be described as works of great erudition.

There are some unsurprising literary debts to such obvious Patristic authors as Cyprian, Ambrose, Jerome, and Augustine, but Leander's primary inspiration is biblical. In this he was very much in the mold of his friend and contemporary, pope Gregory the Great (590-604). The two met in Constantinople in the early 580s, while Gregory was there as *apocrisiarius* or resident papal envoy and Leander was negotiating for imperial assistance for Hermenegild, and they remained in periodic contact by letter thereafter. Gregory dedicated his *Regula Pastoralis* or "Pastoral Rule" of 590 to Leander, and may have sent him copies of at least some of his other exegetical writings. This Gregorian influence in the episcopal library in Seville was one of the few elements that is not traceable to Africa.

It is with his younger brother and successor, Isidore of Seville, that the intellectual revival in the Spanish church becomes most obvious, but as he makes clear in his own *De Viris Illustribus* ("On Famous Men"), there had existed in Leander's day a significant group of bishops in the south, on both sides of the Visigothic/Byzantine frontier, who were exchanging treatises and letters on such topics as baptism, fear of death, the merits of virginity, and the difficulties of the monastic life.[56] None of these has survived, any more than has the short history of recent events in the peninsula composed by bishop Maximus of Zaragoza (died 619).

The network of bishoprics involved in these exchanges included Seville, Cartagena, Málaga, *Ercavica* (Tolmo de Minateda, near Hellín, province of Albacete), Valencia, and Ecija. It also extended to Rome in the person of pope Gregory. While we know next to nothing of the content of their writings, it is worth noting that the geographical breadth of this intellectual ferment is unmatched in later parts of the Visigothic period, in which literary activity tends to be confined to a smaller number of centers, above all Toledo.

With Isidore, who was probably born in the later 560s and died on April 4, 636, the cultural revival of the late sixth century came to

---

[56] All of these are mentioned in the *De Viris Illustribus*, chs. xxviii-xxxiii, ed. Carmen Codoñer Merino, pp. 149-53.

maturity.[57] He may have studied under his brother, but very little is known of the details of his life before he succeeded Leander as bishop of Seville around 599/600. Possibly only one of his works, the *De Differentiis* ("On Differences"), which listed and discussed words that appeared similar but were different in meaning, and ones that meant the same but differed in appearance, may have been written before this time. Thereafter he produced a steady stream of writings, often in more than one version, that continued until his death. This was unmatched in its range and quantity by any of his predecessors or successors in Late Antique and early medieval Spain.

Of the man himself we know little. A few of his letters were collected, but the genuine ones are all so brief and terse that, unlike those of his friend and frequent correspondent Braulio of Zaragoza, they are unrevealing of his personality. All of the longer texts in this collection are of later date, and are essentially treatises from the later Visigothic period that were spuriously assigned to his authorship to give them authority.[58] Isidore's literary style is equally impervious to critical analysis, in that it is extremely fluid, varying from work to work. The most extreme example of this is his "Lamentations of a Sinful Soul," better known from its dependence on one particular figure of speech as the *Synonyma* or "Synonyms."[59] This "synonymous style" was highly influential, and was taken to a new extreme by bishop Ildefonsus of Toledo (657-67) in his "On the Perpetual Virginity of the Blessed Virgin Mary."

The two versions of his chronicle and of his *History of the Goths, Vandals, and Sueves* are, despite their relative brevity, major sources for the history of the the fifth to early seventh centuries in the peninsula.[60] Between writing the first version of the chronicle around 615 and the second by 626 he certainly obtained a copy of John of Biclarum's chronicle. He was also dependent in part on the lost

---

[57] Jacques Fontaine, *Isidore de Séville. Genèse et originalité de la culture hispanique au temps des Wisigoths* (Turnhout, 2000); also Pierre Cazier, *Isidore de Séville et la naissance de l'Espagne catholique* (Paris, 1994).

[58] G. B. Ford Jr. (ed.), *The Letters of St. Isidore of Seville* (Amsterdam, 1970); Roger E. Reynolds, "The 'Isidorian' *Epistula ad Leudefredum*: Its Origins, Early Manuscript Tradition, and Editions," in James (ed.), *Visigothic Spain: New Approaches*, pp. 251-72.

[59] Roger Collins, *Early Medieval Spain* (2nd edn., London, 1995), pp. 63-4 and 75.

[60] *Isidori Hispalensis Chronica*, ed. José Carlos Martín (*Corpus Christianorum, Series Latina*, vol. CXII, 2003).

Historiola or "small history" of bishop Maximus of Zaragoza, which he may have obtained through Braulio.[61]

His best-known and most influential work was his *Etymologiae sive Origenes* ("Etymologies or Origins"), which he may have still been revising at his death.[62] It was given its current 20-book structure by Braulio of Zaragoza. Drawing somewhat indiscriminately on a wide range of classical and Late Antique texts, this attempted to create a systematic survey of knowledge – an encyclopedia, as it has been seen. The controlling principle was that of etymology, with the key words in each topic being dissected to reveal their origins and meaning. Many of the etymologies that Isidore offered were erroneous or far-fetched, but this was a brave attempt to reduce a wide and disparate body of information to a controllable order. As with many of his works, the *Etymologiae* quickly became known outside Spain, and there is evidence for its being read in Francia, northern Italy, Ireland, and in the Anglo-Saxon kingdoms before the end of the seventh century.[63] The precise routes followed remain controversial, but the rapid dissemination of so many of Isidore's writings, even in some cases in his own lifetime, is evidence of closer ties between the church in Spain and several other regions of western Europe than is usually allowed for.[64]

Isidore's *De Viris Illustribus* ("On Famous Men") was a continuation of that of Jerome (d. 419), in the augmented version made by Gennadius of Marseille. It contained very short descriptions of the lives and writings of 33 Gallic, African, Italian, and mainly Spanish authors, in so far as they were known to Isidore. A longer version, containing 46 sections, emerged later in the seventh century, when an African continuation of Gennadius-Jerome was added to Isidore's.[65] He himself was included in continuations made after his own day,

---

[61] Roger Collins, "Isidore, Maximus and the Historia Gothorum," in Anton Scharer and Georg Scheibelreiter (eds.), *Historiographie im frühen Mittelalter* (Vienna and Munich, 1994), pp. 345–58, especially 354.

[62] *Isidori Hispalensis Episcopi Etymologiarum sive Originum Libri XX*, ed. W. M. Lindsay (2 vols., Oxford, 1911).

[63] Bernhard Bischoff, "Die europäische Verbreitung der Werke Isidors von Sevilla," in *Isidoriana* (León, 1961), pp. 317–44.

[64] For aspects of the arguments over the routes of the transmission of Isidore's works see J. N. Hillgarth, *Visigothic Spain, Byzantium and the Irish* (London, 1985), items VI–VIII.

[65] Carmen Codoñer Merino, *El "De Viris Illustribus" de Isidoro de Sevilla* (Salamanca, 1964), pp. 20–41.

initially via an account of his life and works written by his former pupil, Braulio of Zaragoza. However, this failed to become embedded in the main tradition, which is that containing a continuation in 13 sections by bishop Ildefonsus of Toledo.[66] Possibly unaware of Braulio's version, Ildefonsus added his own shorter entry on Isidore to the work.[67]

Braulio, who succeeded his brother John as bishop of Zaragoza in 631, was a member of an ecclesiastical dynasty, in that his father, Gregory, had been bishop of Osma, and another of his brothers, Fronimian, was an abbot of a monastery founded on the site of a late sixth-century hermitage. The *Vita Sancti Aemiliani* or "Life of St. Aemilian" that Braulio wrote at Fronimian's request was crucial in turning one of many such hermits of the Visigothic period into a major saint, whose cult seems rapidly to have eclipsed those of local rivals such as the Late Roman Christian poet Prudentius (died ca.400). This also gave the monastery of San Millán (Aemilian) the chance to develop its economic and spiritual predominance in the Rioja.[68]

Braulio may have studied under Isidore in Seville, and certainly inherited his intellectual leadership of the church in the Visigothic kingdom. In 638 his fellow bishops at the Sixth Council of Toledo asked him to reply to criticism from pope Honorius I (625-38) about their failure to take more repressive measures against the Jews, and late in his life he revised what has been thought to be a law code for king Reccesuinth. This is known from a small collection of 44 of his letters that was put together after his death, and which survives in only one manuscript.[69] Two of these reveal a rather uneasy relationship with his eventual successor, a priest and abbot called Taio.[70]

Before succeeding Braulio as bishop in 651, Taio had been sent to Rome by king Chindasuinth (642-53) to try to obtain works by Gregory the Great that were then not available in Spain, or at least in Toledo. These may have included some parts of the pope's *Moralia*, a huge

---

[66] José Carlos Martín (ed.), *La "Renotatio Librorum Domini Isidori" de Braulio de Zaragoza* (Logroño, 2002), pp. 55-84 and 167-209.
[67] Ildefonsus, *De Viris Illustribus* 8, ed. Codoñer, p. 128.
[68] Santiago Castellanos, *Hagiografía y sociedad en la Hispania visigoda* (Logroño, 1999).
[69] Charles H. Lynch, *Saint Braulio, Bishop of Saragossa (631-51): His Life and Writings* (Washington, DC, 1938), pp. 129-40.
[70] Braulio, *epp.* 11 and 42, ed. Luís Riesco Terreo, *Epistolario de San Braulio* (Seville, 1975), pp. 82-4, 154-63.

commentary on the Book of Job. A legendary account of this visit appears in the *Chronicle of 754*, but more mundanely, it enabled Taio in 653/4 to compose his five books of *Sententiae* or "Sentences," which consist of extracts from Gregory's works, organized thematically.[71] Taio last appears as signatory to the acts of the Ninth Council of Toledo of 655, and little more is known of his diocese for the rest of the Visigothic period. Just as Seville ceases to be a major center of literary activity after Isidore's death, so too does Zaragoza disappear from the intellectual radar in the time of Taio.

The ultimate beneficiary of the learning of Seville, fostered by Leander and Isidore, was to be Toledo.[72] Again the links were essentially personal ones. A royal chaplain called Eugenius left Toledo to enter monastic life in Zaragoza, but was quickly co-opted into the higher clergy of the city by Braulio, who made him archdeacon, and then his personal choice as successor. However, this plan was thwarted in 646, when on the death of Eugenius I (636-46), Chindasuinth had him recalled to Toledo to become bishop as Eugenius II. Braulio's letter collection includes an epistolary exchange between himself and the king, in which he tried unavailingly to persuade Chindasuinth to let Eugenius stay in Zaragoza.[73]

While some of the bishops of Toledo may have been politically influential, they were not yet known for their writings. As Ildefonsus said of a fifth-century bishop called Asturius in his markedly Toledan continuation of Isidore's *De Viris Illustribus*: "he sealed his works of virtue more by the example of his life than with the pen of the scribe."[74] The relative obscurity of Toledo before the mid-sixth century was probably reflected in the history of its church. Of other early bishops, Ildefonsus only had things to say about Montanus, who held the see for nine years in the time of Amalaric and was the author of two letters. There follows a gap until the episcopate of Aurasius,

---

[71] Taio, *Sententiarum Libri V*, ed. M. Risco, *España Sagrada*, vol. 31 (2nd edn., Madrid, 1859), 171-546.

[72] M. C. Díaz y Díaz, "Obra literaria de los obispos toledanos," in his *De Isidoro al Siglo XI* (Barcelona, 1976), pp. 89-115, for an assessment of their achievement.

[73] Braulio, *epp.* 31-3, ed. Riesco Terreo, pp. 132-6.

[74] Ildefonsus, *De Viris Illustribus* 1, ed. Codoñer, p. 116. On this work see Jacques Fontaine, "El *De Viris Illustribus* de San Ifdefonso de Toledo: Tradición y originalidad," *Anales Toledanos III: Estudios sobre la España visigoda* (Toledo, 1971), pp. 59-96, and Carmen Codoñer, "El libro de 'Viris Illustribus' de Ildefonso de Toledo," in *La Patrología Toledano-Visigoda* (Madrid, 1970), pp. 337-48.

bishop for nearly 12 years from 603/4 to 615. Of him Ildefonsus admitted that "the intention of defending virtue mattered more to him than the exercise of writing."[75] In comparison with the subjects of Isidore's *De Viris Illustribus*, who were all noted authors, Ildefonsus's "Famous Men" often had to rely on their moral rather than intellectual weight.

From Aurasius, in whose time Toledo became metropolitan see of the province of Carthaginiensis, Ildefonsus included all the bishops up to his own immediate predecessor Eugenius II. Helladius (615-33), a royal official who had been abbot of Agali before becoming bishop, returned to die there. In his last days he ordained Ildefonsus, a fellow monk of Agali, as deacon. These links created a special devotion on the latter's part to this predecessor, but Ildefonsus had to admit that Helladius "rejected writing, because what might have have been written was made obvious on the page of his daily life" – another elegant circumlocution to justify the bishops of Toledo not matching the literary achievements of those of Seville and Zaragoza.[76]

The importance of Agali continued to be demonstrated with the appointment of Justus. A former pupil of Helladius and monk of Agali from childhood, he succeed his mentor as third abbot in 615 and then as bishop in 633, dying in 636 just 19 days before king Sisenand. He sent Richila, his successor as abbot, a lost treatise, the contents of which are not revealed by Ildefonsus.[77] His successor as bishop, Eugenius I (636-46), was another monk of Agali and pupil of Helladius, whom he accompanied to the city in 615. No writings of his are mentioned, but Ildefonsus reported that he had such a command of computistical details on lunar cycles and epacts as to "stupefy his listeners and to convert them to correct doctrine."[78]

With Eugenius II, the tradition of appointing monks of Agali to the see of Toledo was temporarily broken, but this is not a sign of conflict between secular and monastic clergy. The new bishop was the first to be a significant author as well as an ecclesiastical politician. His pontificate saw a crucial series of councils in Toledo, part of the difficult period of transition marking the death of Chindasuinth and

---

[75] Ibid. 4, ed. Codoñer, p. 122.
[76] Ibid. 6, ed. Codoñer, p. 126.
[77] Ibid.
[78] Ibid. 12, ed. Codoñer, p. 132.

the beginning of the sole reign of Reccesuinth. He was the first bishop of the see to contribute to the liturgy, correcting the singing of chants and adding new texts to the offices. He also made his mark as a theologian, writing a treatise on the Trinity, a copy of which he intended sending to Africa. Although lost, other than a possible fragment in the monastic library of Silos, this may have been a contribution to the Monothelete Controversy, then dividing the church in the Byzantine empire. Maximus the Confessor and other opponents of imperial theology took refuge in Africa, which became a center of resistance as in the time of the Three Chapters controversy a century earlier.

Eugenius is best-known for his verses, though Ildefonsus reports that there existed a parallel corpus of prose writings, which he does not describe. As well as incidental pieces, the verse included a revision of the epic on the six days of Creation by the African poet Dracontius, to which Eugenius added a new part on the Seventh Day. While some of the epitaphs and inscriptions may have been commissioned, many of the small items in the collection were intended for teaching purposes, including a series of two-line versifications of sections of Isidore's *Etymologiae*. A similar collection of anonymous minor poems, once thought to be by Eugenius, has recently been recognized as having a similar purpose in teaching versification. A late Visigothic and Toledan origin for this is likely.[79]

In 657 Ildefonsus was promoted to the see of Toledo from the abbacy of Agali. An account of him was later added to the *De Viris Illustribus* by his eventual successor Julian (680-90).[80] Ildefonsus's most widely disseminated work, on the perpetual virginity of Mary, also influenced by Jerome's abrasive writings on celibacy, owed its literary style to Isidore's *Synonyma*. Each key phrase was reiterated several times, using different but synonymous expressions to produce a rhetorical *tour de force*, one that may seem turgid and unpleasantly vituperative to the modern reader.

As with Isidore's *Synonyma*, this served both as a moral treatise on its subject and as a literary model for teaching. The synonymous style is also found in some of the anonymous prayers of the liturgy, and its

---

[79] Nicolò Messina, *Pseudo-Eugenio di Toledo, Speculum per un nobile visigoto* (Santiago de Compostela, 1984).

[80] On Ildefonsus the main study remains Sr. Athanasius Braegelmann, *The Life and Writings of Saint Ildefonsus of Toledo* (Washington, DC, 1942); see also Juan M. Cascante, *Doctrina Mariana de S. Ildefonso de Toledo* (Barcelona, 1958).

use in preaching and literary composition was actively promoted in the episcopal school in Toledo in the later seventh century. Of other works by Ildefonsus mentioned by Julian, only two short treatises on baptism have survived, composed almost entirely of extracts from earlier Patristic writings on the topic. Little is known of his successor Quiricus (667-80), who was probably translated to Toledo from the see of Barcelona, but as the dedicatee of both Ildefonsus's *De Perpetua Virginitate* and Taio's *Sententiae* he must have been regarded as learned.

Several of the works of Julian (680-90) are still extant, and some were widely read throughout the early and central Middle Ages, but the account of him by his successor Felix (692/3-ca.700) in the last continuation of the *De Viris Illustribus* reveals that a number of others have been lost.[81] Among these was a work on divine judgment, which he dedicated to Ervig, before the latter became king in October 680. After his accession Ervig also received the dedication of Julian's most influential work, the *De Comprobatione Sexti Aetatis* "On the Proof of the Sixth Age," a polemical reply to Jewish arguments against the Messiahship of Jesus.

Other writings credited to Julian by Felix include verses and contributions to the liturgy. The former may be entirely lost, and the latter cannot be identified from the large and anonymous mass of surviving liturgical texts from pre-twelfth-century Spain. As the same is said of both Eugenius II and Ildefonsus, it would seem that poetry and liturgy were central to the literary activities of the later seventh-century bishops of Toledo. Where Julian clearly exceeded his predecessors was in the breadth of his reading, particularly in the works of Augustine, and in his writing of frequently polemical theological treatises.

While attention naturally focuses on identifiable and influential authors, and particularly on the group of bishops linked by the Spanish collection of *De Viris Illustribus*, with its numerous continuations, this is only part of the total picture. There exist a number of minor texts that, like the commentary on Donatus of the reign of Egica, are anonymous, or, like the epistolary treatises wrongly ascribed to Isidore, pseudonymous. Traces of yet other works of probable late Visigothic date can be found in later manuscripts. Several of these anonymous

---

[81] Felix, *Eulogium Sancti Juliani* in *Patrologia Latina*, vol. 96, cols. 445-52.

and other texts seem to be didactic in intent, even if it is not possible to know whether the teaching was to be primarily or exclusively of clerics or if sections of the laity also received instruction in grammar, versification, law, and other subjects.[82]

While there is a narrowing of geographical focus after the time of Isidore, with most known authors being linked to Toledo, this does not necessarily imply that the capital had a monopoly on learning. The monastic rules written by Fructuosus bishop of Braga, the "Life of Fructuosus" written after his death by an anonymous monastic disciple, and above all the extraordinary corpus of texts composed in the last decade or so of the kingdom's existence by the hermit Valerius of Bierzo all testify to the flourishing of a distinctive regional literary culture in part of the northwest of the peninsula in the late Visigothic period. In the case of Valerius it has been shown that not only did he use complex legal metaphors in the construction of his writings about his own ascetic life, but that he may even have quoted the texts of laws found in the *Liber Iudiciorum*, the royal law code.[83]

Questions about the nature and extent of literacy in this society have been raised. Braulio's reference to a count Laurentius owning a library in Toledo, which once contained a copy of the Commentary on the Apocalypse of Apringius of Beja (*c*.550) certainly suggests that the lay elite was literate enough to value the possession of such books.[84] Another of his letters establishes the existence of a royal library, at least in the time of Chindasuinth, but nothing is known of its contents.[85] On the wider dissemination and penetration of literacy outside of the capital a relatively new source of evidence may provide fuller and clearer answers as it continues to be analyzed.[86]

Among the most interesting survivals from the Visigothic period are a number of small pieces of slate on which are carved various

---

[82] Rafael Gibert, "La enseñanza del derecho en Hispania durante los siglos VI al XI," *Ius Romanum Medii Aevi*, pt. I, 5 b cc (Milan, 1967).

[83] Roger Collins, "The Autobiographical Works of Valerius of Bierzo: their structure and purpose," in *Los Visigodos. Historia y Civilización* (= *Antigüedad y Cristianismo* III, Murcia, 1986), pp. 425-42, and Yolande García López, *Estudios críticos de la "Lex Wisigothorum"* (Alcalá de Henares, 1996), p. 30 and n. 73.

[84] Braulio, *ep.* 25, ed. Riesco Terrero, p. 122.

[85] Braulio, *ep.* 26, ibid. p. 124.

[86] Roger Collins, "Literacy and the Laity in Early Medieval Spain," in Rosamond McKitterick (ed.), *The Uses of Literacy in Early Medieval Europe* (Cambridge, 1990), pp. 109-33, provides a survey of the evidence.

figures, letters, and designs.[87] These slate tablets have been discovered at a number of locations across a wide area of the central western regions of Spain, in particular in the provinces of Avila, Segovia, and Salamanca. While some are directly associated with rural settlement sites of Visigothic date, others have been found in the open countryside.[88] Subsequent investigation may reveal traces of habitation so far undetected, as these items must originally have been created in relatively sophisticated contexts.

Despite the surprising nature of the medium, these are documents that served a wide variety of purposes. Over 100 of them are known, and this number might be expected to increase with new discoveries. On the other hand, the friable nature of slate has equally meant that none of them has been preserved complete. Several have broken into separate pieces, and in some cases only small sections of once much longer texts have been found. All of them have lost parts of their inscribed surfaces.

Few are explicitly dated, but some refer to the reigns in which they were written, including those of Reccared (586-601), the joint rule of Chindasuinth and Reccesuinth (649-53), and of Egica (687-702/3).[89] The majority of the pieces have to be dated less precisely on the basis of their paleography, the distinctive characteristics of the script in which they are written. This is not easy, in that those with letters as opposed to numbers are all written in cursive, which was the relatively quickly written script that was used for letters, documents, and essentially ephemeral writings, and not in the more formal handwriting employed in the copying of books. Beyond the slate tablets themselves, relatively few examples of cursive writing have survived from Spain in the Visigothic period. The only documents of the period written on parchment in this script are five badly mutilated fragments, and there are some marginal notes in Visigothic cursive on two manuscripts that have been dated to the early eighth century. Although

---

[87] Isabel Velázquez Soriano, *Las pizarras visigodas. Edición crítica y estudio* (Murcia, 1989).

[88] Ibid. pp. 40-64. For more detail on one such settlement site see Antonio Bellido Blanco, "La ocupación de época visigoda en Vega de Duero (Villabañez, Valladolid)," *Archivo Español de Arqueología* 70 (1997), pp. 307-16.

[89] Velázquez, *Pizarras visigodas*, e.g. No. 8, dated to the first year of Reccared, pp. 160-3; No. 9, undated but in reign of Chindasuinth and Reccesuinth, p. 164, undated; No. 19 is either Sisebut or Sisenand, p. 177.

other cursive inscriptions have been found in cave churches of probably Visigothic date, few of these are dated either.[90]

The tablets themselves are not always easy to read, being carved in thin lines on fragile surfaces, and several errors of transcription and identification were made in the first attempt at editing these texts. To make matters worse, the editor "confirmed" his readings by marking out in white what he thought were the lines of the letters he was copying, only adding to the subsequent difficulty of correcting his transcriptions.[91] However, this has now been achieved, and a secure critical edition of the slate tablets exists.

Even if a precise dating may not be possible in every case, it is clear enough that these texts come from a broad period, extending from around the start of the sixth century to at least the early eighth, coinciding more or less with the Visigothic kingdom in Spain. The inscriptions are of various kinds.[92] Some have been shown to be legal documents that can be compared with model examples of their type contained in the "Visigothic Formulary" or with the far more numerous parchment charters of the immediately subsequent centuries. Slates that fall into this category are therefore legal records, essentially of ownership, but also including judgments given in disputes over property. Not all of the texts of such documents can be completely understood, not least because of their damaged state, but they seem to represent what may be thought of as private archival records that an owner would keep as evidence of his right to his property, and which could be produced as such in court.

Other slates contain numbers, the significance of which is not always immediately obvious, but it may be suspected that many of these were also records, for example, of flock numbers, cereal yields, and so forth. There are also some lists of names with numbers beside them, which may record renders owed to landowners by dependent cultivators. How these types of document were used is not entirely clear, but unlike the charters, they may not have been intended to be permanently preserved. Equally ephemeral may have been what has been shown to be a private letter, a section of which has been discovered.[93]

---

[90] Ibid. pp. 65-140
[91] Manuel Gómez Moreno, *La documentación goda en pizarra* (Madrid, 1966).
[92] Velázquez Soriano, *Pizarras visigodas*, pp. 573-638 for the classification.
[93] Ibid. No. 103, pp. 312-4 and 614.

Yet other texts have been interpreted as having magical significance, and containing curses. Earlier Roman equivalents to these have been found in Bath and elsewhere in the empire, and their existence should not be seen as a sign of mental or other decline.[94]

One class of text is potentially very interesting, not so much for its specific content as for the evidence it may offer of the extent of literacy in this society. This comes from those tablets provisionally identified as "school exercises," which contain pieces of text that seem repetitive or lacking in other obvious intention.[95] It has to be said such a classification may be the paleographer's equivalent of what is often said to be the archaeologist's besetting temptation, which is to label anything whose purpose is not self-evident as "a ritual object." The so-called *probationes pennae* or pen tests and "school exercises" among the slate tablets could have purposes that we have so far failed to understand, especially as some of the texts copied are of a religious character.

Such a classification may also raise over-optimistic assumptions about rural literacy and levels of education. If these slates did have a role in the teaching or practice of writing, it is likely to have been in a monastic or clerical context. But further study of both the texts and the contexts in which they were discovered might produce clarification. There could have been one scribe or many in any given region or locality, producing not only these test pieces, but also the great variety of other documents carved on slate which would have been needed for local legal, administrative, record-keeping, and letter exchanging purposes.

What is certain though is that this was a society in which written title to property and the use of written evidence in legal disputes was regarded as highly important. Not enough survives of any of these texts to be able to reconstruct an actual case, but textual similarities are so strong between the slate tablets recording dispute settlements and the many more numerous and full examples of such documents from later periods, particularly the ninth to eleventh centuries, that it should become possible to get some idea of how the legal system functioned in the Visigothic period itself.

---

[94] R. S. O. Tomlin, "The Curse Tablets," in Barry Cunliffe (ed.), *The Temple of Sulis Minerva at Bath*, vol. 2: *The Finds from the Sacred Spring* (Oxford, 1988), pp. 59–277.

[95] Velázquez Soriano, *Pizarras visigodas*, pp. 624–38.

7

Archaeology: Cemeteries and Churches

Goths in the Ground

Up to the later 1970s the archaeological study of the Visigothic period in Spain focused almost exclusively on two subjects: cemeteries and churches. This is hardly surprising, in that it would have been equally true of the archaeology of all the early medieval societies of western Europe. Of the cemeteries of the Visigothic period, a large number had been known since the end of the nineteenth century, with many being excavated in the 1920s and 1930s.[1] In the early twentieth century attention was particularly paid to a series of relatively large cemeteries located in rural areas, which were held to display various common characteristics. They were found in a number of different parts of the Iberian peninsula, but preeminently on the Meseta, the high plateau in the northwest that lies between the Sierra de Guadarrama and the mountain ranges of the northern coastal regions. The special interest of these cemeteries was seen as lying in the similarities between them and other large concentrations of early medieval burials, particularly the so-called *Reihengräber* or "Row Graves" of the Rhineland. As in the case of the latter, these Spanish cemeteries were taken to be the burial places of the invading Germanic population. In other words, these are the graves of the Visigoths themselves.

Unfortunately, very few of these early excavations of the Meseta cemeteries were either fully or carefully recorded, let alone published at the time. Since then objects from individual burials kept in museum storehouses have often been muddled together, and in many

---

[1] The fullest overall account is still that of H. Zeiss, *Die Grabfünde aus dem spanischen Westgotenreich* (Berlin, 1934).

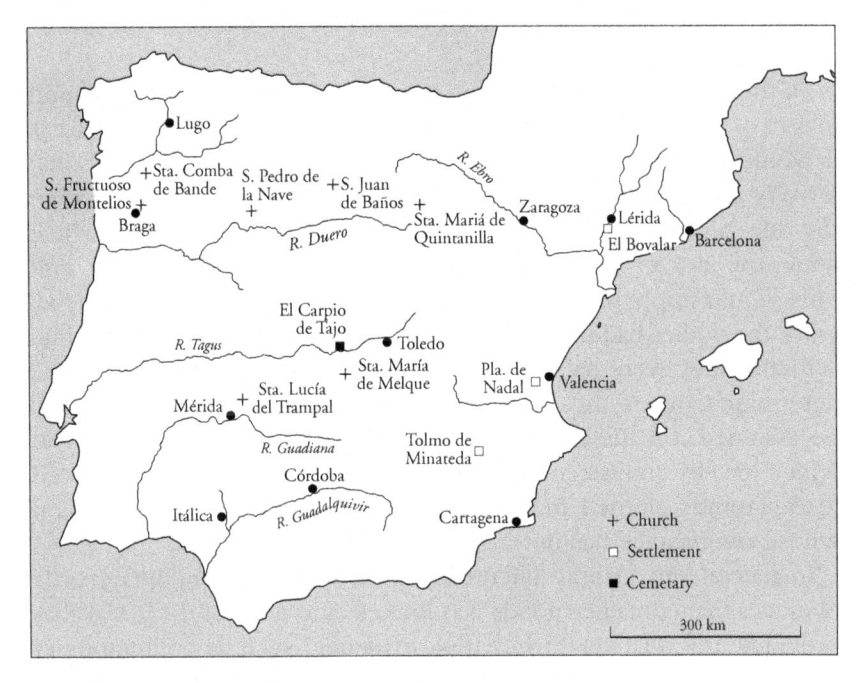

Map 3 Archaeological sites

cases it is not now possible to know the number of burials that once existed in a particular site or to reconstruct the actual distribution of grave goods within the cemetery.[2] Only one of these earlier twentieth-century excavations has left full enough records of itself for the original character and distribution of its contents to be effectively reconstructed and published in a modern study.[3] This relates to the cemetery at El Carpio de Tajo, on the north banks of the Tagus a little to the west of Toledo, on which the original excavator had contented himself with no more than an eight-page article.[4] It is primarily on the basis of the

---

[2] Gisela Ripoll López, "Visigothic Jewelry of the Sixth and Seventh Centuries," in Katherine Reynolds Brown, Dafydd Kidd, and Charles T. Little (eds.), *From Attila to Charlemagne: Arts of the Early Medieval Period in the Metropolitan Museum of Art* (New York, 2000), pp. 188–203.
[3] Gisela Ripoll, *La necrópolis visigoda de el Carpio de Tajo (Toledo)* (Madrid, 1985).
[4] C. de Mergelina, "La necrópolis de Carpio de Tajo," *Boletín del Seminario de Arte y Arqueología (Valladolid)* 15 (1949), pp. 146–54.

reexamination of this site that the evidence of the Spanish "row grave" cemeteries has to be evaluated.

Of the 285 burials recorded, no grave goods of any sort were found in 195 of them, which is nearly 70 percent of the total.[5] On this basis it would have to be said that burying objects and items of personal jewelry along with the body was definitely the exception rather than the rule. Although all evidence of textiles and wrappings is long since gone, the lack of such essential fasteners as buckles, brooches, and pins would imply that in those graves containing no items of metalwork the bodies had not been buried in their normal style of clothing. Whether they were naked or just in some kind of shroud cannot be determined, due to the decomposition of all traces of material. It may be assumed, on the other hand, that in the minority of burials in which jewelry and fastenings were found, the bodies had been placed in the tombs clothed in their ordinary dress. This is a distinction whose significance has never been considered.

In general, the quantity and quality of the items found in the minority of graves that contained goods was limited, and none of the burials has provided any relatively firm dating evidence, such as contemporary coinage. Thus the chronology of these cemeteries has had to be deduced on the basis of stylistic analyses of different categories of object found in the burials.[6] This did not include weapons, which were not found in any of the burials, other than some small knives of probably domestic rather than military value. Although a range of possibilities exist, in practice this attempt to establish stylistic criteria for dating was carried out on the basis of the comparative study of just two types of item, which were held to be particularly useful for this purpose.[7] These are belt buckles and brooches.

Analyses of stylistic changes have to depend upon assessments of how each class of object might have developed over time. Essentially,

---

[5] 68.42%. For a short account see Gisela Ripoll, "The Arrival of the Visigoths in Hispania: Population Problems and the Process of Acculturation," in Walter Pohl with Helmut Reimitz (eds.), *Strategies of Distinction. The Construction of Ethnic Communities, 300-800* (Leiden, 1998), pp. 153-87, at pp. 166-79. For a fuller version see Ripoll, *La necrópolis visigoda* (note 3 above).

[6] Ripoll, "The Arrival of the Visigoths," pp. 171-5.

[7] Gisela Ripoll, "Materiales funerarios de la Hispania visigoda: problemas de cronología y tipología," in P. Perrin (ed.), *Gallo-Romains, Wisigoths et Francs en Aquitaine, Septimanie et Espagne* (Rouen, 1991), pp. 111-32, especially pp. 120-2.

the full range of variant forms has to be classified, and deductions or assumptions made about how all the subdivisions are related to each other. A relative chronology can thus be established on the basis of deciding which styles were ancestral to others, while recognizing that some variants could be contemporaneous. The result is something like a family tree of the particular class of object, covering the period of time within which it is thought the changes occurred. Unfortunately, much of the crucial decision-making ultimately rests upon the subjective assessments made by the classifier. *A priori* decisions have to be made about such questions as whether or not simpler forms and styles necessarily have to precede more complex and elaborate ones. Convenience may also dictate acceptance of the unproven view that artistic development was geographically and chronologically uniform; in other words, that changes in taste occurred almost simultaneously throughout the whole of the Iberian peninsula. These problems affect Merovingian Frankish and Anglo-Saxon archaeology in equal measure.[8] Without external and objective dating criteria, few schemes for dating by stylistic analysis are very credible or should be allowed more than the status of a hypothesis.[9]

In the case of Visigothic Spain it has been claimed that some kind of periodization can be established from the comparative study of belt buckles and brooches, which can then be given a diagnostic value for the dating of the individual graves in which they are found. Four consecutive periods with distinct styles of their own have been identified on the basis of these analyses. The first of these is said to have lasted from the 480s to ca.525; the second from ca.525 to between 560 and 580; the third from ca.560/80 to somewhere between 600 and 640; and the fourth from then up to ca.710/720.[10]

---

[8] Edouard Salin, *La Civilisation mérovingienne* (4 vols., Paris, 1952), vol. II, pp. 223-330; P. Périn, *La Datation des tombes mérovingiennes. Historique, méthodes, applications* (Geneva, 1980).

[9] Guy Halsall, *Early Medieval Cemeteries: An Introduction to Burial Archaeology in the Post-Roman West* (Glasgow, 1995), pp. 38-55, for some trenchant views on the problems of dating.

[10] Ripoll, "Materiales funerarios," pp. 113-23 (based upon her 1991 University of Barcelona thesis: *La ocupación visigoda a través de sus necrópolis*, and *eadem*, "Problemas cronológicas de los adornos personales hispánicos (finales del siglo V-inicios del siglo VIII," in Javier Arce and Paolo Delogu (eds.), *Visigoti e Longobardi* (Florence, 2001), pp. 57-77.

There are a number of obvious difficulties with such a scheme. The view that the starting point has to be around 480/90 derives entirely from the *a priori* assumption that these are the graves of a Visigothic population, the majority of whom are thought to have moved into the peninsula only at that time. Similarly, the end point relies on a quite unproven belief that both the decorative arts and the burial practices of the Visigothic period would have to have been substantially transformed within a decade of the Arab conquest - a view for which there is no evidence either way. As for the internal divisions, that between the second and third phases looks as if it relies entirely upon the historical evidence that suggests significant social transformation taking place around the 570s. But whether the Third Council of Toledo marked a change in fashion consciousness as well as religious allegiance can hardly be said to have been objectively established.

The divide between the ensuing third and fourth periods is far more chronologically vague than the others, which is something that may be refreshingly realistic. However, the items of material culture assigned to the fourth period are so markedly different in appearance to most of those that precede it that it might be wondered if a wholesale sartorial revolution took place in the early seventh century. On the other hand, it may just be that the classification upon which this is based is too doctrinaire, and derives from an assumption that a major change of identity took place among the Gothic population in this time, and in consequence all Byzantine or eastern Mediterranean-inspired styles can be expected to be influential in Spain only after the end of the sixth century.[11]

From all of these difficulties it might be tempting to conclude that cemetery archaeology is of little help in the study of this period, or that it creates more problems than it solves. There would be some justification for these views, especially the second of them. This is thanks not just to the unsatisfactory nature of the methodology that has to be applied, but even more to the way in which the interpretation of the evidence of the cemeteries came to exercise a baleful influence over the understanding of the history of the Visigothic kingdom in Spain in the sixth and seventh centuries.

---

[11] Gisela Ripoll López, "Symbolic Life and Signs of Identity in Visigothic Times," in Peter Heather (ed.), *The Visigoths from the Migration Period to the Seventh Century: An Ethnographic Perspective* (Woodbridge, 1999), pp. 403-31, especially pp. 414-24.

From the work carried out on these sites, not least by German archaeologists in the 1930s, a view was formed not only of the ethnic identity of the people who were buried in them but also of their historical significance, interpretations that have remained almost unchallenged ever since.[12] The nature and decoration of the items buried with the dead in these cemeteries, the lack of weapons in what were otherwise clearly male graves, and the general poverty of the contents, in terms of both artistic quality and the lack of gold and silver, were all seen as indicating that the objects and their owners belonged to a Germanic population of relatively low social status. Their geographical concentration in one particular region, the Meseta, helped confirm the belief that these cemeteries belonged to a free but socially inferior Visigothic population that had migrated into the peninsula, but had been prevented from acquiring lands in the richer southern and eastern parts of the kingdom, where the estates of the Gothic and Hispano-Roman aristocracies were mainly situated.[13]

The occupants of these graves therefore were thought to belong to a Visigothic free peasantry that was not dependent on service to the kings or the nobility, and which had to be given land for settlement, but was otherwise not closely involved in the main currents of the political and economic life of the kingdom.[14] On the other hand, this detachment made them less susceptible to Roman cultural influences and more supportive of such distinctively Germanic aspects of their society as Arianism and Gothic customary law. The presence of large numbers of such relatively unassimilated Visigothic backwoodsmen was also seen as exercising a restraining influence on the more Romanophile tendencies of some of their kings, and their existence was often seen as a major factor in explaining some of the political problems faced by the Visigothic monarchy in the sixth and seventh centuries.[15]

---

[12] Zeiss, *Die Grabfünde*.
[13] W. Reinhart, "Sobre el asentamiento de los visigodos en la Peninsula," *Archivo Español de Arqueología* 18 (1945), pp. 124-39, and idem, *Misión histórica de los visigodos en España* (Segovia, 1951), pp. 16-19; cf. Ripoll, "The Arrival of the Visigoths," pp. 160-4.
[14] E. A. Thompson, *The Goths in Spain* (Oxford, 1969), pp. 147-52.
[15] e.g. ibid. pp. 311-19. For the view that there existed a cultural tension between Romans and Goths in the peninsula, see also P. de Palol, "Esencia del arte hispánico de época visigoda: romanismo y germanismo," in *I Goti in Occidente* (= Settimane di studio del Centro italiano di studi sull'alto medioevo, 3, 1956), pp. 65-126.

Very similar interpretations were advanced by historians who were studying the Ostrogothic kingdom in Italy in the first half of the sixth century. There the markedly pro-Roman cultural enthusiasm displayed by king Theoderic (493-526) and his daughter Amalasuintha was seen as being increasingly out of step with the attitudes of the Gothic rank and file, regarded as being much more suspicious of and hostile to Roman civilization and society. The failure to bring up Theoderic's grandson and successor Athalaric (526-34) in traditional Gothic fashion was thus presented as a direct cause of the reaction that set in following the young king's death, and which led to the murder of his mother and to an ultimately fatal conflict with the empire.[16] It would not be too much of a simplification to say that for this school of thought those early medieval societies in which a Roman cultural element came to the fore were doomed to disaster, as was the case with both branches of the Goths, while the future was predetermined to be bright for those in which the German component predominated, as in the case of the Franks.

Such interpretations largely derived from the intensely Romantic nationalism of nineteenth-century Germany, which generated a tradition of scholarship on the early history of the German peoples as one of its first manifestations. The editing of texts and the writing of national histories came in time to be supplemented by archaeology, which depended upon the historians and upon the literary texts they used for the interpretation of its data. That much of the latter came in the form of burials was largely due to the better chances of survival and of rediscovery of rural cemeteries, which were generally less in danger of being disturbed over the passage of centuries by what took place above them.

Views on the nature and composition of the society that was thought to have produced these cemeteries, both in Spain and in the Rhineland, also took some of its coloring from the ideals of the scholars studying them. German nationalism in the nineteenth and early twentieth centuries was markedly bourgeois in character, even if it could identify itself strongly with hereditary monarchy and heroic leadership, as well as with idealized rural idylls. Therefore the idea that early Germanic societies were dominated by a class of sturdy free peasant proprietors,

---

[16] Herwig Wolfram, *History of the Goths*, trans. Thomas J. Dunlap (Berkeley, CA, 1988), pp. 332-43 provides a modern interpretation.

who were following the lead of an ancient ruling dynasty, but were also retentive of their national culture and suspicious of alien influences, exactly matched the prejudices of those who were studying them.

Since the Second World War a lot of the intellectual stuffing has been knocked out of these myths, and at the same time new ideas on the formation of ethnic identities and on the character and size of the groups that exercised military domination in the west from the midfifth century onward have not only emerged but have gone a long way toward constituting a new orthodoxy. But while historians have bid farewell to the notion of large bodies of Germanic free peasants forming a major and occasionally dominant element in the composition of the societies that emerged after the end of Roman rule, no one seems yet to have told the archaeologists, at least not in Spain. So the belief that these cemeteries were those of a distinctive Visigothic population has never been effectively challenged. The few suggestions to this effect have just been ignored, despite the fact that the theoretical underpinning for the old view has been long since subverted.[17]

This is particularly regrettable when wider issues of burial practices in Spain in these centuries are in urgent need of examination. The Meseta cemeteries have tended to dominate thinking to too great an extent. They need to be got into a new perspective. For one thing, their impression of size is misleading. Taking again the example of El Carpio del Tajo, the only well-documented case, it has been suggested that the cemetery was in continuous use for roughly 200 years.[18] Taking the usual average of 30 years to a generation, which may be a little generous for early medieval populations, this would represent something like seven different generations of inhabitants. As the total number of tombs discovered is 285, this would imply something like 40 graves per generation. As the cemetery includes all ages and both sexes, there is no need to think that any group within the population that used it was excluded. In other words, for all of its apparent size, El Carpio de Tajo may have been the graveyard for a local settlement whose population rarely exceeded 40 people. The image of large masses of unassimilated Goths dwindles in consequence.

---

[17] R. F. Lantier, in *Comptes-rendus de l'Académie des Inscriptions* 1947, pp. 229-35, and 1948, pp. 156-61; see also Roger Collins, "Mérida and Toledo, 550-85," in Edward James (ed.), *Visigothic Spain: New Approaches* (Oxford, 1980), at pp. 199-200.

[18] Ripoll, "The Arrival of the Visigoths," pp. 173-5.

Next to go may be their Gothic identity. This depends partly on *a priori* assumptions previously discussed, which can be disregarded. The nature of the grave goods found in the tombs provides no support one way or another. Partly this is because it is so simple, and partly because there are very few if any items of material culture from early medieval Spain that can be said to be ethnospecific, or in themselves indicators of their owners' ethnic identity. Even if a style or type of object could be traced chronologically and geographically in such a way as to show that it was associated exclusively with a migrating Visigothic population, it would still have to be proved that it remained exclusive to Gothic wearers in a Spanish context. But there is nothing that even approximates to this.

Ultimately, reliance is placed upon one particular argument: the absence of weapons in the graves.[19] This continues to be advanced as the best evidence for the Gothic identity of those buried in El Carpio de Tajo and similar cemeteries. It is said that the two central European cultures that are seen as being ancestral to that of the Tervingi and Greuthungi also had this distinguishing characteristic in their burial practice, and that it remained true of the two Gothic groups both before and after their entry into the Roman empire in the fourth and fifth centuries.[20] This failure to bury weapons with the dead is in marked distinction to the customs of the Franks, Angles, Saxons, Lombards, and others, and is therefore seen as a distinguishing characteristic of the Goths.

That this argument is nonsensical, at least when applied to Spain, should already be apparent. Between the early fourth century and the end of the sixth the Visigoths had transported themselves across several thousand miles in various stages and under different circumstances, had completely changed their name and ethnic identity at least once, had picked up and dropped off numerous different elements of population, intermarried constantly, had changed their political

---

[19] Michel Rouche, "Wisigoths et Francs en Aquitaine," in Périn (ed.), *Gallo-romains, wisigoths et francs en Aquitaine*, p. 144; Michel Kazanski, *Les Goths (Ier-VIIe après J.-C.)* (Paris, 1991), pp. 23-5.

[20] Peter Heather, "The Sîntana de Mures-Cernjachov Culture," in Peter Heather and John Matthews, *The Goths in the Fourth Century* (Liverpool, 1991), pp. 51-101, at pp. 62-3, where it is also pointed out that while deposits of weapons in inhumations may be rare, they have been found in some burials belonging to the same culture; for an example see Kazanski, *Les Goths*, 24.

organization, had lost a supposedly ancestral royal dynasty, had changed their language, had changed their religion twice, and had seen numerous transformations in their material culture. Yet we are asked to believe that the one thing they held on to was a determination not to bury weapons in graves!

Even if this were not preposterous enough in its own right, the evidence from El Carpio de Tajo, which is likely to have been matched by that of the other less well-recorded cemeteries, shows firstly that the people buried in it were in material terms so poor that it would be highly surprising if they could have afforded to bury such relatively luxurious items as spears, let alone swords, along with their other meager personal goods. That they even had weapons to bury is itself an unsubstantiated assumption. Even more significant may be the fact that in this cemetery nearly 70 percent of the inhabitants were buried without any object at all, let alone a weapon. That is far more of a distinguishing characteristic when it comes to making comparisons with the Sîntana de Mures culture, supposed Gothic burials north of the Danube, or the practices of the people buried in the Reihengräber cemeteries of the Rhineland.

To accept that the poorly endowed inhabitants of the Meseta who were buried in these cemeteries may well not have been Goths, and that the lack of weapons in their graves tells us absolutely nothing about their ethnic identity, opens up new possibilities in the interpretation of other burial practices. For example, excavations since 1987 of a number of cemeteries in the Basque province of Alava, which in the early Middle Ages would have been regarded as part of Cantabria, have found weapons in the graves.[21] If it has to be believed that Goths were never buried with weapons, then these cannot be the bodies of Visigoths. The ingenious answer that has been offered instead is that these were the burials of Aquitainian soldiers, sent to garrison this region following its conquest by the Franks.[22]

---

[21] Augustin Azkarate Garai-Olaun, *La Necrópolis tardoantigua de Aldaieta (Nanclares de Gamboa, Alava)* vol. 1: *Memoria de la excavación e inventario de los hallazgos* (Vitoria-Gasteiz, 1999).

[22] Augustin Azkarate Garai-Olaun, "Nuevas perspectivas sobre la tardoantigüedad en los Pirineos occidentales a la luz de la investigación arqueológica," in Arce and Delogu (eds.), *Visigoti e Longobardi*, pp. 37-55 also K. Larrañaga, "El pasaje del pseudo-Fredegario sobre el dux Francio de Cantabria y otros indicios de naturaleza textual y onomástica sobre presencia franca tardoantigua al sur de los Pirineos." *Archivo Español de Arqueología* 66 (1993), pp. 177-206.

Such an interpretation also depends on the view to be taken of a passage in the anonymous *Chronicle of Fredegar*, in its chapter devoted to the Visigothic king Sisebut (611/12-20). In what seems to be a reference to his career prior to his being chosen as king, Sisebut is said to have "won Cantabria, previously held by the Franks, for the Gothic kingdom."[23] This is immediately puzzling, because contemporary references show that Cantabria was clearly already part of the Visigothic kingdom in the time of Leovigild (569-86), and there is no mention by Isidore in either of the versions of his chronicle of such a triumph on the part of Sisebut. This is particularly surprising in the case of the shorter, earlier version of ca.615, as it concluded with praise of the king.

In reality Fredegar's narrative is so confused as to be almost incomprehensible. He goes on to state that "A duke named Francio had conquered Cantabria in the days of the Franks and had long paid tribute to the Frankish kings; but when the province was once more restored to the empire the Goths, as I said above, took possession of it."[24] The order of events he seems to be describing requires Cantabria to have passed from Frankish to imperial overlordship, and then to have become Visigothic. He clearly had no knowledge of where Cantabria was located, as the sentence quoted above continues: "and Sisebut took many cities from the Roman empire on the shore of the sea and destroyed them down to their foundations." This phrase is clearly referring to the capture of imperial towns in the dwindling enclave around Cartagena, and it may just be that Fredegar has confused the latter name with Cantabria. Alternatively or additionally, the name Francio is otherwise found only once in this period, as that of a Byzantine military commander who put up a lengthy resistance to the Lombards in the area of Lake Como.[25] So there could equally well be a confusion with events in Italy in Fredegar's narrative. In general, neither the literary nor the archaeological evidence requires us to believe in the presence of Frankish forces in Alava and the Rioja in the early seventh century.[26]

---

[23] *Fredegar* IV. 33, ed. Wallace-Hadrill, p. 21.
[24] Ibid.
[25] *PLRE* vol. 3: Francio 1, pp. 493-4; see also Wallace-Hadrill (ed.), *Fredegar*, p. 21, note 4.
[26] There may be grounds for suspecting a short lived Frankish presence in Pamplona around 630: Roger Collins, *The Basques* (Oxford, 1986), pp. 91-8 and 104.

The burials in Alava are clearly of great interest, in that they seem to be those of a more militarized and probably wealthier population than that of the typical Meseta cemeteries. Once it is accepted that the latter are not necessarily those of the Visigoths, the evidence of the Alavan ones can be examined without presuppositions. They could indeed be the burial places of military colonies, but not those of Franks or Aquitainiains, but of settlements established by Visigothic kings such as Leovigild or Suinthila, intended to defend the Rioja from the all too frequent raids of the Basques. Whether or not this is the case, predetermining that they can not be Gothic because of the presence of weapons merely serves to limit rational investigation in the interests of ill-grounded dogma.

Freed from preconceptions, what is most striking about the funerary practices of Spain in the Visigothic period is the diversity that can be seen. There are burials with and without grave goods. There are burials with and without weapons, and also with and without ceramics. Some bodies are interred in cists, rectangular funerary spaces delineated by lines of stones placed upright and then covered by larger slabs.[27] Others are buried under tiles leaning together to form a triangular covering over the body. There are numerous burials in sarcophagi.[28] In several places rectangular spaces have been hollowed out of rock to receive bodies, which would then have been covered over with slabs of stone.[29] In probably all of these different types of interment, the grave would have been completed by being covered over by a mound of earth.

Criteria for dating such burials remain difficult to establish, but most of these variant forms of interment seem to have been practiced in the same periods. So it is probably neither necessary nor sensible to assume that there should be one distinctive form of Gothic or of Roman burial. Nor did they have to have separate cemeteries. Some

---

[27] For example, Mercedes López Requena and Rafael Barroso Cabrera, *La Necrópolis de la Dehesa de la Cocosa. Una aproximación al estudio de la época visigoda en la provincia de Cuenca* (Cuenca, 1994).

[28] For example, José Luis Argente Oliver, *La necrópolis visigoda del lugar La Varella-Castellar (Codo, Zaragoza)* (= *Excavaciones Arqueológicas en España* 87, Madrid, 1975), and Martín Almagro-Basch, *La necrópolis hispano-visigoda de Segóbriga, Saelices (Cuenca)* (= *EAE* 84, Madrid, 1975).

[29] For example, Antonio González Cordero, "Los sepulcros excavados en la roca de la provincia de Cáceres," in *Los Visigodos y su Mundo (Arqueología, Paleontología y Etnografía 4*: Madrid, 1998), pp. 271-4.

of the most interesting evidence from the early Islamic period implies that Muslims were using Christian burial grounds, such as the Visigothic cemetery at the old Roman town of Segóbriga (near Uclés in the province of Cuenca), in the early phases of the conquest.[30] In general, a future unprejudiced reexamination of the dating criteria and of the range of evidence available for the study of burial practices in the Visigothic period may be expected to prove highly revealing and illuminating.

A Visigothic Architecture?

As well as the contentious contents of its numerous cemeteries, the material culture of Visigothic Spain used primarily to be defined by its churches. In part this included the fragmentary and dispersed stone carvings that once formed part of the internal decoration of buildings no longer in existence, but above all it was typified by a significant group of small churches that were dated to the seventh century, and which had survived more or less intact. There were five particular examples that seemed to belong to this category: the churches of San Juan de Baños, San Pedro de la Nave, San Fructuoso de Montelios, Santa María de Quintanilla de las Viñas, and Santa Comba de Bande. This represents a high level of survival for such buildings, when compared with their equivalents of the same period in Britain, France, or Italy.

The chronological key to the dating of these buildings was to be found in the inscription set up over the chancel arch in the church of San Juan de Baños de Cerrato, located in the village of Venta de Baños near Palencia. This recorded the fact that the building had been erected in honor of St. John the Baptist, by king Reccesuinth in the year 662.[31] The location of a spring about 100 yards south of the church, the surrounds of which were decorated with a pair of horseshoe-shaped arches similar in style to those found in the building itself, suggested that the healing or other properties of the water may have been the reason for the dedication. The site itself

---

[30] L. Caballero Zoreda, "Pervivencia de elementos visigodos en la transición al mundo medieval. Planteamiento del tema," in *Actas del III Congresso de Arqueología Medieval Española* (3 vols., Oviedo, 1989), vol. 1, pp. 111-34, especially 122-7.

[31] J. M. de Navascues, *La Dedicación de San Juan de Baños* (Palencia, 1961).

was about 20 miles or so west of the location of Reccesuinth's villa at Gerticos, where he died in September 672.

With San Juan apparently so firmly dated, it was possible to develop a stylistic analysis that could offer an approximate chronology for the other churches, based on an interpretation of how the decorative and architectural features seen at Baños might have evolved. On the basis of such comparisons, Santa Comba de Bande, in the south of the Galician province of Orense, was assigned a date of ca.672. This almost matched that of San Fructuoso de Montelios, in the Portuguese town of Braga, which was widely regarded as the mausoleum of the monastic founder and bishop Fructuosus (died ca.670), though this made it not really a church in the fullest sense.[32] San Pedro de la Nave, near Zamora, was held to date from the time of king Egica (687-702/3), while Santa María de Quintanilla de las Viñas, southeast of Burgos, was seen as the last in the sequence, probably having been built around the end of the same reign.[33]

It was recognized that some of these buildings had suffered damage and phases of restoration. Of Quintanilla de las Viñas only the chancel remained, together with some carved stones that may have come from the chancel arch. San Juan de Baños was thought to have been restored in the time of the Asturian king Alfonso III (866-910) after a period of abandonment, but this was felt not to have effected any major changes to its Visigothic original state. Santa Comba de Bande was known from a charter in a Zamora cartulary to have been rebuilt *a fundamentis* - "from its foundations" - in 872.[34] Perhaps surprisingly, this was assumed to be without any loss of its intrinsically Visigothic architectural and decorative characteristics.

It was also generally taken for granted that there would have been no building of new churches after 711 in the areas of the peninsula that fell under Muslim rule. Only in the small Christian kingdom of the Asturias, which came into being around 718/22 would any such construction have been possible. Christians in the south were permitted to go on using churches already in existence, and thus might in

---

[32] A. de Azevedo, *O mausoléu de São Fructuoso de Braga* (Braga, 1964).
[33] P. de Palol and Max Hirmer, *Early Medieval Art in Spain* (London, 1967), pp. 18-20, and pp. 467-8 with references to the older literature.
[34] Manuel Nuñez, *Historia de Arquitectura Galega: Arquitectura Prerománica* (Madrid, 1978), pp. 83-96; Cristina Godoy Fernández, *Arqueología y liturgia. Iglesias hispánicas (siglos IV al VIII)* (Barcelona, 1995), pp. 325-7, with full references.

normal circumstances be allowed to repair them, but even this level of constructional activity was not to be expected in those buildings located between the Duero and the Sierra de Guadarrama, which according to the Asturian chronicles was turned into a depopulated no man's land between the Christian and Muslim realms for most of the eighth to tenth centuries.[35] Most of the extant Visigothic churches are located in this extensive region.

Other buildings that did not seem to fit into the same stylistic categories as those identified as Visigothic, but which were located outside the known borders of the Asturian kingdom, therefore came to be identified as being "Mozarabic" and dated to the tenth century. They were thus thought to be churches built by Christian communities, particularly of monks, fleeing northward. A case in point is that of the church of Santa María de Melque, in open country south of Toledo, which was assigned such a Mozarabic origin and an early tenth-century date.

It was, however, the substantial excavation of this site from 1970 to 1973 that first began to weaken the generally accepted views on the criteria for dating Spanish early medieval churches. These had depended not least on that *a priori* assumption that churches could not have been built in territory under Muslim rule in the period between the end of the Visigothic kingdom and the *Reconquista*. The work done on the church of Melque established archaeologically, on the basis of stratigraphy, that the building had to be older than the tenth century. The surrounding area was also examined, and revealed the presence of subsidiary structures and a boundary wall. There were thus good reasons for arguing that the whole complex was a monastery, something once thought to be true of San Pedro de la Nave, but on dubious grounds. Thus Santa María de Melque was redated to the Visigothic period, and became the best and probably the only candidate for a monastic site of that period.[36]

---

[35] Chronicle of Alfonso III (both versions), ch. 13, ed. Juan Gil in Juan Gil Fernández, José L. Moralejo, and Juan I. Ruíz de la Peña, *Crónicas asturianas* (Oviedo, 1985), pp. 130-1, for the supposed depopulation, on which increasing doubt is being expressed. See the articles in *Despoblación y colonización del Valle del Duero. Siglos VIII-XX* (= *IV Congresso de Estudios Medievales de la Fundación Sánchez-Albornoz*, Avila, 1995).

[36] Luís Caballero Zoreda and José Ignacio Latorre Macarrón, *La Iglesia y el monasterio visigodo de Santa María de Melque (Toledo). Arqueología y arquitectura* (Madrid, 1980).

At the same time, the certainties that had hitherto surrounded the Visigothic origins and character of the five "classic" churches began to be called into question. In particular, the stylistic divergences between two different elements in the decoration of Santa Comba de Bande led to the suspicion that this was far more the product of an Asturian period rebuilding than of its earlier first construction. Similarly, the total stylistic dissonance between the external friezes around the chancel of Santa María de Quintanilla de las Viñas and the carved fragments housed within it led to questioning of its chronological integrity.[37] Interpretations of monograms contained in the very stylized friezes suggested a tenth-century date, which would therefore have to be that of the only part of the building still standing, leaving only the internal carvings as reused elements from a lost earlier construction. Comparable doubts were also expressed about the history of San Fructuoso de Montelios.

In the case of San Pedro de la Nave, often held up as the quintessential example of the seventh-century Visigothic church, its more recent history has cast doubts on some of the claims that used to be made for it. The original site of the church was included in an area that was to be flooded to create a reservoir, and so in 1930 the building was dismantled, moved to a new location about a kilometer away, and rebuilt in accordance with the ideas then current as to what its original state should have been.[38] Photographs taken of it as it was prior to the move and reconstruction show just how dramatic the transformation was. The evidential basis upon which this was undertaken was slight in the extreme, and no account was published of the work carried out and the results achieved.[39] The whole operation can at best be thought of as an experiment, or at worst a flight of fancy.

---

[37] Fontaine, *L'art préroman*, pp. 205-9; Salvador Andrés Ordax and José Antonio Abásolo Álvarez, *La ermita de Santa María, Quintanilla de las Viñas, Burgos* (Burgos, 1982), pp. 11-16; Godoy, *Arqueología y liturgia*, pp. 255-8 with further references. A case for its Visigothic character is made by Achim Arbeiter, "Die westgotenzeitliche Kirche von Quintanilla de las Viñas. Kommentar zur architektonischen Gestalt," *Madrider Mitteilungen* 31 (1990), pp. 393-427.

[38] Miguel Angel Mateos Rodríguez, *San Pedro de la Nave* (Zamora, 1980), pp. 7-61. See also Luis Caballero Zoreda and Fernando Arce, "La iglesia de San Pedro de la Nave (Zamora)," *Archivo Español de Arqueología* 70 (1997), pp. 221-74, for a study of the church in its present state.

[39] Godoy, *Arqueología y liturgia*, pp. 327-32.

This left San Juan de Baños as the only church of definitely Visigothic construction as well as origin, secure in its chronological context thanks to its dedicatory inscription. Even here, though, doubts began to be raised. Eighteenth-century engravings showed that the building had been in a ruinous state at that time, and it was known to have received a major restoration in 1865. This involved the reconstruction of the outer walls of the nave, which were given rather odd decorative niches of semicircular form for which no particular justification can be found, and a whimsical bell-cote was added over the west door. The first serious study of the site was carried out between 1898 and 1903, and the excavator claimed to have found that the original configuration of the east end involved an arrangement of a central chancel being flanked by two detached rooms. The resulting ground plan gave the eastern end of the building three parallel sections, each separated one from the other by small areas of open land; it thus had a three-pronged or trident-like appearance. The two outer chambers had subsequently been demolished, probably in the fourteenth century, with only the inner wall of each being retained. At the same time, the open spaces dividing these rooms from the central chancel were enclosed by new walls across their eastern ends, thus giving the building as a whole a rectangular form. Excavations carried out in 1956, 1961, 1963, and 1983 failed to substantiate all the details of this reconstruction of the building's original shape, but confirmed some of it.[40]

In the meantime, other church sites of Visigothic date had been discovered by excavation, with their dating confirmed by inscriptions and finds. In other cases, sections of buildings normally thought to be later in date were being recognized as showing evidence of Visigothic origin. The best-documented case is that of the church of Santa María de Melque, discussed above. In the same year that the substantial excavation report on Melque was published, another well-preserved if ruinous church, known as Santa Lucía del Trampal and located in the countryside south of Alcuéscar in the province of Cáceres, was identified as being of probably Visigothic origin.[41] It was excavated in

---

[40] Pedro de Palol, *La Basílica de San Juan de Baños* (Palencia, 1988), pp. 5–36; see also Fontaine, *L'art préroman*, pp. 173–7, and Godoy, *Arqueología y liturgia*, pp. 258–61.
[41] Salvador Andrés Ordax, "La basílica hispanovisigoda de Alcuéscar," *Norba* 2 (1981), pp. 7–22.

1986-91.[42] This is a very unusual building with three short parallel chancels running eastward from a small transverse crossing, which opens onto a narrow nave on its west side. Reused Roman stonework in the walls of the church, including altars and other inscribed pieces, suggest the presence of an earlier cult site on this spot, devoted to the divinities associated with a local spring.[43] Similar links with what may have been Roman or pre-Roman sacred springs can also be found at Santa Comba de Bande and San Juan de Baños.

As well as Melque and Trampal, thought to be almost entirely of Visigothic date, other Spanish churches have also been recognized in recent years as containing some features that could come from that period. In some cases, such claims have had to be modified.[44] In general, however, while the purely Visigothic character of the once classic churches assigned a seventh-century date, such as San Pedro de la Nave, has increasingly been called in question, the new discoveries have added to a growing corpus of buildings thought to have originated in this period. In the light of parallels that could be made with the survival of constructions of this period from elsewhere in western Europe, this seems a logical development. Few Frankish, Anglo-Saxon, or Lombard equivalents are as "pure" as the Visigothic ones were once thought to be, while at the same time traces of early medieval construction have been found in a number of buildings not previously suspected of being so early.

It needs to be stressed that much of the evidence for dating remains art-historical rather than strictly archaeological. Few of these buildings have been systematically excavated, and most chronological deductions continue to be made on the basis of comparisons between decorative and architectural features. Simply put, if a particular style of decoration or a specific ground plan in one building is thought to be Visigothic in origin, then the discovery of a similar feature in another one is likely to be taken as evidence that that too belonged to the

---

[42] Godoy, *Arqueología y liturgia*, pp. 313-18.

[43] Juan Manuel Abascal Palazón, "Las inscripciones latinas de Sta. Lucía del Trampal (Alcuéscar, Cáceres) y el culto de Ataecina en Hispania," *Archivo Español de Arqueología* 68 (1995), pp. 31-105.

[44] For example, the church of Sts. Julian and Basila at Aistra in Alava identified as Visigothic in 1970, but now redated to the 10th/11th centuries: Achim Arbeiter, "Die vor- und frühromanische Kirche San Julián y Santa Basila de Aistra bei Zalduondo," *Madrider Mitteilungen* 35 (1994), pp. 418-39.

same period. However, should the Visigothic origin of any of these stylistic clues be called into question, so too would the dating of buildings whose chronological attribution relied on their presence.[45]

A case in point was the suggestion, briefly but pertinently made, that aspects of the architecture of the church of Santa María de Melque, so recently reassigned to a Visigothic from a tenth-century dating, were strikingly reminiscent of that of some of the rural palaces of the Umayyad period in Syria, particularly the one known as Khirbat al-Mafjar, near Jericho.[46] These Syrian Umayyad buildings all belong to the first half of the eighth century, and Khirbat al-Mafjar in particular is associated with the caliphs Hisham (724–43) and al-Walid II (743–4).[47]

That there might have been a current of artistic influence flowing from Visigothic Spain to Umayyad Syria was rightly rejected without serious consideration, and the implication of the relationship was quickly accepted as evidence that Spanish buildings such as Melque, which displayed such symptoms, had to be dated to a period later than the early eighth century. It could be assumed, indeed, that the influence of this particular tradition of Syrian decorative and architectural influence would have made itself most strongly felt after the Umayyads established a new Spanish home for their dynasty in 756.[48] In any event, the establishment of this connection placed the buildings in question into a firmly post-Visigothic context.

While the initial comparisons had been made between Khirbat al-Majfar and Santa María de Melque, the implications of the argument have been taken further in recent years. Because so many early medieval buildings were assigned a Visigothic date on stylistic, not archaeological grounds, the theory of Syrian influence has called into question the chronological and cultural attributions of all other

---

[45] Godoy, *Arqueología y liturgia*, provides details of any archaeological investigation of the churches discussed in her book as part of the individual entries on each of them.

[46] Sally Garen, "Santa María de Melque and Church Construction under Muslim Rule," *Journal of the Society of Architectural Historians* 51 (1992), pp. 288–305. See also Luís Caballero Zoreda, "Un canal de transmisión de lo clásico en la alta Edad Media española. Arquitectura y escultura de influjo omeya en la península ibérica entre mediados del siglo VIII e inicios del siglo X," *Al-Qantara* 15 (1994), pp. 321–48, and 16 (1995), pp. 107–24.

[47] R. W. Hamilton, *Khirbat al-Mafjar: An Arabian Mansion in the Jordan Valley* (Oxford, 1959).

[48] On which see Roger Collins, *The Arab Conquest of Spain, 710–797* (Oxford, 1989), pp. 113–40.

constructions in which the artistic style represented by Melque may be found. Logically, this has led to significant adjustments in the accepted chronology, and to questioning of the very existence of a distinctive Visigothic architecture and decorative tradition.[49]

Simply put, all those buildings that have not now been reassigned to a post-711 date fit perfectly well with the architectural and artistic traditions of Spain in the fourth and fifth centuries. In other words, this evidence indicates that the art and architecture of the Visigothic period were no more than a continuation of their Late Roman equivalents. There is nothing new enough about the buildings of the Visigothic centuries to justify giving them a classification of their own. On the other hand, what does mark a genuine change and break from earlier traditions was the introduction of Syrian architectural and decorative styles in the decades following the Arab conquest. This is where a new departure occurs in Spanish art.[50]

The only possible challenge to this radical revision of the long-accepted belief in the dating of buildings hitherto always assigned an origin in the Visigothic period might be expected to come from the case of the church of San Juan de Baños, where, despite uncertainties about the original configuration of its east end, a firmly dated inscription guarantees its foundation in 661. This would seem to confirm that the decorative style to be seen on the friezes, capitals, and arcading of the church, and which has close parallels with that of other buildings that by the new view would be assigned a post-711 date, must belong to the mid-seventh century.

An exhaustive recent study of the building, looking at its composition, literally stone by stone, has, however, come to the conclusion that there is evidence for a major reconstruction of the church at a relatively early stage in its history. In other words, while there are

---

[49] The process began with comparisons between buildings assigned a Visigothic date and those of the succeeding Asturian period: Luis Caballero Zoreda, "¿Visigodo o Asturiano? Nuevos hallazgos en Mérida y otros datos para un nuevo 'marco de referencia' de la arquitectura y la escultura altomedieval en el Norte y el Oeste de la Península Ibérica," in *39 Corso di Cultura sull'Arte Ravennate e Bizantina* (Ravenna, 1992), pp. 139-90; see now idem, "Sobre la llamada arquitectura 'visigoda': ¿paleocristiana o prerrománica?" in Arce and Delogu, *Visigoti e Longobardi*, pp. 133-60.

[50] Caballero, "Sobre la llamada arquitectura," and idem, "La arquitectura denominada de época visidoda, ¿es realmente tardorromana o prerrománica?" in L. Caballero Zoreda and P. Mateos Cruz (eds.) *Visigodos y Omeyas. Un debate entre la Tardoantigüedad y la alta Edad Media* (Madrid, 2000), pp. 207-47.

genuine components of Visigothic date to be found in its construction, their present location is entirely dictated by a radical program of rebuilding.[51] The inscription is thus genuine in itself, but may not now be in its original place, and so cannot be allowed to prove that the other elements of which the church is now composed are of identical date to it. This view is both so recent and so controversial in its implications that it must be said to be still very much *sub judice*. If accepted, it would certainly remove the authority hitherto granted to San Juan as testimony to mid-seventh-century Visigothic architecture and decorative styles, and would remove the main block on the theory of eighth-century Syrian influence as the inspiration behind many buildings previously accepted as being of Visigothic origin.

While the issue can hardly be resolved here, there is one point that does need to be made. The extensive and detailed work carried out in recent decades on a large number of Spanish buildings is in no way matched by comparable studies of the architecture of the Near East in the Umayyad period. Thus, while there are good grounds for noting various stylistic and structural similarities between Santa María de Melque and Khirbat al-Mafjar, no attention is being paid to the question of the wider context in which the latter stands. The Umayyad palaces do not represent a quintessential Islamic or Arab style of architecture and decoration.[52] Instead they belong more to a Byzantine provincial tradition, which extends back before the Arab conquest of the eastern provinces in the mid-seventh century, and which continued to develop after it.

It thus remains more than possible that the similarities detected between Umayyad constructions in Syria and Spanish buildings hitherto always classified as being Visigothic spring not from a dependence of one upon the other but from a common descent from that Byzantine tradition.[53] The latter was readily accessible throughout the later Visigothic period, via the imperial outposts at Ceuta and

---

[51] Luis Caballero Zoreda and S. Feijoo, "La iglesia altomedieval de San Juan de Baños en Baños de Cerrato (Palencia)," *Archivo Español de Arqueología* 71 (1998), pp. 181-242.

[52] Robert Hillenbrand, *Islamic Architecture. Form, Function, and Meaning* (Edinburgh, 1994), pp. 384-90 also draws attention to similarites with Late Roman fortresses on the eastern frontiers.

[53] For a recent study of Byzantine cultural and economic influences in the West in this period see Anthea Harris, *Byzantium, Britain and the West* (Stroud, 2003), especially pp. 121-30.

the Tangiers peninsula and the Exarchate of Africa, centered on Carthage. Up to around 625 there was a Byzantine presence in Spain itself, and excavations have started to reveal something of the non-military building works undertaken in Cartagena during this time.[54] Were a common debt to the Byzantine tradition to be the real explanation for the similarities detected between Khirbat al-Mafjar and Melque, then the chronological argument requiring the latter to postdate the Arab conquest would lose all validity. It and the other churches that have been shown to display architectural and/or artistic relationships to it could as easily be later seventh-century as eighth in origin, and of the two alternatives the conditions in the earlier period would unquestionably have been the more favorable.

The other difficulty to be faced in accepting the argument currently being advanced for dating such buildings to the post-711 period, and thus for eliminating the whole category of "Visigothic" as a stylistic label is that it is hard to see why the Christian communities in al-Andalus would have been led to adopt features of Syrian secular architectural and artistic traditions for the construction of their churches when there is no evidence that the Muslims themselves did likewise with any of the buildings they erected in the conquered territory. What has survived of early Umayyad construction in Spain shows no influence of the Khirbat al-Mafjar decorative style. Parallels that have been made with the (heavily over-restored) palace complex at Medina Azahara near Córdoba cannot be considered valid, as the buildings in question date from no earlier than the second half of the tenth century.

There is no doubt that the presupposition, which would once have been generally accepted without demur, that no new Christian buildings could be expected to have been built in those areas of the peninsula under Muslim rule is entirely erroneous. Literary references to the construction of new churches and monasteries in the first half of the ninth century, even close to the Spanish Umayyad capital of Córdoba, would demonstrate this.[55] And so it is necessary to take

---

[54] See below pp. 218-20.

[55] For example, the monastery of Tabanos founded near Córdoba a little before the outbreak of the "Martyr Movement": Eulogius, *Memoriale Sanctorum* II. ii, ed. J. Gil, *Corpus Scriptorum Muzarabicorum* (2 vols, Madrid, 1973), p. 402. Several other churches and monasteries of recent construction are mentioned by Euolgius: the relevant texts are usefully extracted in Rafael Puertas Tricas, *Iglesias hispánicas (siglos IV al VIII)* (Madrid, 1975), pp. 253-62.

account of the possibility of a post-711 origin for any such buildings found in the center and south of the peninsula as much as a Visigothic one. However, it is probably premature to dismiss the existence of a distinctively Visigothic style of architecture and decoration just on the basis of the Khirbat al-Mafjar/Santa María de Melque argument. The objections raised above would require the case to be more fully established, and on the basis of a much wider and geographically less disparate body of evidence.

8
Archaeology: Rural and Urban Settlements

Country Dwellers

The limited evidence for the seventh century makes it difficult to see just how much and what kind of new building work may have been undertaken at that time. In later periods, from the end of the eighth century onward, charters provide much information about the construction or repairing of churches and monasteries. However, only five parchment charters of Visigothic date have survived, and all of them are in a damaged and fragmentary state.[1] There are few references in historical or hagiographic texts either.[2] One consequence of this is that virtually nothing is known of royal building programs. It might be assumed that the kings, either through the resources they controlled by virtue of their office or through their family wealth, might have been among the foremost patrons of the kingdom's cathedrals, churches, and monasteries, as well as being responsible for the construction of their own palaces and rural villas. However, the evidence for this kind of activity on their part consists of little more than the references in the *Chronicle of 754* to Wamba's work of renovation in Toledo in the third year of his reign (674/5).[3] This may have been primarily a refortification of the city, as the chronicler quotes the inscriptions the king set up over the gates to commemorate his

---

[1] Angel Canellas López, *Diplomática Hispano-Visigoda* (Zaragoza, 1979), nos. 119, 178, 192, 209, 229. To these can be added those texts identified as charters, also all in a fragmentary state, found on the inscribed slates: see above p. 172.

[2] Such references and the churches that can be identified from these are usefully collected in Rafael Puertas Tricas, *Iglesias hispánicas (siglos IV al VIII). Testimonios literarios* (Madrid, 1975).

[3] Chronicle of 754, ch. 35, ed. José Eduardo López Pereira, *Crónica mozarabe de 754* (Zaragoza, 1980), p. 54.

work. These inscriptions, which were probably still in place 80 years after they were erected, may well have been the source of his all too vague account.

Beyond that, the only other certain information relating to royal patronage comes from the dedicatory inscription of the church of San Juan de Baños. Surprisingly, this survives in two forms: first in the carving still to be seen in the church itself, whether or not it is in its original location, and secondly as written in a tenth-century manuscript containing a collection of verse texts. Known as "the Azagra Codex," this is a very important repository of poetic and other works, and has a complex compositional history.[4]

Some of the components of this collection were put together in the Visigothic period, while others may have been added to the compilation at later dates. Among the original elements is likely to have been the copy of the dedicatory inscription from San Juan de Baños. In other words, this was not just a verse that caught the eye of some medieval traveler who stumbled across it on a chance rural ride to Venta de Baños, but was more likely to have been something composed in Toledo, and may well be a direct copy of the text as commissioned by king Reccesuinth and prior to its being set up in his church.[5] In this sense it is significant that no other comparable texts have been preserved, even in the verse collection of Eugenius II. Royal dedicatory inscriptions may not have been that frequent.

It would seem reasonable to assume that other kings than Wamba ordered the construction or repair of buildings in Toledo, but the very few traces of the art and architecture of the Visigothic capital that have survived provide hardly any clues to the appearance and location of the principal civil and ecclesiastical buildings in the city.[6] The site of the martyrial basilica of St. Leocadia, the patron saint of Toledo, has been located just beyond the medieval walls, but this was so extensively robbed out at some point after the Arab conquest that

---

[4] On this MS see Manuela Vendrell Peñaranda, "Estudio del Códice de Azagra, Biblioteca Nacional de Madrid, Ms. 10029," *Revista de Archivos, Bibliotecas y Museos* 82 (1979), pp. 655-705.

[5] Roger Collins, "Julian of Toledo and the Education of Kings in late Seventh Century Spain," in idem, *Law, Culture and Regionalism in Early Medieval Spain* (Aldershot, 1992), item III.

[6] Isabel Zamorano Herrera, "Caracteres del arte visigodo en Toledo," *Anales Toledanos* 10 (1974), pp. 3-149.

hardly any physical traces survive.[7] It is thought probable, to judge by parallel cases from other cities, that the cathedral church of St. Mary once stood on the site of the present medieval cathedral, which itself replaced the principal mosque in the city following the Castillian conquest of 1085.[8] But when the Visigothic period church was first erected, and what its history may have been prior to the fall of the kingdom is, like so much else, entirely unknown.

Even if hardly anything is known of royal building activities, and uncertainty exists as to the status and chronology of most of the extant early medieval structures that could be of Visigothic date, the survival of a number of inscriptions shows that the seventh century saw quite a lot of church construction. Most of this relates to rural buildings, but this is probably because such inscriptions have enjoyed a better survival rate in the countryside than in towns, where successive phases of construction over the course of a millennium and a half have destroyed so much more of the Visigothic levels lying beneath modern settlements.

Many of the extant inscriptions, which can all too rarely be matched by traces of the buildings in which they were originally erected, refer to local bishops, either as the founders or to provide the chronology for the dedication. Thus, to take the best example, a bishop Pimenius of *Assidona* (Medina Sidonia), whose tenure of office lasted from 629 to possibly as late as 667, dedicated a church in or near his own town in 630, another at Vejer de la Miel in 644, another at Salpensa in 648, and yet another in the vicinity of Alcalá de los Gazules in 662.[9] His successor bishop Theoderax dedicated a second church in the vicinity of Vejer de la Miel in 674.[10] Given the limited chances of survival, these inscriptions testify to a probably considerable amount of episcopal church building and dedicating in this period.

---

[7] Pere de Palol i Salellas, "Resultados de las excavaciones junto al Cristo de la Vega, supuesta basílica conciliar de Sta. Leocadia de Toledo. Algunas notas de topografía religiosa de la ciudad," in Ramón Gonzalvez (ed.), *XIV Centenario del Concilio III de Toledo, 589-1989* (Toledo, 1991), pp. 787-832.

[8] José Jacobo Storch de Gracia y Asensio, "Las iglesias visigodas de Toledo," *Actas del Primer Congreso de Arqueología de la Provincia de Toledo* (Toledo, 1990), pp. 563-70.

[9] José Vives, *Inscripciones cristianas de la España romana y visigoda* (Barcelona, 1969), nos. 304, 305, 306, 309. As the inscriptions are not linked to specific sites, it is possible that they have been moved at some point, so their present locations are not certain guides to the whereabouts of the churches themselves.

[10] Vives, *Inscripciones*, no. 310.

With that said, though, it would be unwise to assume that the constructions themselves were substantial. One of the few cases in which such an inscription can be linked to the remains of a building is that of Ibahernando in the province of Cáceres, where the basilica is recorded as having been consecrated by an otherwise unknown bishop Orontius in the year 635.[11] The excavation of the site in 1973 revealed a very small and simple rectangular building, with a tiny square chancel (1.55 by 1.5 meters) at its eastern end. The nave seems to have been about 7 meters long, and there are traces of a portico or narthex at the west end, that extended beyond the width of the building. On the south side, about 4 meters from the building, the foundations of a circular construction were found, but it was not possible to determine if this was a baptistery or some kind of mausoleum. There were five burials in the nave, covered with stone slabs, and another to the east of the chancel in open ground.[12] In general, Ibahernando can usefully be compared with another small church of similar dimensions and simplicity of plan at El Gatillo, also in the province of Cáceres.[13] This has the interesting distinction of giving evidence of being reused for Muslim worship at some point after the Arab conquest.

The purposes to be served by such small rural churches cannot be easily determined. It should be said that the consecration inscription of Ibahernando, found in 1961, does not refer to any deposition of relics of martyrs, which would normally be placed under the altar of more significant churches. On the other hand, all four churches dedicated by bishop Pimenius of *Assidona* included such relics. This may imply that they were larger or more important constructions than the ones at Ibahernando and El Gatillo. But even king Reccesuinth's church of San Juan de Baños, whatever its original form, cannot have been very big. In its present state it is about 20 meters long, including the chancel and western porch, and with a nave width of about 8.5 meters.[14]

---

[11] Vives, *Inscripciones*, no. 549.
[12] Enrique Cerrillo Martín de Cáceres, *La Basílica de época visigoda de Ibahernando* (Cáceres, 1983), pp. 21-49.
[13] L. Caballero Zoreda, V. Galera, and M.-D. Garralda, "La iglesia de época paleocristiana y visigoda de 'El Gatillo de Arriba' (Cáceres)," *Extremadura Arqueológica* 2 (1991), pp. 471-92; Cristina Godoy Fernández. *Arqueología y liturgia. Iglesias hispánicas (siglos IV al VIII)* (Barcelona, 1995), pp. 318-24.
[14] Pere de Palol, *La Basílica de San Juan de Baños* (Palencia, 1988), pp. 21-31.

Various episodes in the so-called "autobiographical" works of the late seventh-century monk Valerius of Bierzo throw a little light on such rural churches.[15] At an early stage in his career he lived as a hermit in the countryside between Castro Pedroso and Astorga, and after a falling out with a local priest – a frequent element in his narrative – various unnamed well-wishers established him in a church on an estate called Ebronanto, where he lived the life of a recluse in a cell located close to the altar, apparently receiving food and other support from the family owning the estate. However, the head of this household, a noble with the Germanic name of Ricimer, subsequently had the church pulled down and replaced by a new one, apparently with the intention of employing Valerius as its priest. He regarded this as a diabolically inspired attack on his life of contemplation and personal sanctification, from which he was rescued only when the unfinished new church collapsed, killing Ricimer.[16] While this view of his patron may seem to us highly ungrateful to say the least, it is interesting to note that Valerius claimed that the Devil was able to inspire Ricimer to replace the existing church and hermit's cell by showing him that he was soon going to die. The implication must be that this led him to feel that he needed an appropriate burial chapel, and a priest to administer the sacraments in it.

Virtually all of the extant churches of possible or actual Visigothic date contain burials. In most cases these are relatively few in number, and so do not represent cemeteries for large communities. The implication is that at least some of these buildings may have been erected by wealthy families for their own interments; they served as dynastic mausolea for the regional nobility. A definite case in point would seem to be the Late Roman mausoleum of Las Vegas de Puebla Nueva, south of Talavera in the province of Toledo. This was converted into a church and was used for a small number of Visigothic burials in the later sixth century.[17] Whether there was any continuity with the mid-fourth-century Roman family that founded the building as their burial

---

[15] Roger Collins, "The 'Autobiographical' Works of Valerius of Bierzo: Their Structure and Purpose," *Los Visigodos: Historia y Civilización* (= *Antigüedad y Cristianismo III*, Murcia, 1986), pp. 425-42.

[16] Valerius, *Ordo Querimoniae Prefatio Discriminis* 4-5, ed. Ramón Fernández Pousa, *San Valerio, Obras* (Madrid, 1942), pp. 161-5.

[17] Theodor Hauschild, "Die Mausoleum bei Las Vegas de Puebla Nueva," *Madrider Mitteilungen* 10 (1969), pp. 296-316.

place is unknown, but interestingly it seems to have been reused for Muslim worship some time after the Arab conquest.

At a later point in his life, and after various other vicissitudes, Valerius was joined in another hermitage by a nephew of his called John, together with one of his servants. The three of them constructed a small church on the hillside next to their cells.[18] This story would imply another possible origin for some of the small rural churches of Visigothic date: they served the needs of small groups of monks and hermits.

There were certainly a number of larger monastic communities in the Iberian peninsula in the seventh century, but very little is known of them. One of the most important was Agali, which was located close to Toledo, though the actual site is unknown.[19] Several of the abbots of this community became bishops of Toledo, and it must have been highly influential throughout the seventh century. Other monasteries, such as Servitanum and Biclarum, that are known from late sixth- and early seventh-century references do not reappear in the all too meager literary sources, and their subsequent history and significance cannot be assessed.

Slightly better known are a number of monasteries that were founded around the middle of the seventh century by bishop Fructuosus of Braga. Their foundations and locations were recorded in the anonymous *Life of Fructuosus* written by one of his disciples, probably around 680.[20] Something of the life of the inmates can be reconstructed from the two monastic rules that Fructuosus himself composed, but there is no way of knowing the numbers of monks or the physical appearance of their monasteries, other than in the most abstract and theoretical way.[21] While the possible site of *Compludum*, one of Fructuosus's principal foundations, has been located, too little of it has survived to give evidence of its layout or extent.[22] Thus the

---

[18] Valerius, *Replicatio Sermonum a Prima Conversione* 15, ed. Fernández Pousa, pp. 187-9.

[19] For a suggestion as to its site see Francisco de Pisa, *Descripcion de la Imperial Ciudad de Toledo, y Historia de sus Antiguedades... Primera Parte* (Toledo, 1605), p. 102.

[20] Manuel C. Díaz y Díaz (ed.), *La Vida de San Fructuoso de Braga* (Braga, 1974) is the only critical edition of the complete text.

[21] Artemio Manuel Martínez Tejera, "Los monasterios hispanos (siglos V-VIII). Una aproximación a su arquitectura a través de las fuentes literarias," in *Los Visigodos y su Mundo* (= *Arqueología, Paleontología y Etnografía* 4. Madrid, 1991), pp. 117-25.

[22] Florentino-Agustín Díez González, Francisco Roa Rico, Justiniano Rodríguez Fernández, and Antonio Viñayo González, *San Fructuoso y su Tiempo* (León, 1966), pp. 187-9.

only large-scale monastic buildings of possibly Visigothic date to have been identified are the church, perimeter wall, and other associated structures at Melque.[23]

If evidence is limited in terms of the larger monasteries, there would on the other hand seem to be much more available for smaller communities and groups of hermits, such as those described by Valerius. In particular, archaeological investigation in recent years has led to increasing numbers of caves in many parts of the Iberian peninsula being identified as churches and hermits' or monks' cells of Visigothic date.[24] The distribution of these is dependent upon the geology required to produce habitable caves, but they have been found in a number of different locations, and no doubt the number of such sites discovered will continue to grow. Among the largest concentrations of cave churches and cells are those found in Alava and the upper valley of the Ebro.[25] As few of them involve any additional construction, their identification and dating has depended mainly upon the presence of inscriptions and figures carved on their walls, and the writing used in these can be compared with other examples of script, from manuscripts and documents, and shown to belong to the Visigothic period.[26]

The very small number of saints' lives surviving from the sixth and seventh centuries in Spain has limited the amount that may be known about the monastic life of the period and the distribution of monasteries. There are regulations, such as the rules of Fructuosus previously referred to, and a number of aspects of monastic conduct and governance were discussed and legislated for by the bishops assembled at the various plenary and provincial councils.[27] But such normative

---

[23] See p. 188 above.
[24] Mario Jorge Barroca, Manuel Luís Real, and Rui Bastos Tavares, "Escavações arqueológicas nas covas eremíticas de Sabariz (Vila Fria - Viana do Castelo, Portugal)," in *Actas del I Congreso de Arqueología Medieval Española* (5 vols., Zaragoza, 1986), vol. II, pp. 51-71; Rafael Puertas Tricas, "Dos nuevas iglesias rupestres medievales en Málaga," ibid. pp. 73-101; Manuel Riu, "Cuevas eremitorios y centros cenobíticos rupestres de Andalucía Oriental," in *Actas del III Congreso Internacional de Arqueología Cristiana* (Rome, 1972), pp. 431-42.
[25] Agustín Azkarate Garai-Olaun, *Arqueología cristiana de la Antigüedad Tardía en Alava, Guipúzcoa y Vizcaya* (Vitoria-Gasteiz, 1988), pp. 133-498; Luis Alberto Monreal Jimeno, *Eremitorios rupestres altomedievales (el alto Valle del Ebro)* (Bilbao, 1989).
[26] Azkarate, *Arqueología cristiana*, pp. 388-422.
[27] Pablo de la Cruz Díaz Martínez, *Formas económicas y sociales en le monacato visigodo* (Salamanca, 1987) is the best study, drawing on the monastic rules as well as conciliar *acta*.

texts, which lack specific human and geographic contexts, can not provide the detail and sense of reality that can be obtained from, for example, the far larger and more varied body of evidence relating to monastic founders and institutions in Francia in the same period.

In partial compensation for this, it is now possible to envisage many parts of Spain in the Visigothic period as being occupied by hermits, in some cases living separately but in communities, coming together only for occasional worship. Braulio of Zaragoza's *Life of St. Aemilian* may be the only hagiographic text from this period that focuses upon such a figure, but it would be a mistake therefore to think that he was exceptional. For all of what to us appear to be their idiosyncrasies, Valerius of Bierzo's narratives of his spiritual life confirm the presence of many such hermits and holy men in the northwest of the peninsula in the later seventh century. The cave churches and cells of Alava, Málaga, and elsewhere show that Galicia and the Bierzo were not the only parts of the kingdom in which the kind of eremitical life described by Valerius was being led.

As is well known, the cult of St. Aemilian that Braulio helped to foster by the writing of his *Life*, continued to flourish, and the monastery that grew up on the site of his cell became one of the most significant in the Christian kingdoms in the centuries following the Arab conquest.[28] While other cases cannot be so easily documented, due to the lack of literary sources, the close proximity of cave cells and later churches in a variety of locations, both in the north and in those parts of the peninsula that fell under Muslim rule, suggests that similar cults developed around other local holy men, whose former residences were venerated after their deaths, and above or close to which monastic communities came to be established, and churches were built. Valerius indicates that this also happened in the case of Fructuosus of Braga. Unfortunately, in most other such cases these cults died out and the names of the founding saints were lost. But it is necessary to recognize that such sites could once have been numerous and widespread.[29]

---

[28] Santiago Castellanos, *Hagiografía y sociedad en la Hispania visigoda. La Vita Aemiliani y el actual territorio riojano (siglo VI)* (Logroño, 1999) for the origins of the cult in its local context.

[29] Among other examples, see Josefina Andrio Gonzalo, Ester Loyola Perea, Julio Martínez Flórez, and Javier Moreda Blanco, *El conjunto arqueológico del monasterio de San Juan de la Hoz de Cillaperlata* (Burgos, 1992).

While the discovery of rural ecclesiastical sites of this period may be on the increase, secular ones generally remain elusive. In part this may be because they are difficult to detect, as in some cases they may lie beneath later settlements, to which they could even be ancestral, despite the various periods of upheaval that affected many parts of the peninsula in the centuries following the Arab conquest. Additionally, their invisibility would be enhanced if they were originally constructed of wood. The desiccation and deforestation of so much of the Iberian peninsula is largely a post-medieval development, and there would have been a greater availability of timber for construction in many regions than present conditions might suggest.

Fewer rural villa sites of Late Roman date have so far been identified in Spain than in either France or Britain, but it is unlikely that they were less widely distributed. Of those that have been excavated that date from the last centuries of Roman rule in Spain, very few have revealed traces of continuing occupation into the Visigothic period. The main exceptions seem to be ones that have developed into ecclesiastical sites. Thus, in the case of the well known Late Roman "Villa of Fortunatus" at Fraga, near Lérida in Catalonia, the transformation of what was probably the original dining room of the villa into a church in the second quarter of the fifth century was followed by the addition of a baptistery and the abandonment of the living quarters in the sixth century. By this time burials were being inserted both into the church and into former residential parts of the villa.[30] If the process at work here was the transformation of an aristocratic "house monastery" into something more regular, this is one possible and quite credible explanation. Similarly, in the fifth century a bath house that once formed part of a villa complex at Vegas de Pedraza in the province of Segovia was converted into a church, which survived at least to the eighth century. After a possible period of abandonment, this was replaced by a triple-apsed Romanesque church in the twelfth century.[31] The discovery of a Late Roman villa under the site of the tenth-century Mozarabic

---

[30] J. Serra Rafols, "La Villa Fortunatus de Fraga," *Ampurias* 5 (1943), pp. 5-35.

[31] José María Izquierdo Bertiz, "La transición del mundo antiguo al medieval en Vegas de Pedraza (Segovia)," *III Congreso de Arqueología Medieval Española* (3 vols., Oviedo, 1992), vol. II, pp. 89-95.

monastery of San Pedro de Escalada near León may hint at similar continuities.[32]

For the majority of Late Roman villas in Spain that have been excavated, there was no such ecclesiastical reuse, and they appear to have been abandoned, or suffered dramatic internal transformation, involving the degradation of earlier high-status features. Thus in the villa of Torre Llauder, in Mataró north of Barcelona, which was built in the reign of Augustus (27 BC–AD 14) and was substantially restored in the Severan period (193–235), the fifth-century phase is represented by the reuse of once luxurious domestic quarters as agricultural storerooms, with pits being dug through the earlier mosaic floors to house pottery storage jars. Unburied skeletons found in the site have been linked to the Arab conquest of this region in 720.[33]

The only significant villa which may be of Visigothic origin is that found at Pla de Nadal near Valencia, and which was first excavated in 1981.[34] Only a small section of it has been recovered, in the form of what must once have been an impressive entry that was flanked by what are believed to have been towers. Little more than the foundations survive and the dating has to be based on some surviving fragments of decoration. While parallels have been drawn with features of a number of other buildings, almost entirely ecclesiastical, these have been called into question by the arguments previously discussed relating to the nonexistence or otherwise of a distinctive Visigothic style.[35] For those who believe that there was no such thing, the surviving decorative features of Pla de Nadal would date it to after the Arab conquest, and thus make of it the residence of an elite Muslim rather than Visigothic family.[36] For the moment therefore, both its date and its function remain debatable.

---

[32] Hortensia Larren Izquierdo, "Excavaciones arqueológicas en San Miguel de Escalada (León)," *Actas del I congresso de arqueología medieval española* (5 vols., Zaragoza, 1986), vol. 2, pp. 103–23.

[33] M. Prevosti i Monclús and J. F. Clariana i Roig, *Torre Llauder, Mataró, Vil.la romana* (Barcelona, 1988).

[34] Empar Juan and Ignacio Pastor, "Los Visigodos en Valencia. Pla de Nadal: ¿una villa aulica?" *Boletín de Arqueología Medieval* 3 (1989), pp. 137–79.

[35] See above p. 192.

[36] Luis Caballero Zoreda, "Sobre la llamada arquitectura 'visigoda': ¿paleocristiana o prerrománica?" in Javier Arce and Paolo Delogu (eds.), *Visigoti e Langobardi* (Florence, 2001), pp. 133–60, at p. 140.

While it is certain that the court and regional aristocracies of our period must have had rural residences, like that of Reccesuinth at Gerticos, none of these has yet been found. So it is not possible to say in what ways they may have resembled their Roman predecessors. However, other forms of settlement in the countryside are being discovered with increasing frequency, and several of them have been excavated. It may be too early to generalize on the basis of what is still limited and geographically widely dispersed evidence, but some impressions can be given of the results that are now appearing. Most significantly, there is widespread agreement that Roman villas had virtually all been abandoned as residential sites by the end of the fifth century.[37] No rural villa has provided evidence of continuity of such occupation later than this time. Some, such as the villa at Torre Llauder mentioned above, may have been used as storehouses by local agricultural communities. In others the abandoned rooms were turned into places of burial. Interestingly, a similar employment of deserted Roman villa sites as graveyards can be found in several parts of Anglo-Saxon England in the same period.

It has to be asked what this change means, and what alternative forms of rural settlement took the place of the villas. It should first be stressed that while Roman villas are normally thought of in terms of the families that owned and lived in them, their distinctive architectural features, and the quality or otherwise of such decorative features as floor mosaics to be found in them, their wider role in the countryside can sometimes be overlooked. They served as the primary form of rural settlement, in and around which were gathered not only the owning family but also their numerous household and agricultural servants, who in some cases may have been slaves, together with other dependents. They need to be seen as large farmsteads and the basic nuclei of rural settlement, rather than just as country versions of Roman town houses.

---

[37] Antonio Bellido Blanco, "La ocupación de época visigoda en Vega de Duero (Villabañez, Valladolid)," *Archivo Español de Arqueología* 70 (1997), pp. 307-16, at p. 314; J. Gómez Santa Cruz, "Aproximación al poblamiento hispano-romano en la provincia de Soria," in *Actas del 2 Symposium de Arqueología Soriana* (Soria, 1992), vol. 2, pp. 937-56; S. Gutiérrez Lloret, "El poblamiento tardorromano en Alicante a través de los testimonios materiales," in *Arte y poblamiento en el SE peninsular durante los últimos siglos de la civilización romana* (= *Antigüedad y Cristianismo* 5, Murcia, 1988), pp. 323-37; L. Ruiz Molina, "El poblamiento romano en el área de Yecla (Murcia)," in ibid. pp. 565-98.

The pattern of settlement that followed the abandonment of the villas is starting to be recognized on the basis of common features being found in various parts of the peninsula. The main element in this is the proliferation of small groups of houses, often with each having its own stock pens and/or grain silos and other storage facilities.[38] In other words, what seem to be emerging by the end of the fifth century are small villages. Many Spanish examples have been located, though relatively few have been excavated so far. In part this may be due to financial and other pressures on regional archaeological resources, but in many cases only slight traces survive, which may not justify full-scale investigation.[39]

The numbers of buildings found in these sites has been consistently small, and is usually less than a dozen. So, the settlements probably should be called *aldeas* or hamlets rather than villages, which might seem to imply rather larger concentrations of population. That in several of the sites studied numerous small stockyards, grain silos, and possible barns have been discovered would imply that the hamlets consisted of independent households, each depending on its own resources, both in terms of animal husbandry and cereal production.[40] This is a marked difference to the preceding villa economy, in which larger-scale resources were concentrated in a smaller number of hands. Large barns and stock pens were concentrated in and around the villas of the owning families, and few traces have been found of small-scale private ownership of such resources lower down the social ladder.

In the case of the sixth- and seventh-century hamlets, there is of course no way of knowing exactly what quantity of stock or of cereal-producing land would have been associated with each of the households to be found in a typical example. Nor can it be decided if the families in question owned such resources absolutely or if they were subject to economic and other ties of dependence. The probability must be that they did enjoy absolute freedom, but the make-up

---

[38] e.g. J. Francisco Fabian, M. Santonja Gómez, A. Fernández Moyano, and N. Benet, "Los poblados hispano-visigodos de 'Cañal' Pelayos (Salamanca). Consideraciones sobre el poblamiento entre los siglos V y VIII en el SE de la provincia de Salamanca," in *Actas del I Congreso de Arqueología Medieval Española* (5 vols., Zaragoza, 1986), vol. 2, pp. 187-201.
[39] Ibid. pp. 187-8.
[40] Ibid. pp. 188-92.

of these settlements might suggest that their inhabitants' obligations to their landlords would have taken the form of payment of percentages of what they themselves grew or reared. If, as in earlier centuries, the landlords effectively owned most agricultural resources and just depended on their social inferiors for labor, then the concentration of the latter around the lord's villa and an absence of evidence for private agrarian activity might have been expected.

It looks therefore as though the disappearance of the villa economy in the fifth century marks a major social change. A small number of elite families probably still did support themselves from the surpluses that they exacted from those legally dependent on them, but this came in the form of annual renders rather than from having a servile population working permanently for them, and having to be supported by them. This also mirrors changes in the political and economic organization of the Late Roman world, for example, the disappearance of a standing imperial army in the west in the course of the fifth century in favor of reliance on non-Roman mercenary forces that did not require permanent and complex systems of maintenance.[41]

While difficult to quantify, the material evidence for the distribution of villas across the western provinces in the last centuries of imperial rule indicates that there were many such large farmsteads, differing in size, in any given region. This would imply a relatively large number of landowning families, albeit varying considerably in terms of their wealth. There were undoubtedly, as is well known from copious literary evidence, some super-rich families, mostly of senatorial status, many of which held estates in more than one province. The great majority of the Roman villa owners, though, probably owned and worked a single estate. The replacement of the villas by hamlets may also indicate that such families, in so far as they survived the upheavals of the period, failed to be able to support themselves economically, and slid down the social ladder. This would support the impression that in the Visigothic period a rather broader spread of moderately wealthy Hispano-Roman villa-owning families was replaced by a much smaller and wealthier elite that increasingly presented itself as the Gothic aristocracy.

---

[41] Roger Collins, *Early Medieval Europe, 300-1000* (2nd edn., London, 1999), pp. 80-96.

As previously stated, no examples of the country residences of this class have so far been discovered, so it is very difficult to know much for certain about the material aspects of their lifestyle. This secular aristocracy was not the only landlord class, in that gifts of land and other forms of property were continually being made to the church throughout this period. Thus the major monasteries and episcopal households would have to be counted among the main landowners of the kingdom. Lacking the resources to exploit these directly, and with ideological disincentives so to do, such institutions would also have benefited more from receiving surpluses from settlements of small farmers on their lands than from the processes of the old villa economy. Thus the growth of the Christian church in the West may itself have been a further trigger for the change that has been detected in settlement and land-use patterns from the late imperial period onward.

The interesting relationship between abandoned villa sites and burial in subsequent periods is marked but has never been fully explained. In the case of the Visigothic period, such cemeteries have been linked to new settlements of the hamlet type established in the general vicinity of the former villas.[42] It is possible that the inhabitants believed in a continuity between themselves and such abandoned sites, which they regarded as being the burial places of generations of their ancestors. Alternatively, and more mundanely, it could be that the decayed but built-over nature of the villa sites made them unsuitable for agricultural purposes, and that the farmers of the hamlets took their dead to bury them there so as not to have to give over good crop or animal-rearing land for such purposes. If so, it is notable that in some cases this involved traveling some distance, even when other more convenient locations for a village graveyard were available.

Not all of the settlements that followed the abandonment of the villas were of the hamlet type. In various parts of the peninsula earlier fortified or fortifiable sites were occupied from the fifth century onward, including many of the Iron Age castros in the north and west of the peninsula from Portugal to the Pyrenees and from Galicia

---

[42] See, for example, J. A. Arranz Mínguez, S. Carretero Vaquero, S. Repiso Cobo, and L. C. San Miguel Maté, "Arqueología hispanovisigoda en Valladolid. El yacimiento de Piñel de Abajo," *Revista de Arqueología* 104 (1989), pp. 8-12; also Bellido Blasco, "La ocupación de época visigoda en Vega de Duero."

to Castile and La Mancha.[43] In these locations larger numbers of households can be found, more densely packed than in the hamlets. It has been suggested that some of these, such as the castro of Monte Cildá in the province of Palencia, may have served as the fortresses of resident garrisons in frontier regions or in zones requiring special defensive oversight, such as the territory of the former Suevic kingdom.[44] How such a system could have operated in practice is open to question, and most of the reused castros are not located in such areas.

These settlements were clearly more substantial than the hamlets in terms of the numbers of families and the concentrations of resources that they contained, and were thus inevitably more tempting targets for bandits, local potentates, and scavenging armies, and hence needed the capabilities for self-defense. Such refortified settlements were often located on the Roman road network, or close to river crossings, and were thus more conspicuous to those who might threaten them.[45] It is also possible that some of these places may have served as refuges for the inhabitants of the hamlets in times of danger.

One rural settlement in particular needs to be singled out because of the potential importance of the evidence it is said to provide for the social and economic history of Spain in the late Visigothic period. This is the site known as El Bovalar, on the banks of the river Segre near Lérida in Catalonia. The existence of a church of Visigothic date here was first recognized in 1943, and it was excavated in 1963. Little has survived above the level of the foundations, but its rectangular

---

[43] J. L. Avello Álvarez, "Evolución de los castros desde Antigüedad hasta la Edad Media," *Lancia* 1 (1983), pp. 273-82; for some specific examples see E. Rodríguez Almeida, "Contribución al estudio de los castros abulenses," *Zephyrus* 6 (1955), pp. 257-71, and J. Maluquer de Motes, "Excavaciones en el castro de las Merchanas," *Pyrenae* 4 (1968), pp. 115-28. See also Jorge López Quiroga, "Fluctuaciones del poblamiento y habitat 'fortificado' de altura en el noroeste de la Península Ibérica (ss. V-IX)," in Isabel Cristina Ferreira Fernandes (ed.), *Mil Anos de Fortificações na Península Ibérica e no Magreb (500-1500)* (Lisbon, 2002), pp. 83-92.

[44] M. A. García Guinea, *Excavaciones en Monte Cildá* (= *Excavaciones Arqueológicas en España* nos. 61 and 81, Madrid, 1966 and 1973); also Jaime Nuño González and Alonso Domínguez Bolaños, "Aspectos militares del castro del Cristo de San Esteban, en Mulas del Pan (Zamora), un asentamiento en la frontera suevo-visigoda," in Ferreira Fernandes (ed.), *Mil Anos de Fortificações*, pp. 105-20.

[45] Fabian et al., "Los poblados hispano-visigodos de 'Cañal' Pelayos," and the articles cited in note 42 above.

plan, incorporating a chancel between two flanking chambers and a baptistery in its narthex at the west end, is quite clear, as are the large number of sarcophagus burials within it. From its plan this building has been dated to the sixth century.

In 1976 a new campaign of excavation in the church was undertaken, but this was also extended into the adjacent area to the south of it, where the foundations of a series of buildings were discovered. The ground plan of these indicates the existence of what appear to be two adjacent and interconnecting courtyards, running north-south from the church. Each court had irregular-shaped rooms opening off it on all four sides, except in the northern one, where the church itself formed the outer wall on that side. These buildings were identified by their excavators as forming part of a village, largely on the strength of finds of agricultural and domestic implements within the rooms.[46]

More surprisingly, there was also a scattering of gold coins found throughout the site. Several of these were of the late Visigothic king Achila, who reigned in the northeast and in the Ebro valley around the years 711 to 714. The inclusion of Zaragoza within his kingdom was established by the discovery in this site of the first coins in his name from that mint. With this firm dating, added to signs of damage by fire, and the apparently hasty abandonment of a wide range of valuable household implements and agricultural tools, it was not unreasonably concluded that the buildings were destroyed at the time of the Islamic conquest of the Ebro valley in 714.[47]

This precision in dating and the number and diversity of the finds would make this one of the most important and exciting archaeological sites in Spain, certainly as far as the Visigothic period is concerned. It is one, moreover, that should provide evidence of aspects of the domestic and economic life of a section of this society otherwise hardly represented in the archaeological record. It is all the more disappointing, therefore, that other than for a short article and a pamphlet, these excavations have never been published. Now, more than a quarter of a century after they were conducted, there seems little hope that they ever will be.

---

[46] P. de Palol, "Las excavaciones del conjunto de 'El Bovalar'," in *Los Visigodos: historia y civilización* (= *Antigüedad y Cristianismo III*, Murcia, 1986), pp. 513-25, and Pere de Palol i Salellas, *El Bovalar (Seròs; Segrià)* (Lérida, 1989).

[47] Palol, *El Bovalar*, pp. 13 and 27.

Towns in Transition

The depressing fate of El Bovalar, from which so much was promised, can be contrasted with the extremely valuable and well-documented results of several recent excavations of urban sites of Visigothic date. While still limited in number, these have provided much useful information on a range of subjects and over a wide geographical area. Comparisons between the results achieved can provide the beginnings of an overview of how life in towns in Spain changed across the course of this period. One of the best cases is that of Mérida, for which there exist literary sources that can be used in conjunction with and also controlled by some detailed and recent archaeological evidence.

Not surprisingly, most of the textual sources relate to purely ecclesiastical constructions, or ones that were the product of episcopal patronage. Some of the buildings of a succession of later sixth-century bishops of the city are recorded in the anonymous *Vitas Patrum Emeretensium* or "Lives of the Fathers of Mérida," which is usually thought to have been written in the 630s. Although explicitly cast as a Spanish equivalent to the *Dialogues* of pope Gregory the Great (590–604), with its author trying to form a collection of the miraculous deeds of local holy men, it very quickly turns itself into an account of the lives of the bishops of the city from roughly the middle of the sixth century to the beginning of the seventh.[48] There is no absolute evidence for its dating, which just derives from the logic of its own narrative.[49]

According to the *Vitas*, the financial position of the bishopric of what had once been one of the greatest cities of Roman Spain was transformed by an inheritance given to its bishop Paul (540s/550s?) by a wealthy provincial senator, whose wife he had saved by performing a Caesarian operation.[50] Paul's relative and successor Fidelis (550s/560s?) was thus able to restore the episcopal palace after its complete collapse. Even allowing for pious exaggeration, this story

---

[48] *Vitas Sanctorum Patrum Emeretensium*, ed. A. Maya Sánchez (*Corpus Christianorum, Series Latina*, vol. CXVI, Turnhout, 1992).

[49] Joseph N. Garvin, *The Vitas Sanctorum Patrum Emeretensium* (Washington, 1946), pp. 1-6.

[50] *Vitas Patrum Emeretensium* IV. ii, ed. Maya Sánchez, pp. 26-30.

may suggest that even some of the more prominent buildings in the city had been suffering from neglect and lack of repair. The same bishop is also said to have rebuilt the basilica dedicated to the patron saint of Mérida, St. Eulalia. His successor, Masona (570s–c.600), paid for the construction and endowment of a *xenodochium*, a combination of pilgrim hostel and hospital.[51] Neither of the two subsequent bishops, with whom the narrative briefly ends, are credited with any constructions at all, but an inscription uncovered in 1947 records the foundation of a church dedicated to the Virgin Mary, which may be dated to 627.[52]

Unfortunately none of the buildings of Visigothic Mérida have survived intact or anything close to it. The cathedral church of St. Mary may have been demolished as early as the ninth century, but it has also been suggested that some of its fabric was incorporated into the church built on the site following the Leonese capture of the city from the Almohads in 1230. The episcopal palace rebuilt by bishop Fidelis is also long gone, but in its case leaving no identifiable traces at all. The site of Masona's *xenodochium* has almost certainly been located, but it was clearly badly damaged in the Umayyad period.[53] It is possible that some of its internal fittings, in particular some distinctive carved stone pilasters, were reused in the construction of the roof over a cistern in the fortress known as the Alcazaba, that was built by by Abd al-Rahman II in 835.[54]

Rather more has been preserved of the church of St. Eulalia that was restored by Fidelis. The basilica itself was destroyed at some point in the period of Islamic rule, but probably not until after the end of the Umayyad and Taifa periods (that is, after 1090). Following the Leonese capture of the city in 1230 a new church in Gothic style was erected on the site, but recent excavations have shown that much of the foundations of the preceding early Christian and Visigothic buildings have survived under this later construction. The ground plan of the Visigothic church has been fully uncovered, as well as

---

[51] Pedro Mateos Cruz, "*Augusta Emerita*, de capital de la *Diocesis Hispaniarum* a sede temporal visigoda," in Gisela Ripoll and Josep M. Gurt (eds.), *Sedes regiae (ann. 400–800)* (Barcelona, 2000), pp. 491–520, for an overview of recent excavation.
[52] Vives, *Inscripciones* no. 548, pp. 314–15.
[53] Pedro Mateos Cruz, "Identificación del *Xenodochium* fundado por Masona en Mérida," *IV Reunió d'Arqueologia Cristiana Hispànica* (Barcelona, 1995), pp. 309–16.
[54] Mateos, "*Augusta Emerita* de capital de la *Diocesis Hispaniarum*," pp. 516–17.

various burials and inscriptions.[55] This makes it the best surviving example of a major church from any part of Spain in this period.

The lack of detailed and descriptive literary evidence makes it very difficult to visualize what life in a town such as this might have been like, either in the sixth century or the seventh. Mérida again offers some of the best clues from any urban site of the period, largely thanks to recent excavations in the heart of the city, close to the river Guadiana. Here it has been possible to form an overall view of the changes in occupation of what must have been a significant site, close to the great bridge that carried the road to Seville across the river, and located between the cathedral and its adjacent episcopal complex and the southern wall of the city, which paralleled the river bank.[56]

Starting as a prosperous area in the early imperial centuries, and containing at least one substantial town house, it remained so under the Late Empire, when this villa was remodeled and enlarged. This phase of reconstruction and enhancement, probably taking place in the early fourth century, was followed by one of complete abandonment and considerable destruction in the fifth. This phenomenon was clearly not confined to this site alone, as evidence of similar damage and decay has been found in other contexts in the city that can be dated to the same period. This could relate to a Suevic raid in 429, following the departure of the Vandals to Africa, in which their leader Hermigar was said by Hydatius to have offended St. Eulalia, the city's patron saint, but could just as easily be the result of some other unrecorded episode in this obscure period. What is clear, though, is that the city suffered severe and sustained damage at this time. Its physical extent may have been reduced, as burials have been found in the luxurious Roman villas in the vicinity of the amphitheater, which would originally have been located within the urban perimeter.

It is against this background that we have to see the building projects of the bishops of the second half of the sixth century, as reported in the *Vitas Patrum Emeretensium*. It was a ravaged and diminished

---

[55] Pedro Mateos Cruz, *La Basílica de Santa Eulalia de Mérida: Arqueología y Urbanismo* (= *Anejos de Archivo Español de Arqueología* XIX, Madrid, 1999) is the fullest account; see also *Extremadura Arqueológica* III: *Jornadas sobre Santa Eulalia de Mérida* (Mérida, 1992).

[56] Miguel Alba Calzado, "Ocupación diacrónica del área arqueológica de Morería (Mérida)," *Mérida Excavaciones Arqueológicas 1994-1995. Memoria* (Mérida, 1997), pp. 285-315, for the excavations on this site; Mateos, "*Augusta Emerita*," pp. 504-6.

city that benefited from their work. The evidence from the excavations of the basilica of St. Eulalia and the quality of the workmanship of what are thought to be pilasters from the *xenodochium* go some way toward supporting the enthusiastic account of the *Vitas Patrum* of what they achieved.[57] But there is little evidence to suggest that this episcopal patronage and conspicuous magnificence was long sustained. From the later seventh century the only documented construction project is some work done on the entry into the convent attached to the basilica of St. Eulalia, which was carried out in 661 on the orders of its abbess Eugenia.[58]

While ecclesiastical buildings may have been erected in relative profusion in the later sixth century, the evidence of the riverbank site shows this relative opulence did not necessarily extend itself to secular constructions. At some point after the phase of destruction in the fifth century, the Roman town house, or the ruins of it, was reoccupied, but from the evidence of hearth sites within the former public and private rooms, it seems that seven separate households had been established within what had once been a single villa, and that they all shared access to a well. While the chronology cannot be established precisely, it also looks as if the area, once very close to the public heart of the Roman city, became increasingly rural in character, with evidence being found of the practice in it of animal husbandry and agriculture.[59] This is in line with what is known of a number of other once major cities in Spain and elsewhere in the West in these centuries, including the city of Rome itself.[60]

This period of what may be called market gardening within the decaying remains of the reoccupied Roman town houses, roughly datable to the seventh century, was followed by another one of abandonment and destruction, which was reversed only by a resettling of the area in the ninth century. It would be tempting to associate this second phase of apparent disaster with the Arab conquest of 711. Some of the Arab historians record a 13-month siege of the city by

---

[57] María Cruz Villalón, "La escultura visigoda. Mérida, centro creador," in Arce and Delogu (eds.), *Visigoti e Langobardi*, pp. 161-84.
[58] Vives, *Inscripciones* no. 358, p. 124.
[59] Alba Calzado, "Ocupación diacrónica," p. 294; Mateos Cruz, "*Augusta Emerita*," p. 516.
[60] Riccardo Santangeli Valenzani, "Residential Building in Early Medieval Rome," in Julia M. H. Smith (ed.), *Early Medieval Rome and the Christian West: Essays in Honour of Donald Bullough* (Leiden, 2000), pp. 101-12.

Musa ibn Nusayr, but the chronology of this raises considerable difficulties, and it is hard to know how any of the towns of Visigothic Spain would have been capable of putting up such prolonged resistance to the invaders.[61] This episode needs to be treated with some reserve, as do most of the points of detail in the Arab conquest narratives.

It would not have been necessary for the decay and abandonment detected in the archaeology, but not dated precisely, to be the result of war or deliberate destruction. A useful comparison can be made with what is thought to be Leovigild's new city of Reccopolis. Here recent excavations have revealed continuing occupation into the middle of the eighth century, but with the site taking on increasingly rural character. The so-called palace ceased to be properly maintained, and its upper level became unusable, while the ground floor remained in occupation until finally abandoned about 750. Around this time the remaining population seems to have relocated itself to a new, smaller, and more easily defended location about a mile to the west, and the whole site was deserted by the end of the century.[62]

In the same way, parts at least of the city of Mérida may have been progressively abandoned from the seventh century onward, as the population dwindled and problems of defensibility became more acute. One possibility would be that the theater and/or amphitheater provided a new focus of defended settlement until the ninth century. It seems likely that some of the churches of the Visigothic period, including the cathedral and the basilica of St. Eulalia, continued in use for some time after 711, and it has been suggested that some of the decorative stonework fragments found in various locations throughout the city postdate the Arab conquest.[63] If so, there was clearly significant continuity in artistic traditions, and a sufficient demand for building work and restoration to maintain it, but this remains debatable.

If efforts could still be put into maintaining some of the principal Christian buildings - and we know nothing of the new Muslim ones

---

[61] Roger Collins, *The Arab Conquest of Spain, 710-797* (2nd edn., Oxford, 1994), p. 42 and note 57.

[62] Lauro Olmo Enciso, "Proyecto Recopolis: ciudad y territorio en época visigoda," in Rodrigo de Balbín, Jesus Valiente, and María Teresa Mussat (eds.), *Arqueología en Guadalajara* (Toledo, 1995), pp. 211-23.

[63] María Cruz Villalón, "Mérida entre Roma y el Islam. Nuevos documentos y reflexiones," in A. Velázquez, E. Cerrilo, and P. Mateos (eds.), *Los últimos Romanos en Lusitania* (Mérida, 1995), pp. 153-84.

– this needs to be seen against a background of the virtual disappearance of the distinctive features of the Roman city. In the ninth century, when the riverbank area was again reoccupied, it is notable that the Roman road plan had ceased to provide a framework for structuring the buildings that were put up, several of which were erected over what had previously been city streets. These may no longer have been visible to the builders, testifying to the length and severity of the period of abandonment that had preceded the reoccupation of the area.[64]

A rather similar story, though with significant differences, can be told about Cartagena, Roman *Carthago Nova*, which became the administrative center of the Byzantine enclave in Spain after 552. It may have been the last of the imperial fortresses to be recaptured by the Visigothic monarchy, sometime around 625. Like Mérida, Cartagena has benefited from recent campaigns of excavation that have proved particularly revealing of the the city's history over an extended period, at least as far as certain specific sites are concerned.[65] In this case attention has been concentrated particularly on the area around the Roman theater, which, like that in Mérida, was built in the reign of Augustus.

As in the case of many other cities in Spain, evidence of the abandonment of public buildings can be found well before the end of Roman rule; in a few cases this could even be as early as the late first century AD.[66] In the third century a new defensive wall was built, part of which passed through this zone. This construction testifies to the increased level of unease felt in that period, which also saw other such campaigns of wall building around towns such as Braga, Barcelona, and Lugo that were far removed from any known threat of barbarian incursion.[67]

---

[64] Alba Calzado, "Ocupación diacrónica," pp. 295-6; Mateos Cruz, "*Augusta Emerita*," pp. 512-17.

[65] Sebastián F. Ramallo, "*Carthago Spartaria*, un núcleo bizantino en *Hispania*," in Ripoll and Gurt (eds.), *Sedes regiae*, pp. 579-611.

[66] This is true of part of the forum of Ampurias, for example: E. Sanmartí-Grego, "El foro romano de Ampurias," in *Los foros romanos de las provincias occidentales* (Madrid, 1987), pp. 55-60. But this does not necessarily imply significant social and economic decline; see J. M. Nolla, "Ampurias en la Antigüedad Tardía. Una nueva perspectiva," *Archivo Español de Arqueología* 66 (1993), pp. 207-24.

[67] Francisco Sande Lemos, José Manuel de Freitas Leite, and Luís Fernando de Oliveira Fontes, "A muralha de *Bracara Augusta* e a cerca medieval de Braga," in Isabel Cristina Ferreira Fernandes (ed.), *Mil Anos de Fortificações na Península Ibérica e no Magreb (500-1500)* (Lisbon, 2002), pp. 121-32. The dating of the walls of Barcelona remains controversial.

The second half of the fourth century saw a considerable amount of restoration and reconstruction in this zone of Cartagena, the first major program of such works since the Julio-Claudian period. A public bath house was largely rebuilt and several rows of new shops were created. There is also evidence of reconstruction of the interiors of private houses, with new internal walls being created, largely built out of earlier materials. All this positive activity would imply a period of relative wealth and security, a view that might be held of Spain as a whole in the early years of the Theodosian dynasty (379–455).

Unlike Mérida, Cartagena has not so far revealed any evidence of large-scale damage or destruction in the generally far more disturbed fifth century. If anything, the city, which remained under imperial control until the 470s, seems to have continued to prosper. In the later part of the century the theater, which went out of use in the late second century, was redeployed to provide the location and materials for a new commercial quarter. This has been likened to the Markets of Trajan in Rome, and seems to have consisted of a number of large-scale warehouses and trading areas.[68]

This impressive complex did not, however, last long, and had been abandoned either by the end of the century or early in the next one. Whether this relates to a military conquest of the city in the time of the Visigothic king Euric (466–84) or reflects a decline in maritime trade following the end of imperial rule can not be known for certain. Following a short period of abandonment, the theater site was put to quite different uses around the middle of the sixth century. The ruins of the earlier theater and market were covered over and terraced to provide the foundations for a series of new buildings, consisting of two to three small rooms each. Each of these houses opened out onto a communal space, and they were divided one from another by a series of narrow and irregular lanes. Among the pottery found in this area are numerous pieces from distinctively shaped oil amphorae, testifying to active trading links with North Africa.

The houses have been interpreted as being erected for the Byzantine troops who occupied the city in 552. This cannot be confirmed by

---

[68] Sebastián F. Ramallo Asensio, Elena Ruiz Valderas, and María del Carmen Berrocal Caparrós, "Contextos cerámicos de los siglos V–VII en Cartagena," *Archivo Español de Arqueología* 69 (1996), pp. 135–90.

the evidence of what has been found on the site, and can only remain a speculation. It has also not been possible to work out the extent of the city in this period or the nature of its defenses. However, it is highly likely that Cartagena, like Valencia, would have had a much reduced population by this time, and only a limited part of the space of the city in earlier centuries was being occupied.[69] But how important or otherwise this theater zone may have been in the much diminished Byzantine city cannot yet be known.

This whole area, and perhaps much and even the whole of the settlement, was subject to violent destruction in the first half of the seventh century. This has been linked to a Visigothic conquest and sack of the city around 625. While this cannot be confirmed archaeologically, it would seem the most obvious explanation. The theater zone was completely abandoned in the aftermath of this phase of destruction, and the next buildings to be found on the site date to no earlier than the later eleventh century. It would be going too far to say that the whole settlement was completely abandoned in the aftermath of the Visigothic conquest, but it is a definite possibility.

While there are significant differences in detail, the overall pattern of the history of the city in the Visigothic centuries is similar in the cases of Mérida and Cartagena, so far the best examples available. Periods of destruction and abandonment, at least of parts of the settlement, alternate with ones of rebuilding and reconstruction. These latter, however, are short-lived, and the nature of what is attempted and achieved and the quality of the construction work involved tends to decline each time. Smaller towns may have followed similar patterns, and a number of once significant Roman settlements disappear completely either in the seventh or the eighth centuries. In no case can this be linked directly to the Arab conquest.

That the theater in Cartagena remained a focus of occupation within the much diminished city is probably no accident. Other examples exist of large Roman public buildings taking on new significance and purposes in the post-imperial centuries. Another case in point from

---

[69] E. Ruiz Valderas, S. Ramallo Asensio, M. D. Laiz Reverte, and M. C. Berrocal Caparrós, "Transformaciones urbanísticas de Carthago Nova (siglos III-XIII)," in *Sociedades en transición. Actas del IV Congreso de Arqueología Medieval Española* (3 vols., Alicante, 1994), vol. II, pp. 59-65. For Valencia see J. Pascual Pacheco and R. Soriano Sánchez, "La evolución urbana de Valencia desde época visigoda hasta época taifa (siglos V-XI)," in ibid. pp. 67-76.

the Visigothic kingdom is Nîmes, where the amphitheater served for the usurper Paul's last stand against Wamba in 673.[70] While this might seem like a desperate expedient, in a number of other cases, particularly in southern Gaul, it can be shown that the high walls of a Roman theater or amphitheater provided a ready-made defensive structure for a much diminished population.

Its location within what was effectively a militarized zone in the frontier territories between the Visigothic and Frankish kingdoms made defensibility a prime requirement, and it may no longer have been possible to maintain and garrison the much larger urban perimeter defined by the Roman walls. Not all such fortresses in the frontier had to be of Roman origin. A remarkable site in this region is Puig Rom, near Rosas on the Catalan coast, where part of a late Visigothic wall and gate has been excavated. The full extent of the structure has not been recovered, so it is not known whether this formed part of the defensive perimeter of a settlement or of just a garrisoned fortress, but it does testify to the apparent military preparedness of the regions close to the Frankish frontier.[71]

While the evidence is clearly very patchy in terms of detail and geographical distribution, the impression must be that towns, both large and small, in Spain in the Visigothic period were generally rather wretched and squalid places. The great public buildings of the Roman cities had long since been abandoned or had fallen into decay; to be fair, this was a process that can be detected as occurring from the early imperial period onwards. Most such buildings came to serve as quarries for good-quality building stones, and in particular their capitals and columns were prized for reuse in the church buildings that represented the principal construction projects of the Late and post-Roman centuries. The grand private town houses of the early empire do not continue into the Visigothic period. They were either completely abandoned, broken up into smaller units, or transformed, in states of increasing decay, into urban farmhouses. The mosaic and fresco decoration of their grand public rooms, where they survived at all, appear in almost all cases to have been hidden

---

[70] Julian of Toledo, *Historia Wambae* 18 (*Corpus Christianorum, Series Latina*, CXV), p. 234: ... *in castro illo arenarum* ...

[71] P. de Palol, "Castro hispanovisigodo de Puig Rom (Rosas)," *Informes y Memorias* 27 (1952), pp. 163–82.

under levels of detritus, and their existence was probably unrecognized by most of their new occupants.

As in this period there is strong evidence of decline in the size of population in the former Roman towns and cities, together with increasing ruralization, in terms of crop-growing and animal husbandry taking place within their walls, it may be better to think in terms of a spectrum of settlement types rather than of a marked dichotomy between town and country. At one end were the tiny hamlets of half a dozen or so small farmhouses, and at the other the former large cities, in which the inhabitants were supporting themselves increasingly from what they raised on land that had once been purely urban in character and use. The towns probably continued to serve as centers for production and distribution in the localized trade in such necessities as ceramics (all coarse wares) and metalwork. These items would have been sold both to the inhabitants of the smaller civil settlements, if they did not make their own, and to rural ecclesiastical centers such as monasteries.[72]

Between the two extremes of the decaying or metamorphosing towns and the *aldeas* were a variety of other settlements of different sizes, which might have included towns that had shrunk to small fortified nuclei, centered possibly in a former theater or amphitheater, and also other relatively densely populated locations, such as the reoccupied hill-top fortresses of pre-Roman origin. There may have been a number of new small-scale fortified centers, such as the site at Puig Rom. Ongoing and future excavations will add depth, detail, and inevitably correction to the brief outline attempted here of some of the results achieved so far in trying to recapture aspects of the social and economic life of Spain in this period.

---

[72] Lauro Olmo Enciso, "Nuevas perspectivas para el estudio de la ciudad en la época visigoda," in *Los Visigodos y su mundo* (= *Arqueología, Paleontología y Etnografía 4*, Madrid, 1998), pp. 259–69. Much work remains to be done on such local distribution networks in this period. See Elías Carrocera Fernández and Otilia Requejo Pagés, "Producciones cerámicas tardía en castros y villas asturianas," *Boletín de Arqueología Medieval* 3 (1989), pp. 21–30, and Ramón Bohigas Roldán and Alicia Ruiz Gutiérrez, "Las cerámicas visigodas de poblado en Cantabria y Palencia," ibid. pp. 31–51 for some regional studies.

9
Law and Ethnic Identity

The Fog of the Law

In recent years it has become standard to regard the various codes of law created in the kingdoms that succeeded the Roman empire in western Europe as having more of a symbolic than a practical value. They are seen as manifestos of a new royal authority that emerged almost in imitation of that of the emperors, and whose growth was fostered and sustained by the leaders of the church in each realm.[1] The crucial element is seen to be the writing down of laws that in large part may have represented the customary practices of the peoples whose rulers were thereby acquiring control over processes that had originally been more popular or even democratic in character. This creeping Romanization, largely under the influence of the church, of earlier Germanic traditions of government and law-making is seen as a crucial step in the bringing together of the two elements in the population and as being an essential stage in the transmission of Roman culture across the divide represented by the "barbarian" conquests of the former empire.[2]

Reasons given for seeing the numerous Anglo-Saxon, Frankish, and other codes as being less intended for practical use in courts and more as statements of royal law-making authority, even in the area of long-established custom, include the small size, lack of comprehensiveness, and poor organization of the contents of many of them. In

---

[1] J. M. Wallace-Hadrill, *The Long-haired Kings and Other Studies in Frankish History* (London, 1962), pp. 179-81, and idem, *Early Germanic Kingship in England and on the Continent* (Oxford, 1971), p. 44.
[2] Patrick Wormald, "*Lex Scripta* and *Verbum Regis*: Legislation and Germanic Kingship, from Euric to Cnut," in P. H. Sawyer and I. N. Wood (eds.), *Early Medieval Kingship* (Leeds, 1979), pp. 105-38.

themselves they would be insufficient to provide a full and coherent statement of current law that would offer authoritative guidance for judges and lawyers in their work. Some of the contents of codes such as the Frankish *Lex Salica* also seem to be archaic in character; presenting themselves as written statements of ancient custom rather than legal solutions to contemporary problems.[3]

There is some sense in this line of argument, though some features of it would be weakened if comparison is made with processes of law-making in the church. Individual councils, whose acts were always separately recorded, produced briefly worded sets of rulings that were usually few in number and seemingly random in their contents. They were responses to current issues that required regulation, but also contributed to the growth of the much larger body of canon law created by the acts of all ecclesiastical councils held to be orthodox. Likewise, revealing comparisons can be made between the smaller Germanic law codes and the edicts that could be issued by Late Roman Praetorian Prefects, whose successors the kings were in many respects.[4]

Whatever the merits of the arguments about the primarily symbolic nature of many of the Germanic law codes, it has been recognized that those of the Visigoths and of the Lombards do not fall into this category.[5] The code calling itself the *Liber Iudiciorum* ("Book of the Judges"), also known as the *Lex Visigothorum* ("Law of the Visigoths"), is very substantial, being by far the largest of any of these early collections of law issued by non-Roman rulers.[6] It is coherently organized into 12 books, an arrangement that has itself been seen as a reflection of Roman legal tradition, and subdivided into titles and numbered individual laws (which are called *eras* in the earliest manuscript).[7] It abrogates all earlier codes, giving itself unique authority, and contains explicit instructions on procedures to be followed in obtaining legal rulings on issues that were not already included in its

---

[3] Ibid. pp. 109-10.

[4] Roger Collins, "Law and Ethnic Identity in the Western Kingdoms in the Fifth and Sixth Centuries," in Alfred P. Smyth (ed.), *Medieval Europeans* (Basingstoke and New York, 1998), pp. 1-23.

[5] Wormald, "*Lex scripta*," pp. 114-18.

[6] Karl Zeumer (ed.), *Leges Visigothorum* (= *MGH Legum, sectio* I, vol. 1, Hanover, 1902); see p. xix for the title.

[7] MS Vatican Reg. lat. 1024 (7th/8th century), f. 138r.

contents. It even stipulates the maximum price to be charged for a copy of itself.[8] Beyond the internal evidence of the contents, evidence exists in the form of hundreds of records of legal cases from later centuries of how these laws worked in practice. In many such documents explicit reference is made to the *Liber Iudiciorum*.[9]

In terms of its scale, organization, and practical applicability this code matches official Roman legal compilations, such as *Codex Theodosianus* or the Theodosian Code of 438 in most respects. Furthermore, it remained in force for centuries, modified only by the local privileges known as the *fueros*. Its authority should have been eclipsed in Catalonia by the issue of the *Usatges* of Barcelona around 1150, and in Castile by the promulgation of the *Siete Partidas* of Alfonso X the Wise (1252-84), but in neither case was this effect immediate or absolute.[10] Manuscripts of it were still being written as late as the fourteenth century.[11]

Similar practical utility is also seen as a major function of the earlier law codes of the Visigothic kings, but with the difference that they may not have been applicable to all inhabitants of the kingdom. These include a code by Euric (466-84), of which only a fragment may survive. A revised and augmented version of this may have been promulgated by Leovigild (569-86), but this does not survive in its original form. Still extant is an abridgment of the imperial Theodosian Code issued by Alaric II (484-507) in 506, known as *Lex Romana Visigothorum* ("The Roman Law of the Visigoths") or as the Breviary of Alaric.[12]

The question of whether or not these codes really had "personal" as opposed to "territorial" application has been warmly debated. By these terms are meant the difference between laws that apply to an individual by virtue of his ethnic identity and those that were issued

---

[8] Law V. iv. 22: *Quo presens liber debeat pretio conparari*, ed. Zeumer, p. 226.
[9] Roger Collins, "*Sicut lex gothorum continet*: Law and Charters in Ninth and Tenth-century León and Castile," *English Historical Review* 100 (1985), pp. 489-512.
[10] Adam J. Kosto, *Making Agreements in Medieval Catalonia: Power, Order and the Written Word, 1000-1200* (Cambridge, 2001), pp. 278-81; in the case of the *Siete Partidas* this remains controversial: J. F. O'Callaghan, *The Learned King: The Reign of Alfonso X of Castile* (Philadelphia, 1993), pp. 36-7.
[11] Zeumer (ed.), *Leges Visigothorum*, his MSS 9, 16, 19 of the "V" class, pp. xxiii-xxiv.
[12] For a useful overview of Visigothic legal history see José Manuel Pérez-Prendes Muñoz-Arraco, "Historia de la legislación visigótica," in *San Isidoro Doctor Hispaniae* (Seville, 2002), pp. 50-67.

for all of a ruler's subjects, irrespective of their sense of racial or other separateness.[13] Traditionally the codes of Euric, Alaric II, and Leovigild have been seen as intended for the use of Goths in the case of the first and third of them, and for Romans in the second. The code of Euric also contains rulings on the settlement of disputes to which both Goths and Romans were party, which might seem to confirm this distinction. By this view, the first "territorial" code of the Visigothic monarchy, applicable to Goths and Romans alike, was the *Liber Iudiciorum* of Reccesuinth, promulgated in 654.

This interpretation has been contested by those who would see all of these codes as being territorial.[14] The issue can never be settled to the satisfaction of all on the basis of the available evidence. The older view of the separation of Roman and Gothic legal systems relies upon contradictions between the codes, and thus expects a clarity and coherence that is usually impossible to find in Late Antique and early medieval law. The existence of contradictions and conflicts between the contents of the codes is not in itself enough to show that they must have been intended for different elements of the population, because Roman legislators found it impossible to eliminate such features in the imperial law.[15]

Similarly, the modern expectation that there should have been separate codes of law for different ethnic groups under a single political authority may be conditioned by what happened in the Carolingian empire in the eighth and ninth centuries rather than by the realities of the immediate post-Roman centuries. Under the Carolingians many supposedly "national" codes were effectively invented and imposed upon the subject peoples, in order to reinforce their separateness from the Franks; the latter's failure to even attempt to assimilate their subjects into a new all-embracing and cohesive identity contributed to the rapid disintegration of their empire. On the other hand, in the

---

[13] For these arguments see Alvaro D'Ors, "La territorialidad del derecho de los visigodos," in *Estudios Visigóticos* I (Rome, 1956), pp. 91-150, and A. García Gallo, "Nacionalidad y territorialidad del derecho en la época visigoda," *Anuario de historia del derecho español* 13 (1936-41), pp. 168-264.

[14] P. D. King, "King Chindasvind and the First Territorial Law-code of the Visigothic Kingdom," in Edward James (ed.), *Visigothic Spain: New Approaches* (Oxford, 1980), pp. 131-57, especially pp. 131-42.

[15] A. H. M. Jones, *The Later Roman Empire, 284-602* (3 vols., Oxford, 1964), vol. 1, pp. 470-9.

Late Roman period what can be found is evidence for different legal rules for military and civilian elements in the population, and it was as soldiers that the Germanic groups were regarded and treated by the imperial administration. So laws about resolving Gothic-Roman disputes were really concerned with conflicts over military and civil jurisdiction.[16]

Whatever may be thought of the primary Frankish and Anglo-Saxon codes, the earliest Visigothic one does not consist of a writing down of traditional Germanic laws or customs. The text that has been identified as the only surviving section of of the Code of Euric is predominantly, even exclusively, Roman in its contents and its structure. It may not be identical in its rules and wording to the law set out in the imperial edicts and *rescripta*, as contained in the Theodosian Code, but it belongs to the category of what is called "Roman Vulgar Law," provincial practice that was not always written, and which covered many areas ignored or only lightly touched upon by imperial law.[17]

The Code of Euric raises other problems, as some scholars see it as infringing an imperial monopoly on legislating, and thus insist it could not possibly predate the end of imperial rule in the West in either 476 or 480. This ceases to be a problem if it be accepted that this text represents a codifying of Roman provincial legal practices, together with some new regulations dealing with relations between the military and the civil population, as this was perfectly within the competence of a Roman Praetorian Prefect, and such a code or *Edicta* would have currency within the territory under his authority.

Euric may also not have been the first Visigothic king to issue laws in his own name. Evidence for such activity on the part of his father Theoderic I (419–51) could come from a statement in a letter by the Gallic aristocrat and later bishop of Clermont, Sidonius Apollinaris. Criticizing a Roman official called Seronatus, who was accused of collaborating with the Goths, he described him as "spurning the Theodosian laws and promoting those of Theoderic."[18] By *leges*

---

[16] Collins, "Law and Ethnic Identity," pp. 3–4.
[17] Roger Collins, *Early Medieval Spain, 400–1000* (2nd edn., London, 1995), pp. 24–31 for a brief account; see also Pablo C. Díaz and Raúl González Salinero, "El Codigo de Eurico y el derecho romano vulgar," in Javier Arce and Paolo Delogu (eds.), *Visigoti e Longobardi* (Florence, 2001), pp. 93–115.
[18] Sidonius Apollinaris, *Epistolae* II. i. 3, ed. W. B. Anderson, *Sidonius, Poems and Letters* (2 vols., London and Cambridge, MA, 1936), vol. 1, p. 416.

theudosianas was obviously meant the Theodosian Code of 438. So it is argued that Sidonius's jibe would only make sense if a parallel code of Gothic law existed, named after either Theoderic I or his son Theoderic II (453-66). However, this may be to take sarcasm too literally, and allowance has to be made for the exaggerated argumentative style of the Roman rhetorical tradition, of which Sidonius was a noted exponent.[19]

As there are no extant laws of either Theoderic I or Theoderic II, this argument's significance really lies in its role in identifying the sole surviving section of the Code of Euric. This may be uniquely preserved in a palimpsest manuscript now in the Bibliothèque Nationale in Paris.[20] Only 11 folios survive, written in a sixth-century uncial script that cannot be located geographically. The manuscript was lightly erased in northern France in the late seventh or early eighth centuries, when another work was written over the top of the original text.[21] It is thus still possible to read that original undertext despite the later rewriting.

What is preserved is a corpus of numbered laws, of which only items 276 to 336 are contained here. Even within this group some complete laws and phrases of others have been lost due to the damaged state of the manuscript. The material has been organized systematically and divided into sections called "Titles," of which several headings survive: *De Commendatis vel Commodatis* "On Deposits and Loans" (items 278-85), *De Venditionibus* "Concerning Sales" (286-304), *De Donationibus* "Concerning Gifts" (305-19), *De Successionibus* "Concerning Inheritances" (320-36). The first two laws belong to a section dealing with boundaries of which the rest is lost.

Lacking the opening of the text in the manuscript, there are no explicit indications of the origin, date, or purpose of this code, but as several of the laws relate to legal relations between Romans and Goths, it must be put into a Visigothic or Ostrogothic context. That this is almost certainly a Visigothic one is indicated by the fact that some of the laws found here later reappear in the *Liber Iudiciorum* issued by Reccesuinth in 654.

---

[19] Jill Harries, *Sidonius Apollinaris and the Fall of Rome* (Oxford, 1994), pp. 1-19.
[20] E. A. Lowe, *Codices Latini Antiquiores*, vol. 5, no. 626 (Oxford, 1950), p. 31.
[21] Ibid. p. 624: a 7th/8th century cursive copy of Jerome-Gennadius, *De Viris Illustribus*.

This still leaves the question of which Visigothic king may have been responsible for it. The only internal evidence with a bearing on this question is the instruction in law 277 that old boundaries are to be retained "just as our father of good memory ordered in another law."[22] Thus, this legislator's father had also issued laws. This information fits Sidonius's possible evidence that Theoderic I had done so. His sons Theoderic II or Euric would therefore be the possible authors of this law 277.

In favor of Theoderic II may be another remark by Sidonius Apollinaris in a poem, in which he speaks of the king giving laws "to the Getae," an archaizing term for the Goths.[23] Again, too much may be read into a purely rhetorical phrase. Of greater weight may be a statement by Isidore of Seville, describing the reign of Euric in his *Historia Gothorum*, in which he says "under this king the Goths began to have ordinances of the laws in writing, for before this they were bound by customs and habit."[24] This is generally taken to mean that Euric was the first of the Visigothic kings to issue laws in writing in the Roman fashion, which would imply that his predecessor could not be the author of the "Code of Euric."

Caution is required in interpreting Isidore's remark, as he was writing a century and a half later, and would have known Euric's law-making activities only through traditions current in the early seventh century. He is not a first-hand witness to more than the fact that the Visigoths in his own day looked back to Euric as the first of their kings to issue written laws. His claim would also seem to undermine the view that Theoderic I had issued laws. So, if Isidore is thought to be authoritative, then Sidonius's references to law-making on the part of either or both of the two Theoderics are being misinterpreted. If, on the other hand, Sidonius is to be preferred, then Isidore was wrong.

Similarly, the logic of Isidore's remark would involve accepting that the text contained in the Paris manuscript, and normally called the Code of Euric, could not have been produced by that king, as the author of law 277 refers to a previous law of his father. If Euric was indeed the very first Visigothic king to issue legislation, then he would

---

[22] Zeumer, *Codicis Euriciani Fragmenta*, 277, in *Leges Visigothorum*, p. 5.
[23] Sidonius, *Carmina* V, line 562, ed. Anderson, p. 108.
[24] *Historia Gothorum* 35, ed. C. Rodríguez Alonso, *Las Historias de los Godos, Vándalos y Suevos de Isidoro de Sevilla* (León, 1975), pp. 228-9.

have to be the person indicated, and law 277 would then be the work of his son Alaric II. It should also be noted that Isidore merely refers to the first making of written law, and is not claiming that Euric had such laws codified.

Some scholars have therefore argued that the compiling of the laws contained in this manuscript was actually carried out in the time of Euric's son Alaric II (484-507).[25] This would make the earliest stages of law-making among the Visigoths very similar to those of the Burgundians. The code known as *Lex Burgundionum* or the *Liber Constitutionum* was long thought to be by king Gundobad (473-516), but it is now generally recognized that while most of the individual laws may date from his time, the collecting and codifying of them was carried out in the second year of the reign of his son Sigismund (516-23).[26]

The questions concerning the origins, authorship, nature, and applicability of the text known as the Code of Euric are not going to be solved to everyone's satisfaction, and the evidence is insufficient to provide the answers required. That fifth-century Visigothic kings issued laws that were Roman in character and content seems certain, though when and why they were first codified is not. By the time of Leovigild and Isidore, this process was regarded as having been started by Euric.

If the date, origins, and purpose of the so-called the Code of Euric remain controversial, there are fewer problems with the next Visigothic code. This is the abridged compilation of Roman law and jurisprudence put together in the Gothic kingdom of Toulouse and now known as the *Breviarium* or "Breviary of Alaric." Its dating is uncontroversial, in that the work itself, which survives in numerous manuscripts, records that it was published at an assembly of nobles and clerics meeting in Toulouse on February 2, 506, by the authority of king Alaric II and under the direction of a Count Goiaric.[27]

Copies must have been issued to royal officials throughout the kingdom in the aftermath of its promulgation, as all but one of the manuscripts of it derive from examples sent by the king to a count

---

[25] H. Nehlson, *Sklavenrecht zwischen Antike und Mitttelalter* (Göttingen, 1972), pp. 153-5.
[26] Collins, "Law and Ethnic Identity," p. 8.
[27] T. Mommsen and P. M. Meyer (eds.), *Theodosiani Libri XVI cum Constitutionibus Sirmondianis*, vol. 1 pt. 1 (Zurich, 1905), pp. xxxiii-xxxiv.

Timotheus, while the exception descends from one sent to a count Nepotian.[28] The primary contents of the Breviary consist of an abbreviated version of the Theodosian Code, together with a selection of imperial *Novellae* or "New Laws" issued by the emperors in the fifth century. To most of these *interpretationes* have been added. These were codicils that were intended to clarify the meaning of the original law or to adapt its application to contemporary circumstances.

Adding such "interpretations" to imperial laws had long been a privilege and responsibility enjoyed by Praetorian Prefects. So, constitutionally this hardly marked a break with Roman legal tradition or infringed an imperial monopoly on the making of new law. The *interpretationes* themselves were largely taken from the writings of earlier Roman jurists, and in any case may have been attached to the laws at an earlier date and prior to their incorporation into the Breviary.[29] Alaric's code ended with abridgments of some classic Roman jurisprudential texts, including the *Institutes* of Gaius and the *Sententiae* attributed to Julius Paulus, and with much shortened versions of two late third-century privately made collections of earlier imperial laws.[30] The general purpose of this compilation would seem to have been to prune and simplify the existing body of Roman law and some of the texts currently used to interpret it.

That it was seen as more than just a convenient abridgment of the Theodosian Code is clear from the text of the law of king Theudis (531-48), discussed in an earlier chapter. This was "to be added to the fourth book of the Theodosian corpus under title sixteen."[31] As it has survived uniquely in the León palimpsest of the Breviary, the only Spanish manuscript to contain that work, the implication would seem to be that Theudis regarded what we call the *Breviarium* or the *Lex Romana Visigothorum* as the authoritative text of the Theodosian Code. In other words, this was the official version of that code for the Visigothic kingdom. The applicability of the law it contained depends, as with the Code of Euric, on the view taken of the

---

[28] J. Martindale (ed.), *Prosopography of the Later Roman Empire*, vol. 2 (Cambridge, 1980): Timotheus 4, p. 1121.
[29] W. W. Buckland, *A Text-Book of Roman Law from Augustus to Justinian* (3rd edn., Cambridge, 1963), p. 36.
[30] J. Baviera (ed.), *Fontes Iuris Romani Antejustiniani*, pt. ii (Florence, 1968), pp. 321-417, 669-75.
[31] *Leges Visigothorum*, ed. Zeumer, p. 469.

arguments over the personal or the territorial character of these early Visigothic codes.

Isidore of Seville is the only witness to the next legal reform by a Visigothic king. He says of Leovigild in the *History of the Goths* that "in the laws too he corrected those things which had been set up inadequately by Euric, adding very many laws that had been omitted and removing some superfluous ones."[32] This has been taken to mean that Leovigild carried out a major revision of Euric's laws, and that the result was a new "Code of Leovigild."[33] If so, this has not survived independently. However, a revised version of it may have been subsequently absorbed into the *Liber Iudiciorum* of Reccesuinth. The only attempt made to try to reconstruct Leovigild's lost code has had to be abandoned, as there is no real way of deconstructing the Reccesuinthian version so as to recover the original form of the text.[34]

The lack of Spanish manuscripts of Euric's code and of the Breviary, other than for a fragment of the latter, and the complete loss of Leovigild's code, all result from the replacement of these once authoritative sources of law by the *Liber Iudiciorum* in 654.[35] This rendered all such earlier texts obsolete and outlawed their use. Not surprisingly, copies of them were then destroyed or written over. The Code of Euric survived only partially and by chance, though it did influence the later law code of the Bavarians. The Breviary continued as the main source of Roman law in Francia, and has thus been preserved complete and in several good manuscripts.[36]

It is with Reccesuinth's *Liber Iudiciorum* that the legal history of the Visigothic kingdom in Spain really takes on its distinctive character, because of the survival of so many complete manuscripts. The history of its formation and revision and reissue has long seemed relatively uncomplicated. The key stages were worked out in a series

---

[32] Isidore, *Historia Gothorum* 51, trans. Guido Donini and Gordon B. Ford jr., *Isidore of Seville's History of the Goths, Vandals, and Suevi* (Leiden, 1970), p. 24. This statement appears in both versions of the *Historia*: ed. Rodríguez Alonso, p. 258.
[33] Pérez-Prendes, "Historia de legislación," pp. 59-60.
[34] Rafael Gibert, *Código de Leovigildo I-V* (Granada, 1968).
[35] There is a transcribed facsimile of the León MS of the Breviary in *Legis Romanae Wisigothorum Fragmenta ex Codice Palimpsesto Sanctae Legionensis Ecclesiae* (Madrid, 1896); see also Lowe, *CLA* vol. XI, no. 1637, p. 17.
[36] Ian Wood, "The Code in Merovingian Gaul," in Jill Harries and Ian Wood (eds.), *The Theodosian Code* (London, 1993), pp. 161-77. For surviving early MSS see the index to the supplementary volume of *CLA*.

of lengthy articles by Karl Zeumer (1849-1914), the German scholar also responsible for establishing the regnal chronology of the kingdom, preceding the publication of his edition of the Visigothic codes.[37] His views on the formation and history of *Liber Iudiciorum* survived almost unchallenged for a century or more, with only minor modifications to them being suggested.

From comparing the contents of the manuscripts Zeumer deduced that they fell into three different classes. The first he thought represented the original form of the code as promulgated by Reccesuinth in 654. The second class he regarded as containing a revised and expanded version, issued by king Ervig in 681. The third and largest class, which he called the *Vulgata* or "Common," was not linked to any specific royal initiative, but was distinguished by the presence of various additional items not contained in the other two versions, such as a handful of laws of Egica (687-702/3) and Wittiza (693/4-710). These he saw as having been added in a piecemeal way and as the result of private initiative. So while of interest for these few extra texts, this class of manuscripts did not represent an official version, and was therefore less worthy of study than the other two.

Zeumer did not attempt to establish the textual tradition of the manuscripts, and classified them purely according to their contents, without detailed comparisons and the creating of a stemma. So his classification is not confirmed by proven relationships between the manuscripts thought to belong to each class. Furthermore, his interpretation of the "V" or *Vulgata* group meant that he gave it little attention compared to the other two.[38] As his intention, following the editorial practices of the time, was to create a text that was as close as possible to the first version of the work, he concentrated on the manuscripts of the first two classes: the "R" or "Reccesuinthian," and "E," the Ervigian. In 1895 he published an edition just of the "R" version, and followed this in 1902 by a larger one in which both "official" forms were edited in parallel.

While his views were generally accepted, some criticism focused on the failure to identify a version that correspond to the one Egica

---

[37] Karl Zeumer, "Geschichte der westgothischen Gesetzgebung," *Neues Archiv* 23 (1898), pp. 419-516, 24 (1899), pp. 39-122 and 571-630, 26 (1901), pp. 91-149.
[38] Yolande García López, *Estudios críticos de la "Lex Wisigothorum"* (Alcalá de Henares, 1996), pp. 14-17.

was known to have issued in the fifth year of his reign (691/2), and it was suggested this might be what the "V" class really represented.[39] Views on this issue continue to be mixed. It seems surprising, if this were the case, that this new version would contain only three laws of the king held responsible for it, one of which is explicitly dated to the sixteenth year of his reign (702/3). This argument also ignores the great variety in text and content between the manuscripts of the "V" class, which is inconsistent with it being an authorized version.[40]

The only other significant modification that has been proposed to Zeumer's interpretation of the history of the code relates to the first stage of its compilation. Reccesuinth's version contains 88 laws in his name, but an even higher number, 99, in that of Chindasuinth (642-53). This has led to the argument that Reccesuinth incorporated into his own code an earlier one formed by his father. It is allowed that this hypothetical "Code of Chindasuinth" may have never been completed or officially promulgated, but the argument that it contributed to the larger code that was actually issued in 654 has attracted support.[41]

In addition to laws of Chindasuinth and Reccesuinth, the *Liber Iudiciorum* also included 315 other laws lacking royal attribution, but which are headed *Antiqua* or "Old." These have been accepted as deriving from the otherwise lost "Code of Leovigild," and include revised texts of items that can also be found in the "Code of Euric." So they may be royal laws of the period from the reign of Euric to that of Leovigild, which the latter incorporated into his code. But just as Leovigild was said by Isidore to have corrected the laws received from Euric, and as Ervig revised those of Reccesuinth, it is likely that the *Antiquae* in the *Liber Iudiciorum* had been subjected to a similar editorial process. A letter of bishop Braulio of Zaragoza to king Reccesuinth may even refer to this.[42]

---

[39] R. de Ureña y Smenjaud, *La legislación gótico-hispana* (Madrid, 1905), pp. 203-5.
[40] García López, *Estudios críticos*, p. 16; Pérez-Prendes, "Historia de la legislación," p. 64.
[41] King, "King Chindasvind and the First Territorial Law-code," especially pp. 142-57.
[42] Braulio, *Ep*. 38, ed. Luís Riesco Terrero, *Epistolario de San Braulio* (Seville, 1975), p. 150. The suggestion of a relationship between letter and code was made in Charles H. Lynch, *Saint Braulio, Bishop of Saragossa (631-651): His Life and Writings* (Washington, DC, 1938), pp. 135-40. It should be noted that Braulio died in 651 and the code was not promulgated until 654.

From the end of Leovigild's reign in 586 to the beginning of that of Chindasuinth in 642, the evidence for royal law-making is surprisingly slight. In the code issued by Reccesuinth in 654 laws of only two kings from this period appear: three of Reccared (586-601) and two of Sisebut (611/12-20). Their presence may mean that the term *Antiqua* was only applied to laws earlier than the reign of Reccared.[43] But why the legal compilers of Reccesuinth's time were apparently so much more interested in the laws of the fifth- and sixth-century kings than those of the immediately preceding half-century has never been adequately addressed.

This problem raises another. There seems to be no disagreement that Reccesuinth promulgated *Liber Iudiciorum* in 654, soon after his father's death.[44] The latter's presumed laws are indicated by the presence of his name in the margin next to them in the manuscripts. So those laws with the name of Reccesuinth similarly attached to them must have been issued after Chindasuinth's death. But there are 88 of them, out of a total of about 500 contained in the whole code in its first version.[45] So we are required to believe that nearly a fifth of the laws in *Liber Iudiciorum* were drawn up and issued in the few months before its official promulgation in 654. This can be contrasted with 99 laws of Chindasuinth from the 11-year period of his reign.

Even stranger must be the fact that Ervig's version of 681 contains no laws of Reccesuinth not already to be found in the original code of 654. Several of the latter's laws have been revised, but there is nothing in Ervig's code that represents legislation issued by Reccesuinth after 654. It strains credibility that Reccesuinth should have rushed out the prodigious quantity of 88 laws in the first few months of his sole reign, and then entirely given up legislating for the next 18 years. In fact there is evidence that he did indeed issue laws after 654, in that at least two of his that were not included in the first issue of *Liber Iudiciorum* appear in some of the manuscripts of the *Vulgata* class.

Moving on to Ervig's version does not raise the level of credibility. He ascended the throne in October of 680, and by the time that the Twelfth Council of Toledo assembled in early January 681 had a

---

[43] García López, *Estudios críticos*, p. 10
[44] Ureña, *Legislación gotico-hispana*, pp. 458-61.
[45] King, "King Chindasvind and the First Territorial Law-book," p. 142.

collection of 28 new laws ready to put before them, all of which dealt with the status and treatment of the Jews. That these were prepared for him by bishop Julian of Toledo, to whom this was a subject of almost fanatical interest, is highly probable. When his revised version of *Liber Iudiciorum* was ready to be promulgated in November 681, Ervig only had another six new laws to add to the 28 on the Jews, and together these 34 rulings constitute his only original contribution to the code. No trace can be found of any laws that he might have made after 681, other than for the one confirming the acts of the Thirteenth Council of Toledo of 683. That the latter is included in one of the only two complete manuscripts of the "E" version indicates that this does not represent a wholly pure and uncontaminated version of the code promulgated in 681.

Eighty laws of Reccesuinth were revised for inclusion in Ervig's version of the code, which also includes three laws of Wamba (672-80). Almost uniquely, these three are preserved in full, with their dates and place of issue. The only other exception is a law of Egica (687-702), the king who issued a further revision of *Liber Iudiciorum* in the fifth year of his reign, thus before late November 692.[46] That this version should have vanished without trace seems improbable, and, despite the arguments to the contrary, it may indeed be represented by some of the manuscripts of the *Vulgata* class, even though that means that it may not have contained more than two new laws of the king promulgating it.

The strongest reason for saying this is the dating of the three known versions of the code: 654, 681, and 692. Each of these coincided exactly with a period of crisis for the monarchy, in which conspiracies and revolts had been detected and crushed or (in 681) soon after a palace coup had been carried out. On each of these occasions there had been criticism of royal policies and fiscal practices, which had been openly aired in councils held in Toledo.[47] The political contexts for each of these acts of codification have been reviewed in detail in earlier chapters. Examination of the versions of the codes themselves only adds to the clear sense that their purpose was primarily symbolic and political.

---

[46] The *Chronica Regum Visigothorum* states that Egica was anointed king on VIII of the Kalends of December in era 725: November 24, AD 687, ed. Zeumer, p. 461.
[47] See above pp. 86, 96, 112.

As has been seen, in each case the bulk of the legislation included was ancient, deriving from the late fifth century. Roughly three fifths of Reccesuinth's version and half of Ervig and Egica's were laws thought to date back to the time of Euric. If some of them had indeed been revised by Leovigild, no mention was made of this. They were *Antiquae*, ancient laws of the people. The rest of the contents of the code consist of an extraordinarily ill-assorted mixture. There is virtually no legislation dating from between 586 and 642, but this is followed by large clutches of laws made by Chindasuinth in the 640s(?), and by Reccesuinth, but in his case only before the end of 654. Then there are just three laws from the 670s, a handful of new ones issued in 681, almost entirely to do with the Jews, but possibly nothing more from the 680s Finally there comes a tiny smattering of laws issued at various points between circa 692 and 710.[48] Taken as whole or in the parts represented by the three versions, this hardly looks like a coherent program of the codification of existing royal law.

One of the problems with the seeming wealth of Visigothic legislation from the seventh century, and the apparent sophistication and practicality of the codes in which it is to be found, is that these features obscure the greater weight of what we do not know. In the case of Frankish law, as well as possibly symbolic codes of supposedly ancestral "tribal" law, such as *Lex Salica*, there have survived a large quantity of what are called capitularies.[49] These are the records of legal decisions and legislative acts made at royal assemblies, at which the Frankish kings and their lay and ecclesiastical magnates debated a wide range of current issues. There are no Spanish equivalents.

In consequence we lack any evidence of the initial stages of lawmaking, although it is known from *Liber Iudiciorum* that this was done at the king's court. There are the three dated laws of Wamba and one of Egica already referred to, which have been incorporated into the code in fuller textual form than is the case with the others.[50] It is possible to say that Wamba issued two laws on December 23, 675, one dealing with the conduct of bishops and the other about

---

[48] The laws of Egica and Wittiza should now be consulted in the critical edition, with commentary, of García López, *Estudios críticos*, pp. 209-590.

[49] F. L. Ganshof, *Recherches sur les capitulaires* (Paris, 1958) remains the classic account.

[50] Wamba: IV, v. 6 and 7, IX. ii. 8; Egica: IX. i. 21: given at Córdoba in the 16th year of his reign. This began on November 24, 702, and must have been soon before his death.

freed slaves formerly belonging to the church, as well as issuing another one on the army on November 1, 673. Although a very small sample, this looks like the kind of pattern one would expect, with laws being made individually or in small numbers on a wide variety of dates and occasions throughout a king's reign. It would be odd in the extreme to believe that these were the only laws that this king issued. The presence of an extract from another otherwise unrecorded law of Wamba, uniquely preserved in two manuscripts of the *Vulgata* class, would prove this not to be so.[51]

Therefore there were once many more royal laws of the Visigothic kings that were never included in any of the codes or in individual manuscripts containing them. It might be suggested that only those of particular importance were collected and codified, but if so it is hard to believe that Reccesuinth did all his best law-making in 654 and then never produced another useful one for the remaining 18 years of his reign.

It is also notable that no version of *Liber Iudiciorum* gives any indication of how it was to be disseminated. Unlike the Breviary of Alaric, none of the extant manuscripts can be shown to have descended from copies sent to royal officers. Like Roman imperial legislation, the onus seems to have been left entirely upon those who needed to know the current state of the law to try to inform themselves of it. This might apply to both judges and those who appeared in their courts as advocates for parties to a dispute. No attempt seems to have been made to indicate that the version of the code issued by Ervig in 681 had in any way superseded that of Reccesuinth of 654. Surprisingly, the two versions survive in the same number of manuscripts and fragments: a mere four in both cases, to be compared with more than 20 of the *Vulgata*.

The only concession that may have been made to facilitate the distribution of the code was the law setting a maximum price to be charged or paid for a copy of it. This was six *solidi* in the Reccesuinthan version, but had risen to 12 in that of Ervig.[52] Extraordinarily, a penalty of 100 lashes was set not only for anyone trying to

---

[51] VI. v. 21, found now in only MS Madrid, Univ. Compl. 89 of 13th/14th-century date. Its presence was also recorded in a lost manuscript of uncertain date from San Juan de los Reyes in Toledo.

[52] V. iv. 22.

demand more than than this price, but also for anyone misguided enough to pay more for a copy. The kind of private enterprise that was required for obtaining one may have resulted in the proliferation of copies containing additional and later laws, represented by the unstandardized *Vulgata* class of manuscripts. These latter have been the focus of recent study, which has also drawn attention to the importance of the geographical distribution of the codices of this class in the centuries after the Arab conquest.[53]

It must now be clear that Zeumer's century-old synthesis is in need of revision, and that the principles underlying his edition, good as it still is in many ways, are not as sound as often assumed, especially in the light of his relative neglect of the *Vulgata* manuscripts. Among other features that need to be taken into account are the differences between manuscripts in the assigning of individual laws to kings, and greater weight needs to be given to textual variants. As the *Liber Iudiciorum* continued in use for centuries without formal revision or expansion after the Visigothic period, subtle but significant changes to its contents might have been effected by alterations in wording.[54] Of the extant manuscripts, only one could date from before the Arab conquest, and even that may have been written in Francia. The majority of the rest come from the later ninth to eleventh centuries. Grounds for confidence that the "R" and "E" classes represent uncontaminated texts of Reccesuinth and Ervig's versions of the code are also less strong than seemed the case in the late nineteenth century. Reexamination of these and other related issues will lead to better understanding of the strengths and weaknesses of the evidence for the understanding of the law of the Visigothic kingdom.

Gothia and Hispania

The Arab conquest of Spain in 711/12 put an end to what in many respects had been a largely successful military and political unification of the Iberian peninsula on the part of the Visigothic monarchy in the late sixth and seventh centuries. Never again, with the exception of

---

[53] García López, *Estudios críticos*, pp. 41-205.
[54] These questions are currently being investigated by Dr. Jérome-Emanuel Bepoix of the University of Nice.

the years from 1580 to 1640, would all of the peninsula be under the rule of a single authority. However, the events of the conquest could only complicate but not reverse the emergence of a new sense of common ethnic identity among the upper classes, which seems to have been taking place in the later Visigothic period.

As also in Francia in the sixth to eighth centuries, the achievement of stable monarchical rule within more or less fixed territorial boundaries seems to have initiated a process of reformation of ethnic identity.[55] This has probably been more clearly understood in the case of the Frankish kingdoms than in that of Spain. The problem is partly one of mistaken assumptions as to the nature of the change and the degree of resistance that it might have faced, but it is also related to the fact that the process was derailed by the Arab conquest and by the fragmentation of political unity in the peninsula that then ensued. Simply put, while Roman Gaul turned into *Francia*, the territory ruled by the kings of the Franks, *Hispania* never became *Gothia*. The reasons for this are less obvious than often assumed.

One tradition of interpretation of the internal development of the Visigothic kingdom in Spain between 589 and 711 has been concerned almost exclusively with the dichotomy between Roman and German.[56] This approach to the period that emphasizes contrasts and conflicts between two sections of the population has been challenged, but is not entirely superseded.[57] In part it reflects a mistaken assumption of the existence of inevitable cultural friction between Romans and Germans in a kingdom in which the latter were a numerical minority but exercising political and military predominance. By this way of thinking, a supposed decline in the intellectual and disciplinary standards of the episcopate in this period is directly paralleled and occasioned by a rise in the number of bishops of Visigothic origin.[58] Similarly, influential interpretations of both the legal history and the archaeological evidence of the Visigothic period, which have

---

[55] Suzanne Teillet, *Des Goths à la nation gothique* (Paris, 1984), pp. 503-36 and 637-44; Peter Heather, *The Goths* (Oxford, 1996), pp. 276-98.

[56] E. A. Thompson, *The Goths in Spain* (Oxford, 1969) is the best example of this tradition in English historiography.

[57] R. Collins, "Mérida and Toledo, 550-585," in Edward James (ed.), *Visigothic Spain: New Approaches* (Oxford, 1980), pp. 189-219.

[58] Thompson, *Goths in Spain*, pp. 289-96; José Orlandis, "El elemento germánico en la iglesia española del siglo VII," *Anuario de Estudios Medievales* 3 (1966), pp. 27-64.

been critically examined in previous chapters, have depended upon the supposed antagonism of Roman and German elements in both population and culture.

That the latter constituted the numerical minority would seem clear, even accepting older arguments that suggested a population size of around 100,000 for the Goths who entered the peninsula in the middle of the fifth century. However, recent views on the formation of the barbarian or Germanic confederacies would see this as far too large a number, and the reappraisal of the evidence of the Spanish cemeteries given in chapter 7 above removes any need to believe in the existence of large settlements of unassimilated Goths in the sixth or seventh centuries. What the actual size of the Gothic population may have been is impossible to estimate with any confidence. A figure of around 20,000 would at best be a guess, but is probably much more realistic than the older one of five times that number. This has to be seen in the context of a Hispano-Roman population whose numbers are equally difficult to estimate, but which almost certainly exceeded a million.[59]

In general, what has been evoked as evidence of decadence, division, and inter-ethnic conflict within this society is far from unequivocal.[60] The ultimate fate of the Visigothic kingdom played a part in making historians in the twentieth century, both in Spain and elsewhere, look for deeper structural causes to explain its swift and dramatic overthrow, even after the search for such explanations fell from favor in the study of other societies that were equally quickly and decisively defeated by the Arabs.[61]

There are no good reasons to deny the possibility of the development of a common Gothic ethnic identity in later seventh-century Spain. To some extent there was hardly any alternative. There was no

---

[59] A. E. R. Boak, *Manpower Shortage and the Fall of the Roman Empire in the West* (Ann Arbor, MI, 1955), pp. 5-6 discusses some of the rival theories for the total size of the population of the Roman empire.

[60] For the idea of decadence see Luís A. García Moreno, *El fin del Reino Visigodo de Toledo. Decadencia y catastrofe* (Madrid, 1975); P. D. King, *Law and Society in the Visigothic Kingdom* (Cambridge, 1972), pp. 1-51, and for an extreme example: R. D. Shaw, "The Fall of the Visigothic Power in Spain," *English Historical Review* 21 (1906), pp. 209-28.

[61] Walter E. Kaegi, *Byzantium and the Early Islamic Conquests* (Cambridge, 1992); George Huxley, *Why did the Byzantine Empire not fall to the Arabs?* (Athens, 1986).

need for a separate Roman identity to be preserved once the major religious differences between the indigenous population and the Gothic minority had been resolved in the late sixth century. Indeed, it must be asked to what extent there could be such a thing as a Roman ethnic identity by that time. To be a Roman was to have the full legal rights of a citizen. This had mattered particularly in the early imperial period in which there had been different grades of citizenship, with that of *civis Romanus* conferring the fullest rights.[62] But the extension of full citizenship to all free inhabitants of the Empire by Caracalla in 212 AD did not thereby transform a distinction in terms of legal status into one of ethnicity. It is interesting to see how, in the aftermath of the disappearance of the Roman empire in the West, in some regions a Roman ethnic identity had to be deliberately fostered, and just as origin stories were developed for the Germanic peoples, so too were some classical historical texts recast as the *origines gentis Romanorum*.[63] In Spain the process went the other way, and the abrogation of the authority all previously functioning codes of law in by Reccesuinth's *Liber Iudiciorum* in 654 must have marked the end of any form of distinct Roman citizenship in the Visigothic kingdom, if it still existed.

What could have been a major barrier to integration, separate languages, never even seems to have existed in Spain. Had the Gothic language survived in use, it is hard to see how a large-scale absorption of the Hispano-Roman upper classes into a new sense of identity could have occurred. However, there is no evidence for the use of Gothic in Spain in the sixth and seventh centuries.[64]

Overall, in the way that the Gallo-Romans north of the Loire and in the Rhineland gradually came to think of themselves as Franks, so did

---

[62] Peter Garnsey, *Social Status and Legal Privilege* (Oxford, 1970); Thomas Wiedemann, *Adults and Children in the Roman Empire* (London, 1989), pp. 113–42. It is notable that the discussion of Roman citizenship was retained, if in reduced form, in the epitome of the *Institutes* of Gaius incorporated into the Breviary of Alaric: J. Baviera (ed.), *Fontes Iuris Romani Ante Justiniani*, pt. ii (Florence, 1968), *Gai Institutionum Epitome* I.1: "de statu hominum," pp. 232–3.

[63] A good example is that of Aquitaine: see M. Rouche, *L'Aquitaine des Wisigoths aux Arabes, 418–781: naissance d'une région* (Paris, 1979), especially pt. II, chs. 3 and 5.

[64] An attempt to justify the contrary position, that the Gothic language was indeed still in use in Spain under Visigothic rule, could only suggest two possible indicators of its survival, neither of which is at all convincing: H. Reichert in *Linguistica et Philologica. Gedenkschrift für Björn Collinder* (*Philologica Germanica* vol. 6) (Vienna, 1984).

the Hispano-Romans become Goths. That this had happened is clear both from the absence of reference in the later seventh-century sources to a separate Roman population, and the very clear indicators of extensive "Gothicization" of the indigenous population at all levels of society in the Visigothic period.[65] One simple indicator is the extraordinary prevalence of names of Gothic origin in the copious documentation of the centuries following the Arab conquest in both north and south.[66] This does not relate just to possible descendants of a small genetically Germanic pre-conquest population. The majority of Christians in Spain after 711 had names of Gothic origin, several of which, such as Alfonso, have survived to the present. While there were also numerous Basque names in use, and even Arab ones, as well as common Christian ones of primarily New Testament origin, there are hardly any classical Roman ones to be found among the populations in the north of the peninsula.[67] The few that do appear tend to be deliberately archaic, such as that of a count Scipio, and testifying to learned affectation.[68]

In the succeeding Asturian (718-910) and Leonese (910-1037) kingdoms in the north, there is only one context in which the word *Romanus* appears. In a number of documents of manumission from these centuries, the freed slave is invested with Roman citizenship, thus allowing him to own property, marry freely, and give legal testimony. In part this was antiquarian.[69] There are other similar features, such as anachronistic references to the *Lex Aquila*, in the notarial practices of this time, but it is also testimony to the fact that "Roman-ness" was seen, as under the empire, as a form of

---

[65] The last reference to *Romani* is to be found in a law of Ervig (680-7): *Liber Iudiciorum* IX. 2. 9, ed. Zeumer, *Leges Visigothorum*, pp. 374-9, where it appears be a rhetorical flourish to emphasize the comprehensive nature of this law on military obligations. All other mentions of *Romani* in the Visigothic codes are to be found in the *antiquae*, dating to before 586.

[66] Cf. Victoria Aguilar and Fernando R. Mediano, "Antroponomia de origen árabe en la documentación leonesa, siglos VIII-XIII," *El Reino de León en la alta Edad Media*, vol. 6 (1994), pp. 499-633, for texts and methodology.

[67] José J. Bautista Merino Urrutia, *La lengua vasca en La Rioja y Burgos* (2nd edn., Logroño, 1978), pp. 77-85.

[68] Count Scipio: *Chronicle of Alfonso III* xxiii (both versions), ed. Juan Gil in *Crónicas Asturianas* (Oviedo, 1985), pp. 142-3.

[69] e.g. MS Madrid, Archivo Histórico Nacional 986 B (Cartulario de Celanova), folios 60^v-61^r.

legal status and not as an ethnic determinant.[70] These texts also closely follow the text of documents of manumission of the Visigothic period. No practical examples of the latter survive, but a number of model forms are preserved in a collection of notarial formulae put together in the Asturian kingdom from a range of Visigothic examples, some at least of which came from Córdoba.[71] These again would seem to imply that "Roman citizenship" was regarded in the late Visigothic kingdom as a category of status, rather than as a form of ethnicity.

The ideology of a new Gothic political and ethnic identity in seventh-century Spain is articulated most clearly in some of the acts of the plenary ecclesiastical councils that were held in the kingdom between 589 and 711. The Fourth Council of Toledo of December 633, presided over by Isidore of Seville, referred to a single *gens et patria* ("people and homeland"), without any suggestion that there might be different *gentes* within the one *patria*.[72] The realm is further characterized in these decrees as being that of the Gothic people. The full phrase *gens et patria Gothorum* first appears in the acts of the important Seventh Council of Toledo of October 646, and may be found thereafter as the principal way of referring to the territory and the inhabitants of the Visigothic kingdom, both in the conciliar *acta* and in royal legislation of the later seventh century.[73] At the same time, the kings were entitled *rex Hispaniae atque Galliae*. The *patria Gothorum*, which they ruled, was thus geographically defined as *Hispania* and *Gallia*; the latter referring to the former Roman province of Septimania, which remained under Visigothic control when the rest of their kingdom in Gaul was conquered by the Franks

---

[70] For example, references in such documents to the *Lex Aquila*: see docs. I, VI, and VII in Juan Gil (ed.), *Miscellanea Wisigothica* (Seville, 1972), pp. 71, 77, and 79.

[71] *Formulae* in Gil, *Miscellanea*, pp. 70-112. These survive only in one 16th-century manuscript: Madrid Biblioteca Nacional MS 1346, copied by Ambrosio de Morales from a lost original that he found in Oviedo. Documents II to VI (pp. 72-77), each of which is a *cartula libertatis*, include reference to Roman citizenship in the grant of freedom.

[72] IV Toledo c. lxxv, ed. Gonzalo Martínez Díez and Felix Rodríguez, *La colección canónica Hispana*, vol. V (Madrid, 1992), pp. 248-53. The same canon also characterized unfaithfulness to their monarchs as an alien trait: *non sit in nobis sicut in quibusdam gentibus infidelitatis subtilitas* (ibid.).

[73] e.g. VII Toledo c. 1, ed. Martínez Díez and Rodríguez, vol. V, pp. 338-47 (3 appearances); XVI Toledo (of May 693), ed. José Vives, *Concilios visigóticos e hispano-romanos* (Barcelona, 1963), p. 487.

in 509.[74] This equation of the *Regnum Gothorum* with a clearly defined geographical area, primarily constituted by the old Roman *Hispania*, was an important ideological determinant for future centuries; all the more so as the *Liber Iudiciorum* and the *acta* of the ecclesiastical councils of the Visigothic kingdom continued to be authoritative under the succeeding Asturian and Leonese monarchies.[75]

There is no way, in the light of the very limited nature of the evidence surviving from late Visigothic Spain, to be certain just how far the process of the reforging of ethnic identity had reached in practice by the time of the Arab conquest of 711. Certainly, a comparable process within Francia had more than achieved critical momentum by this time, and, at the very least, it must be said that none of the evidence relating to the late seventh and early eighth centuries indicates the presence of a separate Roman population in Spain at this point. The anonymous author of the *Chronicle of 754*, writing in Toledo around that year, speaks only of Goths in his account of the conquest.[76] Likewise, in the late ninth or early tenth centuries an Asturian author referring to a Muslim of indigenous origin, in the person of Musa ibn Musa of the Banu Qasi, who died in 863, refers to him as *natione Gotus sed ritu Mamentiano*.[77] Whatever his religious and political affiliations as a subject (albeit rebellious) of the Umayyads and as a Muslim, he was regarded, at least by a Christian author in the north, as being a Goth by birth.

Although a move toward a new Gothic identity for the upper classes of Hispano-Roman/Visigothic society was clearly well under way by the late seventh century, there are no contemporary indications that this was leading toward a change in geographical nomenclature, of

---

[74] e.g. the formula *religiosissimus Sisenandus rex Spaniae atque Galliae* used in the acts of IV Toledo, ed. Martínez Díez and Rodríguez, vol. V, p. 179.

[75] IV Toledo canon lxxv, ed. Martínez Díez and Rodríguez, p. 252; V Toledo: the edict of Chintila, ed. Vives, p. 231; VI Toledo canon 12, ed. Vives, p. 241; VII Toledo canon 1, ed. Vives, pp. 250-1; *Liber Iudiciorum*, VI.i.2-3, VI.i.6-7 etc. For the continued application of the laws see Roger Collins, "Visigothic Law and Regional Custom in Disputes in Early Medieval Spain," in Wendy Davies and Paul Fouracre (eds.), *The Settlement of Dispute in Early Medieval Europe* (Cambridge, 1986), pp. 85-104 and 252-7.

[76] José Eduardo López Pereira (ed.), *Crónica mozárabe de 754* (Zaragoza, 1980), chapters 53-54, pp. 68-72.

[77] *Adefonsi Tertii Cronica - versio Rotensis* 25, ed. Gil, p. 144. On Musa and his family see A. Cañada Juste, "Los Banu Qasi (714-924)," *Príncipe de Viana*, vol. 158/9 (1980), pp. 5-90.

the kind that turned Gallia into Francia. The famous remark of king Ataulph (410-16), reported by Orosius, about the possibility of turning *Romania* into *Gothia* was not to be given geographical expression in the far more integrated society of the seventh-century Spanish kingdom.[78] *Hispania*, together with its small Gallic appendix across the eastern Pyrenees, remained the *patria* of the *gens Gothorum*.

This conservatism in geographical nomenclature is in part a testimony to the legacy of Isidore of Seville and the high regard that continued to be afforded some aspects at least of classical culture in Spain in the later Visigothic period.[79] Isidore popularized and through his *Etymologiae* maintained a somewhat archaic taste in literary style, which continued to make itself felt in Spanish Latin texts for centuries to come. The geographical book of the *Etymologiae* helped to make permanent the use of even anachronistic topographical terms.[80] It was no accident that it was under his presidency, and no doubt thanks to his drafting of the conciliar acts, that the Fourth Council of Toledo frequently employed the archaic political terminology of *Hispaniae*, "the Spains," thus referring back to the early Roman division of the peninsula into the two parts of *Citerior* and *Ulterior* ("Nearer" and "Further" Spain), rather than the simpler unitary term *Hispania*.[81] The name in both its single and plural forms continued not only to define the geographical area known as the Iberian peninsula, but also to influence conceptions of political authority within it. These become clearer once the political and cultural unity imposed on the peninsula was destroyed by the unforeseen consequences of the Arab and Berber invasion.

---

[78] Orosius, *Libri septem historiarum contra paganos* VII. 43, ed. Karl Zangemeister (Vienna, 1882), p. 560; see J. M. Wallace-Hadrill, "Gothia and Romania," *Bulletin of the John Rylands Library*, 44 (1961), reprinted in his *The Long-haired Kings* (London, 1962), pp. 25-48.

[79] Teillet, *Des Goths*, pp. 463-502; H. Messmer, *Hispania-Idee und Gotenmythos* (Zurich, 1960).

[80] Isidore, *Etymologiae* bk. XIV, ed. W. M. Lindsay (Oxford, 1911).

[81] IV Toledo canons v, vi, x, xii, xli; the single form, *(Hi)spania* is also used: canons ii, iii, v, viiii, xi, lxxv, ed. Martínez Díez and Rodríguez, vol. V, pp. 161-274.

Bibliographical Essay

A marvellous introduction to some of the most interesting topics and to the historiography of the Visigothic period can be found in the first three chapters of Peter Linehan's *History and the Historians of Medieval Spain* (Oxford, 1993). For bibliographical guidance to almost everything published on the subjects covered by this book up to the year 1984 recourse can be made to Alberto Ferreiro's splendidly comprehensive and well-organized *The Visigoths in Gaul and Spain* A.D. *418-711: A Bibliography* (Leiden, 1988), which contains well over 9,000 items. The year 1984 also saw the death of Claudio Sánchez-Albornoz (1893-1984), who, despite spending much of his later career in political exile in Argentina, was the unchallenged doyen of Spanish historians. His pupils and their pupils after them filled many of the leading posts in this field in Spanish universities, and he browbeat them with vitriolic replies if they were ever impudent enough to disagree with him; for how could the disciple know better than the master? A flavor of this can be found in his *Estudios polémicos* (Madrid, 1979).

His frequently republished articles are a bibliographer's nightmare, as they were constantly reprinted in ever-changing combinations. Virtually all of his books are now, at last, out of print, but several of his articles relating to Visigothic Spain can be found in collections such as his *Investigaciones y documentos sobre las instituciones hispanas* (Santiago, 1970). His successor, at least for the Visigothic period, is the Majorcan Jesuit José Orlandis, whose own voluminous writings include the autobiography *Años de Juventud en Opus Dei* (Madrid, 1993). Author of at least two general surveys, *Historia del reino visigodo español* (Madrid, 1988) and *Historia de España: la España Visigótica* (Madrid, 1977; reissued 1990), he has also produced *Semblanzas visigodas* (Madrid, 1992), which depicts 14 individuals from the period. A selection of social and economic themes are examined in *La vida en España en tiempo de los Godos* (Madrid, 1991).

The principal cooperative survey is that contained in the *Historia de España Menéndez-Pidal*, volume III (Madrid, 1991), edited by J. M. Jover Zamora, replacing the first edition whose main value now is to show what Visigothic studies were like in 1940. Written by the leading Spanish authorities of the 1980s, and very well illustrated, this new version in two volumes is sound and sensible rather than challenging. A much shorter survey from the same time is Luís García Moreno's *Historia de España Visigoda* (Madrid, 1989). His earlier *El Fin del Reino visigodo de Toledo* (Madrid, 1975) is a classic of the "decadence and catastrophe" school of interpretation of the late Visigothic kingdom. More practical is his *Prosopografía del reino visigodo de Toledo* (Salamanca, 1974). A prolific author of often lengthy articles, which have not yet been collected, he may be seen as Orlandis's heir as the main Spanish authority on this period, which now tends to be regarded in Spain more as a branch of ancient than of medieval history.

This denies the legacy of Sánchez-Albornoz, who happily wrote on periods extending from the Roman Republic to the twelfth century, if not later, and ignored most boundaries of specialization. Best known as a historian of institutions, he gave enormous impetus to the study of Visigothic and medieval Spanish law through his founding of the journal *Anuario de Historia del Derecho Español*, which first appeared in 1924 and still continues. Scholarly interest in the Visigothic law codes had existed in Spain since at least the publication by the Real Academia Española of *El Fuero Juzgo en latín y castellano cotejado con los más antiguos y preciosos códices* (Madrid, 1815), and manifested itself not least in the unjustly ignored *Historia de las instituciones sociales de la España goda* (four volumes, Valencia, 1896) of Eduardo Pérez Pujol. Renewed attention followed the publication of Karl Zeumer's studies and editions of the codes between 1895 and 1902. Not surprisingly, they were thenceforth seen in the light of contemporary German scholarship that emphasized their supposedly Germanic elements. One product of this was *El elemento germánico en el derecho español* (Madrid, 1915) by Eduardo de Hinojosa, who was also Sánchez-Albornoz's teacher.

While the codes, especially the *Liber Iudiciorum* or *Fuero Juzgo*, as its medieval vernacular version was known, have frequently been used as a source of evidence for the study of detailed aspects of the social and legal history of the Visigothic period, the question of their own nature and purposes was effectively not reopened after 1915. This has now changed, thanks not least to the publication of the ground breaking article "La *Lex Visigothorum* y sus manuscritos. Un ensayo de reinterpretación," by M. C. Díaz y Díaz, in *Anuario de Historia del Derecho Español* 46 (1976), pp. 163-224, which has been followed up and expanded on in Yolanda García López, *Estudios críticos de la "Lex Wisigothorum"* (Alcalá de Henares, 1995).

The archaeological study of the Visigothic period paralleled its legal history in owing a considerable debt to early twentieth-century German scholarship, and also in failing to break free of interpretative models that had become outmoded. Cemetery archaeology is the most obvious case in point, and this subject requires radical rethinking. At the opposite extreme, the classification and dating of the churches once confidently assigned to the Visigothic period has recently become highly controversial, thanks to challenging new interpretations. The bibliography relating to both of these areas will be found in the references to chapter 7 in this book. While primarily concerned with the relationship between architecture and liturgy, Cristina Godoy Fernández, *Arqueología y liturgia. Iglesias hispánicas (Siglos IV al VIII)* (Barcelona, 1995) provides a very useful survey of the churches assigned to these centuries and a comprehensive bibliography on them.

New areas of investigation have been opened up by the general improvement of techniques in medieval archaeology. While there is a great deal of local publication of results, which is not always easy to track, much of it appears in the journal *Archivo Español de Arqueología*, and a number of sites have been given full treatment in the monograph series *Excavaciones Arqueológicas en Espana*, both of which are published in Madrid. Another very valuable source of information on current work are the proceedings of the irregularly held *Congressos de Arqueología Medieval*. Even so, it is notable that in all of these so far published there are fewer contributions relating to the Visigothic period than to ones after the Arab conquest.

The editing of major historical and literary texts of Visigothic date has flourished in recent years. The highly expensive but excellent *Corpus Christianorum* series, published by Brepols in Turnhout in Belgium, now includes an edition of Isidore's Chronicle by José Carlos

Martín in volume CXII (2003), as well as ones of his *Sententiae* by Pierre Cazier in volume CXI (1998), and of his verses by J. M. Sánchez Martín in volume CXIIIA (2000). A project initiated in France in 1975, to publish a new edition of Isidore's *Etymologiae* in 20 volumes in the *Société des Éditions "Les Belles Lettres"* would now have to be described as limping, with no more than a quarter of them having appeared nearly 30 years later. The same series includes editions of Isidore's *De ortu et obitu patrum* by César Chaparro Gómez (1985), which is important not least for its evidence on the cult of Santiago, and of the first book of his *Differentiae* by Carmen Codoñer Merino (1992). Isidore's *De Viris Illustribus* should be read in Carmen Codoñer Merino, *El "De Viris Illustribus" de Isidoro de Sevilla* (Salamanca, 1964), and Ildefonsus's continuation in her *El "De Viris Illustribus" de Ildefonso de Toledo* (Salamanca, 1972). For Braulio's account of Isidore see José Carlos Martín (ed.), *La "Renotatio Librorum Domini Isidori" de Braulio de Zaragoza* (Logroño, 2002).

While most of the works of Julian of Toledo were published by J. N. Hillgarth in *Corpus Christianorum*, volume CXV (1976), a second part, being edited by Adolfo Robles Sierra and containing his *Antikeimenon*, shows no sign of ever appearing. Other important texts of this period in the *Corpus Christianorum* include the Chronicle of John of Biclarum, edited by Carmen Cardelle de Hartmann in volume CLXXIIIA (2001), and the *Vitas Patrum Emeretensium*, edited by A. Maya Sánchez in volume CXVI (1992); others are in preparation. The poetic works of Eugenius II are accessible in F. Vollmer's edition in *Monumenta Germaniae Historica, Auctores Antiquissimi*, volume XIV (1905), while Ildefonsus, other than his *De Viris Illustribus*, should be read in Vicente Blanco and Julio Campos (eds.), *San Ildefonso de Toledo* (Madrid, 1971), which is volume 320 of the *Biblioteca de Autores Cristianos* series. The companion volume 321, Julio Campos and Ismael Roca (eds.), *Reglas monásticas de la España visigoda* (1971) provides texts of the monastic regulations of Fructuosus of Braga, but the anonymous life of this indefatigable founder of monasteries needs to be consulted in the edition by M. C. Díaz y Díaz, *La Vida de San Fructuoso de Braga* (Braga, 1974), which includes a section lacking in previous versions. Finding this book may not be easy. Even rarer is the only modern edition of the works of Valerius of Bierzo, Ramón Fernández Pousa (ed.), *San Valerio,*

Obras (Madrid, 1942), which was published at a time when most parts of the world were otherwise engaged.

The Visigothic liturgy, of which only some sections date to this period, is contained in numerous manuscripts. The problems of dating and authorial attribution of the contents limit the use that has been made of this wonderful resource, full of evidence on the ideas and language of those who created it, if only they could be identified. For the contents of some of the manuscripts containing it see the nine volumes of *Monumenta Hispaniae Sacra* (Madrid and/or Barcelona, 1946–72), and the volumes of the *Serie Liturgica* published by the Instituto de Estudios Visigótico-Mozarabes de Toledo.

In better state is the *Hispana* canon-law collection, in which the acts of the Visigothic councils were included and transmitted to other parts of western Europe. Unfortunately the project to produce a critical edition that was initiated by Gonzalo Martínez Díez, *La Colección Canónica Hispana*, volume I (Madrid, 1966), seems to have come to an abrupt end with volume V in 1992, leaving the last seven Councils of Toledo still awaiting inclusion. For them recourse has to be made to José Vives (ed.), *Concilios visigóticos e hispano-romanos* (Barcelona and Madrid, 1963), which is based upon a much smaller number of manuscripts. For the history of the councils see José Orlandis and Domingo Ramos-Lissón, *Historia de los concilios de la España romana y visigoda* (Pamplona, 1986).

Outside interest in the history of Spain in the Visigothic period is long-standing but intermittent. The contribution made by the new critical editions of the law codes and other texts from the *Monumenta Germaniae Historica* was matched by the teaching that a number of leading Spanish scholars received in German universities at various points throughout the twentieth century. However, relatively few German historians devoted themselves to Hispanic subjects. An exception was Wilhelm Reinhart, who pioneered the modern study of Suevic history in his *Historia general del reino hispánico de los Suevos* (Madrid, 1952). On the ecclesiastical side, this has been matched by Knut Schäferdiek, *Die Kirche in den Reichen der Westgoten und Suewen bis zur Errichtung der westgotischen katholischen Staatskirche* (Berlin, 1967). The same could be said for more recent years of Dietrich Claude, author of *Adel, Kirche und Königtum im Westgotenreich* (Sigmaringen, 1971), as well as of several articles. On the other hand, the German archaeological Institute in Madrid has always played a significant role in promoting excavation and research in Spain in the Roman and Visigothic periods, and several distinguished contributions to these areas can be found in its journal *Madrider Mitteilungen*.

In the case of France, the discovery of the Visigothic period came later than in Germany, and was primarily the work of Jacques Fontaine. His thesis *Isidore de Séville et la culture classique dans l'Espagne wisigothique* (two volumes, Paris, 1959; second edition with new third volume, 1983) really put Isidore, who had long been neglected or even derided, onto the intellectual map of western Europe in the post-Roman centuries. This was followed by a critical edition of the *De Natura Rerum* in *Isidore de Séville, Traité de la Nature* (Bordeaux, 1960), and then by numerous contributions to conference proceedings and other collections of articles, and most recently by a general survey of Isidore's achievements in *Isidore de Séville. Genèse et originalité de la culture hispanique au temps des Wisigoths* (Turnhout, 2001). He also regularly contributed review articles on recent work on the period to the *Revue des Etudes Augustiniennes* or to the *Bulletin Hispanique*, thus continuing the tradition established by Baudouin de Gaiffier in his "*Hispana et Lusitana*" articles in *Analecta Bollandiana*. Although he also wrote an excellent and well-illustrated survey of the art and architecture of the period, Fontaine's interests have always been essentially literary, as have those of such disciples as Pierre Cazier, author of *Isidore de Séville et la naissance de l'Espagne catholique* (Paris, 1994), Suzanne Teillet, who wrote *Des Goths à la nation gothique* (Paris, 1984), and Marc Reydellet, editor of book IX of the *Etymologiae*. At the moment they have no successors, and although French archaeologists have made vital contributions to the emergence of the revitalized study of the Spanish Middle Ages, this has been entirely in the context of the period after 711.

In Britain, where Spanish history was scarcely to be found in the syllabus at any level for any period, the turning point came with the publication of E. A. Thompson's *The Goths in Spain* (Oxford, 1969), which carried forward work he had previously done on the Visigoths in earlier periods. Its interpretations of this society were imbued with his characteristic Marxism, but it was not a subject that seems to have really fired him, and the book is unusually dull for an author normally so spirited and lively. In later years his attention turned to the Sueves, on whose kingdom he left a small group of articles, usefully collected in his *Romans and Barbarians* (Madison, WI, 1982). A very different approach was taken by P. D. King, a pupil of Walter Ullmann, who subjected the seventh-century law codes to detailed examination in his *Law and Society in the Visigothic Kingdom* (Cambridge, 1972), which is full of useful analysis and insight, if generally rather too much in thrall to the then current view of the kingdom as "demoralised . . . and bent on self destruction" (p. 22). A perhaps overly optimistic counter to this tendency was offered in Roger Collins, *Early Medieval Spain, 400-1000* (London, 1986; second edition, 1995). More recently, Peter Heather has specialized in the earlier history of the Visigoths in such works as *Goths and Romans 332-489*, but has extended his scope to include the Spanish kingdom in his survey *The Goths* (Oxford, 1996).

In the USA the Visigothic period has not attracted as much interest as have some later ones in Spanish history. Jeremy du Quesnay Adams has been one of those most active, producing several articles, mostly on the councils. Some of these appeared in a useful but now defunct journal, *Classical Folia*, founded by Joseph Marrique. Alberto Ferreiro produced his monumental 1988 bibliography as his thesis, and since then has written several articles on Martin of Braga, among other topics. The most recent American contribution is that of Rachel L. Stocking, *Bishops, Councils, and Consensus in the Visigothic Kingdom, 589-633* (Ann Arbor, MI, 2000). Jocelyn Hillgarth has worked indefatigably in the UK, Boston, and then Canada on both Visigothic and later medieval Spanish history. As well as his edition of Julian of Toledo, he is noted for valuable articles on a range of topics, a good number of which will be found in his volume of collected studies *Byzantium, Visigothic Spain, and the Irish* (London, 1984).

Index

Abd al-Aziz ibn Marwan, *wali* of Egypt 127, 129
Abd al-Malik, Umayyad caliph 127
Abd al-Rahman II, Umayyad amir 214
Abu al-Mujahir, *wali* of *Ifriqiya* 126, 127
Abu Bakr, caliph 118
Achila, Visigothic king 131, 133, 137, 139-40, 212
Adrianople, battle of (378) 18, 23
Aemilian, St. 53, 165, 204
Aetius, *Magister Militum* 30, 31
Africa *see* North Africa
Agali: monastery 76, 153, 167, 168, 202
Agathias, Byzantine historian 48, 62
Agila, Visigothic king 46-7, 48, 52, 54, 62
Agilulf, Lombard king 74
Alamans, the 36
Alans, the 11-12, 13, 14, 15, 24, 25, 29
Alaric I, Visigothic king 18, 20, 22, 23, 26, 40, 42, 45, 87
Alaric II, Visigothic king 33-4, 41, 45, 225, 230, 238
Alava, modern province 183, 184, 185, 203
Alcalá de los Gazules 199
Alcazaba of Mérida, the 214
Alchadra 134
Alexandria, city 120, 121, 122, 128
Alfonso III, Asturian king 136, 187

Alfonso X, Castilian king 225
Algeria 125
Almohads, the 214
Amalaric, Visigothic king 41-2, 166
Amalasuntha, Ostrogothic queen 43
Ambrose of Milan, St. 158, 162
Ammianus Marcellinus, Roman historian 19-20
Amr 123
Anglo-Saxons, the 4, 164, 177, 182, 191, 207, 223
Annales School of French historians 4
Antiquae in the *Liber Iudiciorum* 234
Apollonia 122
Apringius of Beja, *Commentary on the Apocalypse* 170
Aquis: site of bishopric 100
Aquitaine 27, 183, 185
Aquitaine, duke of 141
Arab Conquest of Spain 2, 5, 37, 111, 113, 117, 133-43, 147, 151, 202, 204, 205, 216-17, 239, 241, 245, 246
Arabia 118
Arabs 117-30, 133
Aragón, kingdom 1, 2
archaeology of the Visigothic period 3-4, 7-8, 174-222, 240-1
architecture, Umayyad 192, 194, 195

INDEX

architecture, Visigothic 186-96, 206
Ardabast, father of Ervig 102
Ardo, Visigothic king 140
Argimund 69
Arianism 57-8, 61, 64-7, 68, 73, 115, 153, 157-9, 160, 161, 179
Arles, city 14
Asinoda (Medina Sidonia) 52
Aspendius, local ruler 54, 62
Astorga, city 31, 201
Asturian chronicles 76-7, 98-9, 102-3, 109, 135-6, 137, 138
Asturias, kingdom 1, 75, 76-7, 137, 189, 243, 244, 245
Asturius, bishop of Toledo 166
Ataulph, Visigothic king 18, 26, 34, 246
Athalaric, Ostrogothic king 43, 180
Athanagild, Visigothic king 44, 47, 48, 49, 50, 52, 54, 57, 59, 61
Athanagild, son of Hermenegild 59
Athanaric, Visigothic "judge" 18
Attila, Hun king 31
Augustine of Hippo, St. 156, 158, 162
Augustus, emperor 206, 218
Aurasius, bishop of Toledo 166-7
Austrasia, Frankish kingdom 59, 73
Auvergne, the 33,
Avars, the 118-19
Avitus, bishop of Vienne 159
Avitus, emperor 31, 35
Awraba, Berber confederacy 126
Azagra Codex, the 150, 198

Baddo, queen 67, 73
Baetica, province 29, 58, 80, 131, 154
Bagaudae 27-8, 31, 53, 55, 62
Balkans, the 22, 24, 50, 118
Balt dynasty 45, 87
Baltic Sea 24
Banu Qasi, the 245
Barcelona, city 14, 36, 41, 99, 206, 218

Barqa/Barce, city 122, 127
Basques 58, 75, 77, 84-5, 93, 94, 142, 183, 185
Bastitania 52
Bavarians: law code 232
Berbers, the 117, 124, 133, 134, 139, 140, 151, 152, 246; *see also* Awraba; Luwata
Biclarum, monastery 202; *see also* John of Biclarum
Bierzo, the 204; *see also* Valerius of Bierzo
Boniface, *Magister Militum* 30
Braga, city 51, 187, 218
Braulio, bishop of Zaragoza 53-4, 82-3, 163, 164, 165, 170, 234
Breviary of Alaric, the 225, 230, 238
Britain 13, 25, 26, 28
Brunechildis, Frankish queen 57, 74
Bulgar, count 75
Burdunellus 35, 36
Burgos, city 187
Burgundians, the 36, 230
Burgundy, kingdom 59, 66, 74
burials 201-2
Byzantine empire 102, 118, 119, 148, 152
   army 63, 73, 75, 109
   fleet 109, 122
   influence 58, 194
   in Italy 62, 152, 184
   in the Mediterranean 72, 109
   in North Africa 42, 84, 109, 122, 194
   in Spain 47-9, 51-2, 55, 74, 77, 195, 219-20

Cáceres, modern province 190, 200
Caesarius, bishop of Arles 160
Cantabria 53, 62, 75, 183, 184
capitularies 237
Caracalla, emperor 242
Carcassonne, city 68
Carolingians, Frankish dynasty 226

Cartagena (*Carthago Nova*), city 7, 32, 48, 74, 77, 134, 154, 162, 184, 218-21
Carthage, city 30, 59, 109, 123, 126, 128, 130, 195
Carthaginiensis, province 69, 99, 101, 154, 167
Castile, kingdom 1, 2, 211
Castinus, *Magister Militum* 29
Castro Pedroso 201
castros, reuse of 210-11
Catholicism 64-7, 154, 159-60
Celsus, count 83
Celtiberia 53
cemeteries 174-86
Ceuta, town 42, 45, 109, 129, 130, 134, 139, 194
Chalcedon, Council of 149
charters 197
Childebert I, Frankish king 46
Chilperic, Frankish king 74
Chindasuinth, Visigothic king 81, 82-3, 88, 102, 103, 112, 113, 114, 155, 165, 166, 167-8, 170, 171, 234, 235, 237
  possible law code 234, 237
Chintila, Visigothic king 80-1, 82
Chronica Regum Visigothorum 98, 105, 109, 111, 112
Chronicle of Albelda, the 135
Chronicle of 754, the 85, 97, 100, 109, 110, 111, 112, 132, 133, 137, 139, 142, 166, 197, 245
church, Catholic 147-61
citizenship, Roman 242
Cixilo, queen 109, 138
Claudius, *dux* 68
Claudius II, emperor 17
Clermont-Ferrand 227
Clovis, Frankish king 36, 37
Codex Euricanus see Euric, code of
Codex Theodosianus 225, 227, 231
coinage 71-2, 78, 82, 107, 131, 212
Como, Lake 184
Compludum, monastery 202

Constans II, emperor 122, 123
Constantine I, emperor 160
Constantine III, emperor 13, 14-15, 25
Constantinople, city 109, 110, 118-19, 120, 148, 149, 150
Constantius III, emperor 15, 27, 29
Consularia Caesaraugustana 33, 34, 51
Contra Varimadum, anonymous 157
Córdoba, city 46-7, 48-9, 58, 111, 134, 136, 195, 244
Corippus, Flavius, poet 148, 150
councils 71, 79, 156, 236; see also Lérida; Tarragona; Toledo
Crete 109
Ctesiphon, Sassanian capital 119
Cyprian, bishop of Carthage 156, 162
Cyprus 121-2
Cyrenaica 120, 121, 122, 123, 124, 125

Dagobert I, Frankish king 76, 78
Danube, river 17, 19, 20, 22, 24, 183
Desiderius, *dux* 69
dhimmis 124
Donatism 157
Donatus, abbot of *Servitanum* 153
Donatus, grammarian 156-7, 169
Dracontius, poet 155, 168

Eboric, Suevic king 60
Ebro, river 29, 31, 32, 35, 75, 78, 83, 93, 139, 142, 153, 203, 212
Ebronato, estate 201
Ecija (*Astigi*), city 162
Edicta, prefectural 227
Egica, Visigothic king 72, 105-7, 108, 111, 112, 114, 115, 133, 134, 137, 138, 157, 169, 171, 187, 233-4, 237
Egitania (Idanha a Velha), city 131
Egypt (*Misr*) 118, 120, 125

El Bovalar 211-12, 213
El Carpio de Tajo, cemetery 175-6, 181, 183
El Gatillo, church 200
Ercavica, Roman and Visigothic town 7, 162
Ermenberga, Visigothic princess 73, 74
Ervig, Visigothic king 97, 98-9, 102-3, 104, 105, 106, 107, 108, 112, 114, 115, 138, 233, 234, 235-6, 237, 238, 239
ethnogenesis 23
Eugenia, abbess 216
Eugenius I, bishop of Toledo 80, 166, 167, 198
Eugenius II, bishop of Toledo 88, 91, 99-100, 155-6, 166, 167-8, 169
Eulalia, St. 65
Euric, code of 226, 227, 228-30, 231-2, 234
Euric, Visigothic king 32-3, 225, 229-30
Eusebius of Caesarea 149
Eutropius, bishop of Valencia 82-3, 153

Facundus of Hermiane 151
Felix, bishop of Seville and Toledo 107, 110
Felix, *Magister Militum* 30
feudalism 4-5
Fidelis, bishop of Mérida 213, 214
"Florinda" or "La Cava," spurious daughter of "Count Julian" 129
Fraga: Villa Fortunatus 205
France 228
Francia 84
Francio 75, 184
Franco, Francisco 1, 3
Franks, the 40, 43, 142, 177, 221
  and Catholic church 158
  customs 180, 182
  defeats 46, 68-9

identity 240
kings 49, 59, 73-4, 78, 184, 237
law codes 223, 224, 237
raids 59-60
victories 12, 36-7, 38, 41-2, 183, 244-5
"Fredegar," chronicler 70-1, 74, 75, 81, 82, 93, 94, 105, 184
Froia, rebel 84-5
Fronimian, abbot of San Millán 165
Fructuosus, bishop of Braga 147, 170, 187, 202, 203, 204
Fulgentius, bishop of Ecija 154
Fulgentius of Ruspe 157-8, 159

Galicia, province 29, 32, 50, 55, 60, 61, 131, 187, 204
Galla Placidia, empress 26, 29
Gaul 12, 13, 14, 15, 18, 22, 25, 26, 28, 31, 34, 36-7, 38, 79, 92, 160, 244
Gennadius of Marseille 164
Germany 180-1
Gerona, city 41, 94, 131
Gerontius 14, 15, 25
Gerticos: royal villa 92, 93, 187, 207
Gesalic, Visigothic king 50, 55, 60, 61
Gibraltar 135
Goiaric, count 230
Gosuinth, Visigothic queen 50, 56-7, 68
Gothic identity 182-3, 240-6
Gothic language 242
grammarians 156-7
Gregory, bishop of Osma 165
Gregory, exarch of Africa 123-4
Gregory the Great, pope 51, 57, 65, 84, 100, 162, 165-6, 213
Gregory of Tours, Frankish historian 42, 46, 59-60, 69, 70, 93
Greuthungi, the 19, 22, 23
Guadalquivir, river 52, 55, 58
Gumild, bishop of Maguelonne 93
Gundemar, Visigothic king 74, 101

INDEX

Gunderic, bishop of Toledo 110, 111
Gundobad, Burgundian king 66, 230
Gunthamund, Vandal king 156
Guntramn, Frankish king 59

Hasan ibn al-Nu'man, *wali* of Ifriqiya 128, 129
Hasdings 11, 29; *see also* Vandals
Hejaz, the 118
Helladius, bishop of Toledo 76, 79, 167
Heraclius I, emperor 76, 119, 120, 123,
Hermenegild, Visigothic prince 56-9, 60, 62, 158, 159-60, 162
Hermigar, Suevic king 30, 215
Hisham, Umayyad caliph 192
Hispana, canon law collection 147, 156
Hispanidad 1, 3
Honorius, emperor 13, 15, 26, 29
Honorius I, pope 165
Hormisdas, pope 160
Hosius, bishop of Córdoba 160
Huns, the 11-12, 17-18, 22, 31
Hydatius, chronicler 14, 160, 215

Ibahernando: church 200
Ibba, Ostrogothic general 41
Ibn Abd al-Hakam, Egyptian historian 134, 135, 136
Ibn Khaldun, Berber historian 128
Ildebad, Ostrogothic king 43
Ildefonsus, bishop of Toledo 147, 152, 163, 165, 166-7, 168-9
Ilderic, bishop of Nîmes 93
Ingundis, Frankish princess 57
Ireland 164
Isidore of Seville 79, 80, 147, 162-5, 166
  chronicle 51, 61, 69-70, 73, 163-4
  church council decrees 79, 110

De Differentiis 163
De Natura Rerum 75
De Viris Illustribus 50, 154, 155, 162, 164-5
Etymologiae 75, 81, 164, 168
Hispana 110, 156
History of the Goths 42, 47-8, 69-70, 76, 77-8, 79, 163, 229, 232
"Isidoran Renaissance" 148, 161
Synonyma 163
Italy 5, 15, 18, 22, 26, 30, 32, 34, 38, 43, 49, 51, 62, 164
Iudila, king 72, 80

Jerome, St. 158, 162, 164, 168
Jews 76, 236, 237
Johannes, emperor 29-30
John, bishop of Zaragoza 165
John of Biclarum, chronicler 50-1, 52, 53, 54, 55-6, 60, 61, 64, 68, 69, 148, 150, 151-2, 153, 163
John, *Magister Militum* 151
Julian, bishop of Toledo 70, 71, 92, 93, 97-8, 99, 103, 105, 106, 108, 109, 110, 147, 151, 157, 168, 169-70
Justin II, emperor 148, 149, 150
Justinian I, emperor 38, 47, 49, 149, 150, 152
Justus, bishop of Toledo 167

Kahina, Berber prophetess 128
Kasila, Berber king 126, 127
Khirbat al-Mafjar: Umayyad palace 192, 194, 195-6
Khusro II, Sassanian shah 119

La Mancha 211
Lactantius, Christian author 156
Laurentius, count 170
law, Visigothic 3, 6, 44, 87, 90, 103, 111-12, 165, 170, 172, 179, 223-39
laws, codes of 223-6

Leander of Seville 58, 153, 154, 161-2, 163
learning, classical 6-7
legal documents 7
León, kingdom 2, 44, 243, 245
Leontius, emperor 109, 128
Leovigild: presumed code of 232, 234, 237
Leovigild, Visigothic king 48, 50-63, 66, 67, 68, 72, 73, 75, 82, 94, 158, 159, 184, 185, 217, 225, 232, 235
Lepcis Magna, city 123
Lérida, city 205, 211
Lérida, Council of 153
Levante, the 152
Lex Aquila 243
Lex Romana Visigothorum 225, 231
Lex Salica 224, 237
Liber Iudiciorum 224, 225, 226, 228, 232-9, 242, 245
library, royal 170
liturgy, Visigothic 147, 157, 169, 170
Liuva I, Visigothic king 50, 54, 87, 94
Liuva II 73, 75, 81, 115
Liuvigoto, queen 104, 106
Loire, river 27, 28, 36, 242
Lombards, the 152, 182, 191
Lugo, city 218
Lusitania, province 29, 32, 68, 99, 100, 131
Luvilana 106
Luwata, Berber confederacy 124, 131

Majorian, emperor 32
Málaga, city 52, 162, 204
Malaric, Suevic king 60-1
Martin of Braga 50-1
Maslama ibn Muhallad, *wali* of Egypt 126
Masona, bishop of Mérida 64, 65, 68, 73, 155, 214

Mataró: villa near 206
Maurice, emperor 58, 72
mawali 126
Maximus, bishop of Zaragoza 47, 162, 164
Maximus, emperor 14, 15, 26, 29
Maximus the Confessor 168
Medina Azahara, palace city 195
Medina Sidonia 48, 199, 200
merchants 155
Mérida, city 7, 30, 31, 47, 51, 65-6, 72, 152, 153, 159, 213-18, 220
Merovingian kingdoms 4, 5, 177
Meseta, the 174, 181, 185
Miro, Suevic king 54, 60, 75
missorium of Aetius, the 78
monasticism, Visigothic 152-3, 170, 188, 202-4, 205-6
Monophysites 119, 149
Montanus, bishop of Toledo 166
Morocco 125
"Mozarabic" style 188
Muhammad, prophet 118
Musa ibn Musa 245
Musa ibn Nusayr, *wali* of *Ifriquiya* 129, 133

Narbonensis, province 59, 70, 92, 93, 94, 131, 139, 140
Narbonne, city 50, 94, 131
Navarre, kingdom 1, 77
Nepopis, bishop of Mérida 65
Nepotian, count 231
Neustria, Frankish kingdom 74
Nîmes, city 93, 94, 95, 221
nobility, Visigothic 34, 59, 82, 87, 88, 96, 105, 113, 115-16, 132-3, 209
North Africa 14, 41, 45, 148
and Arab conquest 117-21
and Byzantine empire 25, 30, 31, 42, 51, 84, 109, 122, 194
and Catholic church 79, 149-52, 153, 154-7, 161, 168

Novellae 231
Numidia 126, 128

Oea, city 123
Olite, town 77
Oppa, son of Egica (?) 133, 134, 137, 139
Orbigo, battle of the (456) 31
Orense, modern province 187
Orosius, historian 13, 14, 26, 160, 246
Orospeda 54
Ostrogoths, the 4, 17-18, 19, 25, 37, 38, 42, 43, 62, 180, 228

Pacian, bishop of Barcelona 160
Palencia, city 186
Paul, bishop of Mérida 213
Paul, count and rebel 93-4, 95, 139, 221
Persians 118, 119
personal names 243
Peter, "tyrant" 35, 36
Phocas, emperor 123
Pimenius, bishop of *Asidona* 199, 200
Pla de Nadal: villa site 206
plague 110
poetry 148, 150, 168, 169
  see also Corippus; Dracontius; Eugenius II; Verecundus
population sizes 25, 241
Portugal, kingdom 1, 131, 216
Potamius, bishop of Lisbon 160
pottery 219
Praetorian Prefects 224, 227, 231
Priscillianism, heresy of 160
Procopius, Byzantine historian 42, 43, 48, 62
Prosper, Roman chronicler 51, 149
"protofeudalism," spurious concept 4-5
Provence 37
Puig Rom, fortress 221, 222
Pyrenees, the 11, 12, 13, 37, 77, 140, 210

Qayrawan 127
Quiricus, bishop of Barcelona and Toledo 84, 93, 100

Ranimir, abbot 93, 94
Ranosind, *dux* 94
Reccared: laws of 235
Reccared I, Visigothic king 51, 55, 59, 61, 64-9, 72, 113, 115, 132, 147, 171
Reccared II, king 76-7
Reccesuinth, Visigothic king 92, 93, 102, 186-7, 207
  brothers 88
  and the church 99, 198, 200
  law code 90, 228, 232-3, 234, 235, 237, 238, 239
  property 89-90, 112
  reign 82-3, 85, 90-1, 104, 114, 115, 168, 171
Recciberga, queen 90-1
Reccopolis, city 7, 55-6, 217
Rechiarius, Suevic king 31, 32
Rechila, Suevic king 31
Reconquista, the 1
Rhine, river 11, 12, 19, 174, 183, 242
Rhône, river 36, 37, 60
Riccimir, king 78
Richila, abbot of Agali 167
Ricimer, *Magister Militum* 32, 35
Ricimir, Visigothic noble 201
Rioja, the 53, 55, 75, 94, 157, 165, 184
Rome, city 13, 18, 21, 111, 219
Rosas 221
Ruccones the 75
Ruderic, Visigothic king 113, 115, 131, 132, 133, 134-5, 136, 138, 139, 143

Sabaria 53, 54, 55
Sabratha 123
Sagunto, city 73
Sahara, the 122-3
Sahel, the 121, 126

Salamanca 53, 92
Salpensa 199
San Juan de Baños: church 186-7, 190, 191, 193-4, 198, 200
San Millán: monastery 157, 165
San Pedro de Escalada: church 205
San Pedro de la Nave: church 186, 188, 189, 191
Santa Comba de Bande: church 186, 187, 191
Santa Eulalia, Mérida: church 214-15, 216, 217
Santa Leocadia, Toledo: church 198-9
Santa Lucía del Trampal: church 190-1
Santa María de Melque: church 188, 190, 191, 192-3, 194, 195-6, 203
Santa María de Quintanilla de las Viñas: church 186, 187, 189
Santander 53
Sao Fructuoso de Montelios: church 186, 187, 189
Sappos 53
sarcophagi 185
Sassanians, the 118, 119
Sbeitla (*Sufetula*) 124
Scipio, count 243
Segga 68
Segobriga, Roman city 186
Segovia, modern province 205
Septimania 244
Septimius Severus, emperor 123
Seronatus, prefect 227
Servitanum: monastery 152, 202 see also Donatus; Eutropius
Severianus, father of Leander and Isidore 154
Severus, bishop of Málaga 158
Seville, city 46, 47, 49, 58, 137, 162, 167, 215
Seville, Second Council of 79
Sicily 122, 128
Sidonius Apollinaris, bishop of Clermont 227-8, 229

Sierra de Guadarrama 174, 188
Sigebert I, Frankish king 49, 57
Sigeric, Visigothic king 26
Sigismund, Burgundian king 66, 230
Silings, the 11, 26, 29; see also Vandals
Silos: monastery 168
Sindered, bishop of Toledo 111
Sîntana de Mures culture 183
Sisbert, Visigothic noble 59
Sisebert, bishop of Toledo 106, 107, 108
Sisebut, Visigothic king 69, 75-6, 184
Sisegutia 60
Sisenand, Visigothic king 72, 85
slate documents 4, 170-3
springs, sacred or medicinal 186, 191
Sueves, the 11, 12, 14, 15, 24, 25, 26, 27, 29, 30-1, 32, 54, 60, 160, 215
Suevic kingdom, the 54, 55, 60-1, 62
Suinthila, Visigothic king 69, 77-8, 88, 102, 119, 185
Suniefred, Visigothic king 72, 107
Sunna, Arian bishop of Mérida 65, 68
Sweden 17
Syagrius, Roman ruler 36
Symmachus, pope 160
Syria 120, 121, 128

Tagus, river 56, 175
Taio, bishop of Zaragoza 84, 100, 165-6
Talavera, town 201
Tangiers, city 42, 120, 121, 129, 130, 139
Tariq ibn Ziyad, Berber general 130, 134, 135, 139
Tarraconensis, province 29, 31, 32, 46, 94, 131, 139, 153
Tarragona, city of 7, 14, 41, 59, 153

Tarragona, Council of 153
Teruingi, the 19, 22, 23
Thecla, rebel 106
Theodefred, count 136
Theodegotho, Ostrogothic princess 41
Theodemir, count 143
Theodemir, rebel 106
Theoderax, bishop of *Asidona* 199
Theoderic, Ostrogothic king 33, 40-1, 42, 43, 180
Theoderic I, Visigothic king 29, 74, 227-8, 229
Theoderic II, Visigothic king 31-2, 33, 73, 74, 228, 229
Theodore Ascida, bishop of Caesarea 149, 150
Theodosian dynasty 45, 219
Theodosius I, emperor 18, 20
Theudis, Visigothic king 42, 43, 44, 45, 46, 231
Theudisclus, Visigothic king 46
Thorismund, Visigothic king 78
Thrasamund, Vandal king 66
Three Chapters Dispute, the 149-51, 168
Timotheus, count 231
Tokra, city 122
Toledo, Arian synod of 57, 64
Toledo, city 3, 85, 132, 136, 175, 245
   as capital 44, 50, 68, 69, 74, 83, 94, 95, 105, 139
   and the church 71, 79, 83, 92, 100-1, 111, 137, 153, 166, 167, 202, 236
   coins 72
   fall 133-4, 142, 143
   library 155
   as literary center 162
   renovation 197, 198-9
Toledo, Eighth Council of 86-9, 94, 98, 99, 114
Toledo, Eleventh Council of 99, 100
Toledo Fifteenth Council of 104, 105, 107
Toledo, Fifth Council of 80, 104
Toledo, Fourteenth Council of 103-4
Toledo Fourth Council of 76, 79-80, 244, 246
Toledo, Ninth Council of 89, 99, 166
Toledo, Second Council of 41
Toledo, Seventh Council of 83-4, 86, 244
Toledo, Sixteenth Council of 95, 106-7
Toledo, Sixth Council of 80-1, 98, 165
Toledo, synod of 610 101
Toledo, Tenth Council of 89, 93
Toledo, Third Council of 67, 69, 73, 79, 115, 153, 154, 155, 162, 178
Toledo, Thirteenth Council of 103-4, 105-6, 107
Toledo, Twelfth Council of 96, 97-9, 100, 101, 103, 106, 235-6
Tolmo de Minateda (*Ercavica*) 55
Torre Llauder: Roman villa 206, 207
Toulouse, city 33, 35, 36, 37, 41, 230
towns in Visigothic Spain 213-22
treasure 40, 47
Tripoli, city 123
Tripolitania 122-3, 124, 125
Tulga, Visigothic king 81-2, 115
Tunisia 121

Ugernum: fortress 60
Uldila, bishop 68
Umayyad dynasty 245
   architecture 192, 194, 195
Uqba ibn Nafi, *wali* of *Ifriquiya* 125, 126, 133
Usatges of Barcelona, the 225
Uthman, caliph 124

INDEX

Valencia, city 59, 153, 162, 206, 220
Valens, emperor 18
Valentinian III, emperor 29, 30, 31
Valerius of Bierzo, hermit 170, 201, 202, 204
Vandals, the 11, 12, 13, 14, 15, 24, 25, 26, 27, 29, 30-1, 38, 49, 66, 151, 152, 156, 160, 215
Vegas de Pedraza: villa 205
Vegas de Puebla Nueva: mausoleum 201
Vejer de la Miel 199
Venta de Baños 186, 198
Verecundus of Junca, bishop 150-1
Verona, city 151
Victor of Tunnunna, chronicler 51, 149-50, 151
Victoriacum, new town 58
Vigilius, bishop of Thapsa 156
Vigilius, pope 150
Villa Fortunatus, Fraga 205
villages 208-9, 210-11
villas 197, 205-9, 215
Vincent, bishop of Zaragoza 64, 158
Viseu, town 136
Visigothic Formulary, the 172, 244
Visigoths: origins 15-26

Vitas Patrum Emeretensium, the 68, 73, 159, 213, 215, 216
Vouillé, battle of (507) 36, 38, 42
Vulgar Law, Late Roman 227

Walid I, Umayyad caliph 129
Walid II, Umayyad caliph 192
Wallia, Visigothic king 26
Wamba, laws of 236, 237-8
Wamba, Visigothic king 70, 71, 93-5, 96, 97-8, 99, 100, 101-2, 104, 112, 115, 139, 197-8, 221
Witteric, Visigothic king 73-4, 75
Wittiza, count 106
Wittiza, sons of 136, 137, 138
Wittiza, Visigothic king 108-9, 111-13, 115, 130, 131, 132, 133, 136, 138, 233
writing 171-2, 173

Yarmuk, battle of (635) 119
Yazid II, Umayyad caliph 126

Zamora, city 187
Zaragoza, city 32, 33, 38, 46, 85, 166, 167, 212
Zeumer, Karl 72, 233-4, 239
Zorita de los Canes (site of *Reccopolis*) 56